D0513810

013431376 5

MY STORY Dwain CHAMBERS

Race Against Me

Libros
INTERNATIONAL

The right of Dwain Chambers to be identified as the Author of this Work has been asserted by him in accordance with the Copyright, Designs and Patents Act 1998.

Copyright © Dwain Chambers 2009

All rights reserved. No part of this publication may be reproduced, stored in a retrieval system, or transmitted, in any form or by any means without the prior written permission of the publisher, nor be otherwise circulated in any form of binding or cover other than that in which it is published and without a similar condition being imposed on the subsequent purchaser. Any person who does so may be liable to criminal prosecution and civil claims for damages.

ISBN: 978-1-905988-75-4

Cover design by Kelly Leonie Walsh
Cover photograph by Edwin Cole Photography
www.edwin-cole.blogspot.com

Published by Libros International

www.librosinternational.com
www.dwain-chambers.com

FSC

WARWICKSHIRE COUNTY LIBRARY	
013431376 5	
Askews	
796.422	£18.99

Acknowledgements

Thanks to the author Ken Scott for his patience and sheer determination to try and make a writer out of me. On more than one occasion he threatened to walk away from the book if a thousand words weren't in his e-mail inbox at a certain hour. On more than one occasion he told me that this book is Dwain Chambers' and not Ken Scott's. At times I thought it was beyond me, a real chore, but now I look on writing as a pleasure and a therapy. Thanks, Scotty.

To the great journalists who were not afraid to voice their opinions, especially to Oliver Holt and Peter Hildreth.

To my editor Carol Cole and my designer Kelly Walsh. Not forgetting my great friend and agent Simon Dent who despite all the odds pulled the book deal together in the first place. I also want to thank my own personal A Team: Nick Collins, my great friend Jonathan Crystal and their families.

I have many friends and members of my family who have supported me throughout my life. I cannot list them without the risk of forgetting someone. You know who you are anyway. In bringing this section to a close I would just like to thank especially my mum and dad, Lascelle, and apologise to those who I may have hurt along the way. Please find it in your hearts to forgive me.

I dedicate this book to my baby Leonie. I know I've added a few more grey hairs to your head, but it's all in the name of love. Thank you for your support, patience and understanding. Jayon, Skye and Rocco Star, I'm proud of you all. One day I will make you proud of me.

CONTENTS

Foreword by Oliver Holt
Chief Sports Writer of The Daily Mirror
Sports Journalist of the Year 2005 and 2006

Ghostwriter of:
Stan: Tackling My Demons by Stan Collymore (2004)
Left Field by Graeme Le Saux (2007)

It is, I accept, a skewed kind of morality that lauds a former drugs cheat as a hero of his sport. Nonetheless, I have come to believe that Dwain Chambers' belated candour in admitting his crimes against sprinting has set him apart as a man to be admired. It has also distinguished him from the rump of liars and dissemblers who have run and won with the aid of performance-enhancing drugs and have eventually been caught doing so but continue to live their lives in a state of miserable and preposterous denial.

Chambers cheated. He was caught. He was punished. And then he did a very strange thing, a thing that makes him uniquely valuable in the post-innocence era of athletics. Instead of crying foul, instead of saying his sample must have been contaminated, instead of saying one of the lozenges he bought at his local sweet shop was infected by a stray impurity, he volunteered that he had given in to temptation and self-doubt and joined forces with Victor Conte, sport's most loquacious rogue and purveyor of the famously illicit substances, The Cream and The Clear.

His sport hated that. Athletics loves denial because it allows it to try to claim that cheating is not endemic and that many positive drugs tests and missed drugs tests are just a series of terrible mistakes. When, for instance, sports writers from outside athletics' magic circle questioned Christine Ohuruogu's excuses for her missed tests, we were condemned as 'football hacks' and 'curtain-twitchers' by some of those who have borne witness to the steady destruction of their sport for decades without exposing the problems that have crippled the credibility of athletics.

So when Chambers went one step further and suggested in an interview with Sir Matthew Pinsent that a drug cheat would have to have a 'real bad day' to lose to a clean athlete at the Beijing Olympics, athletics fell into a state of apoplexy. Chambers had broken the code. He had brought the sport's practice of 'plausible deniability' a giant step closer to obsolescence. And so, rather than seek to learn from him or applaud him as someone who was finally speaking out, someone who had finally defied the omerta, the British Olympic Association sought to punish him again, this time for his honesty.

They chose to make a distinction between him and people like Ohuruogu, triathlete Tim Don and judoka Peter Cousins who had all committed drugs offences by missing three random tests but who had all had their lifetime Olympic bans waived by the BOA because each of them said it had all been a terrible mistake. Three times.

Never mind that it seemed nobody from the BOA had actually

sought to test the validity of their various excuses. Out of curiosity, I tried out the route between Ohuruogu's home in Stratford and the Olympic Medical Institute at Northwick Park in north London, where she missed one of her tests. When she didn't turn up, the testers telephoned her at home to tell her she had an hour to get there. She said there was no way she could make it. I drove it in a few minutes under the hour. Comfortably. Without breaking any speed limits on the North Circular, either.

 And yet when people like me pointed out these reservations, we were roundly condemned by those in athletics and accused of pursuing a vendetta against Ohuruogu. Not simply trying to find the truth but acting maliciously. And then we were told that Ohuruogu's case was quite different from Chambers', merely because he had admitted what he had done was wrong and she had said it had all been a terrible mistake.

 A few morons even trotted out the pathetic line that Ohuruogu, for instance, had never failed a drug test. Dear me. Whatever happened to the principle that a missed test, or three, is equivalent to a failed test? Otherwise, what's the point in conducting random tests in the first place? Even Lord Coe was unable to accept that there was no conflict between questioning Ohuruogu and campaigning for Chambers to have his lifetime ban overturned. But all we vendetta-pursuers were arguing for was that the two of them should be treated the same.

 But then there are many monuments in British athletics that have been built by being economical with the truth. The London Olympics, for whom Lord Coe was such a skilful, passionate and effective proselytizer, was won partly because London 2012 provided grossly inaccurate estimates of how much the Games would cost. Had we and the IOC delegates known the bill would soar to almost 400% more than the original £2bn estimate, Paris, not the English capital, would be hosting the 2012 Games.

It is within this context of systemic self-delusion and denial that Chambers' admissions should be viewed. Voices like his are often condemned as unreliable and sensationalist by those who wish that it were so. The same happened when the former baseball great, Jose Canseco, wrote a memoir about steroid use in baseball called Juiced. When it was first published, many within the sport sought to dismiss it as the ramblings of an attention-seeking ex-player. The subsequent revelations of wrongdoing in baseball, though, have made Canseco's claims appear rather modest.

I wish that Chambers' honesty had been rewarded instead of scorned. I wish that the athletics community had welcomed him back instead of shunning him. I wish they had learned lessons from what he told them instead of suggesting they did not recognise the picture he was painting of the ugly face of their sport. Because until athletics stops paying lip-service to the fact that it has a problem, until it acts consistently to punish cheats, until it tries to force those who expose the issue into exile, the problem will not get any better.

Dwain Chambers' willingness to expose the truth about modern athletics could have been a turning point for the sport in Britain. Instead, athletics heard what he had to say and turned away.

Preface by Ken Scott
Author of:
Jack of Hearts (2005)

A Million Would Be Nice (2007)

The Sun Will Still Shine Tomorrow (2009)

Ghostwriter of:
Do The Birds Still Sing In Hell by Horace 'Jim' Greasley (2008)

Cheating or gamesmanship?

Key 'the definition of cheat' on a standard Google search and you will be presented with nearly three million results all of which proffer an opinion as to what the term actually means. There are many forms of cheating and the 'cheats' operate on every level known to mankind and in every business ever created by the human form. Cheats have won medals and cups, world trophies, world titles, made vast fortunes, bankrupt individuals and companies, won world wars, lost world wars, conquered countries. Hollywood has glamourised the con man, the swindler, the charlatan, the trickster...the cheat.

There are big cheats, little cheats, cheats that brought multinational corporations and even countries to their knees, cheats that ruined governments and, of course, cheats that maimed and murdered individuals and whole nations. Throughout history cheats have been chastised and yet applauded in the same breath. Depending on where you were looking in from, your man, your leader could be a devious, cunning, tactically brilliant individual or, in the eyes of the opposition, a cheat.

For the purpose of the next few paragraphs we won't pull any punches: we will lose all of the adjectives and simply call that devious, cunning individual a cheat.

There is no greater arena where the cheat operates than in the sporting world. Sport today goes beyond local or national pride, irrespective of the individual or team. Today sport is about money… big money. No matter what the motive or spur of the individual sportsman, someone somewhere stands to benefit financially. In every country, on every playing field, pitch, stadium, arena, wicket, therein lurks a cheat in waiting, a man or woman seeking to gain an unfair advantage over the opposition.

The definition of cheating is generally unanimously defined, no matter which dictionary or thesaurus it comes from. Give or take a few different adjectives, a comma or a full stop in a different place, it generally follows the same pattern. That is:

"To break the rules in a game, examination, or contest, in an attempt to gain an unfair advantage."

There you have it, breaking the rules to gain an unfair advantage. But what exactly is unfair and just how thin is that non-existent line where gamesmanship to seek an unfair advantage is classed as downright cheating? How many sportsmen and women have we looked up to or put on pedestals who have gained an unfair advantage over their rivals? How many athletes with an unblinking desire and passion to win have we admired over the years and, because of that desire and passion, have been prepared to go that step further in the quest to train harder, run faster, compete longer.

In recent years, particularly in the English Premiership a new expression has emerged among the tabloids and broadsheets gracing our breakfast tables after the weekend's fixtures. The commentators and so-called professional pundits utter the word carefully, always in the right context, and generally at a level two or three decibels lower than the sentence in which it has been included.

I'm talking about *gamesmanship*.

And in sporting clubs and pubs and restaurants after every game, in the lounge of every suburban home, the arguments rage over whether the grossly overpaid megastar taking a dive after a knock that wouldn't have felled a ten-month-old toddler taking their first tentative steps on the living room carpet was in fact cheating or whether he was simply deploying a little 'gamesmanship'.

In every walk of business life, the rules are bent. Insider trading, corporate bullying, industrial espionage, spying, lying, phone tapping, fiddling, meddling, nepotism, corruption, dishonesty, scams, shams, falsification, avoidance; the list goes on and on.

The great Douglas Bader uttered these immortal oft-used words: "Rules are for the obedience of fools and the guidance of wise men."

To the supporters of Manchester City and Chelsea, Ronaldo is a cheat. To his loyal followers from Old Trafford he is a genius at trickery and gamesmanship. Likewise, Didier Drogba is a cheat at Old Trafford and The Emirates and St James's Park and Anfield, but when the said six foot two, fourteen-stone man of muscle cartwheels to the ground from a waft of air from an opponent's boot six inches away, forty-two thousand 'fans' at Stamford Bridge turn to each other, smile and collectively whisper *gamesmanship*.

Therein lies the problem. When does a gamesman push the rules to such a limit he oversteps the mark and becomes a cheat?

The great coaches and journalists will tell you that the individual sportsman with an overwhelming stop-at-nothing attitude, with a fierce desire to win, is the sportsman that will generally make it to the top.

The greatest Formula One driver of our generation was Michael Schumacher. End of debate. No one could touch him. His focus and desire was unquestionable. But occasionally Michael Schumacher could be a little naughty and he had a certain fondness for barging rivals off the track. He didn't need to knock Damon Hill, David Coulthard or Jacques Villeneuve into the middle of next week as he had the skill level and the car to more than compete on an even keel.

Certain championships were slightly tainted as he took his main rivals onto the gravel or the grass with a careless or, some would say, reckless manoeuvre. The really unkind would declare to anyone that would listen that he had cheated, calculated the maths and, because he was so far ahead in the championship, been prepared to sacrifice his points along with that of the main contenders. In reality he had a stop-at-nothing overwhelming desire to win; that's why he risked his life on the F1 circuit for so long; that's why he won the F1 title an incredible seven times.

Who can forget viewing the BBC footage of 1963? That Muhammad Ali moment when Henry Cooper had him seeing stars. Cooper had floored Ali in the fourth round with a powerful left hook. Ali barely made it to his corner man Angelo Dundee. Dundee was a seasoned trainer and err... a gamesman. The footage from the BBC that night clearly shows two intact gloves as Ali wobbled towards his stool. But incredibly... to the astonishment of Ali, Cooper and the ringside spectators (but not the admirable Angelo) the miracle of the split glove occurred during the twenty seconds or so Ali sat on the stool wondering which of the two Angelos to look at. Ali recovered in the time it took to find a new glove from the dressing room and came out fighting in the fifth round. Cooper's eye was badly gashed and Ali set to work landing as many punches as possible into the swollen bloody mess of raw meat until Cooper couldn't go on. The fight was stopped and Ali awarded a TKO. The rest they say is history. The two careers of Ali and Cooper could have taken a totally different direction had events been different that night on the 18th June 1963, had a certain individual not taken the law into his hands and played with the rules.

The term 'sledging' is part and parcel of the modern game of cricket. For the uninitiated amongst you, 'sledging' is a bowler's or batsman's way of bending the rules in order to seek an unfair advantage (where have I heard that before?); in this case, abusing their opposite number in order to affect the concentration needed to compete in the modern game. When Botham walked towards the crease in an Ashes match many moons ago, Rodney Marsh grinned, welcomed him to the wicket and said, "So how are your wife and my kids?"

Some were not so polite. Glen McGrath was liberal with the F-word in many a Test. During one memorable occasion he shouted down the wicket during a Test match with Zimbabwe to the slightly overweight Eddo Brandes.

"Hey, Eddo, why are you so fucking fat?"

Eddo Brandes replied with a straight face, "Because every time I fuck your mother, she gives me a biscuit."

So it seems 'sledging' works, otherwise they wouldn't do it. But sometimes it backfires. Ramnaresh Sarwan came back with a corker when asked by Glen McGrath again (he's a glutton for punishment is old Glen): "What does Brian Lara's dick taste like?"

Sarwan replied, "I don't know. Ask your wife."

Alas it seems it was Glen McGrath who then lost his concentration threatening to rip Sarwan's fucking throat out if he ever mentioned his wife again. The whole incident was captured for posterity on live television microphones.

Throughout sporting history, the cheat and the rule-bender have flouted and played with the spirit of the game. We are lucky to be able to live in an environment of free speech and one of the great after-events of a sporting occasion is the debates that go on afterwards in the bars and cafés of the world. Was it a goal or not? Did he tamper with the ball, a penalty or take a dive?   One of the arguments against the introduction of trial by television is that it would put an end to all these healthy and passionate debates.

And if he or she did tamper with the ball, dive in the box or deliberately trip an opponent on the final bend of a 3000 metre race in the European Championships is it any less of an offence than an athlete seeking to improve muscle definition through a banned substance? Cheating is cheating. Who are we to say X form of cheating is worse than Y?

Ask any forty-something English male what is the worst case of cheating they have ever seen and I'd take a quick walk along to Ladbrokes and bet that they'd mention a certain deliberate attempt to guide the ball into the opponents' net, costing an England team a place in the semi-final of the world's biggest competition.

114,000 spectators and 350 million people worldwide witnessed Diego Maradona's blatant handball on the 22nd June 1986. The world-governing body of football witnessed it and played it back in slow motion countless times. The Football Association of Argentina cringed, I assume, as time after time, no matter how often they rewound the tape, the cheat known as Maradona deliberately guided the ball illegally with his hand past the stranded England goalkeeper Peter Shilton and straight into the onion bag.

Tunisian referee Ali Bin Nasser did not see the infringement and allowed the goal. The Argentine players and fans celebrated.

Television footage shows Maradona looking towards the referee who, for a split second, was puzzled by the Argentine players' lack of response. Spur of the moment his hand of God may well have been, and he might have been forgiven for a winner's instinct.

What happened next was not.

The ball was in the net, Peter Shilton, arms raised, pleaded with the referee, several players ran to the linesman believing at least one official must have witnessed the blatant act of cheating?

It appeared not.

Maradona would later say, "I was waiting for my teammates to embrace me, and no one came. I told them, 'Come hug me, or the referee isn't going to allow it.'"[1]

Yes, England were cheated, Sir Bobby Robson was cheated, the captain, the team and the whole of the nation were cheated by that infamous hand of God. Everybody in the civilized world apparently witnessed that despicable act and Maradona was labelled (in the British press at least) a cheat!

Now most of you reading this will be of a certain age to remember that incident with clarity, albeit possibly through a beer-filled alcoholic and dejected haze. Some of you however are too young. Let me tell you what happened to Diego Maradona:

There was an almighty uproar that reverberated throughout the footballing world. FIFA and the Asociación del Fútbol Argentino immediately stripped the cheat known as Maradona of his captaincy. Within twenty-four hours FIFA had nullified the result and ordered the two teams to replay. Forty-eight hours after the incident Maradona was humbled on world television and made to apologise to the world. He was given a five-year ban and sent back home to Argentina in disgrace. The Argentinean FA claimed he would never play for Argentina again and his club at the time, Napoli, immediately placed him on the transfer list. A record fine of one million US dollars was imposed, a record that still stands today.

Well, actually no… I'm sorry… but none of the above ever took place.

Maradona was not stripped of the captaincy, he did not receive a fine and, although he did appear on world television, he gloated and smirked and, when asked about the cheating incident, smiled and claimed it was the hand of God. FIFA sat back with their fingers up their rectums and smiled nervously, mumbling on about the best player in the world which Maradona undoubtedly was. Maradona in my eyes was the greatest footballer on the planet at the time. Not only did he have a God-given gift, but also an overwhelming desire to win at all costs. In Maradona's mind the hand of God was gamesmanship, pushing the rules to the limit. In the eyes of the watching world (excluding Argentina) he was a cheat.

What sticks in the throat of the general sports fan so much is that he went unpunished. He went on unhindered, captained Argentina and lifted the greatest trophy in world sport. Maradona used his hand, he was not malicious, nor did he set out to deliberately hurt an opponent but he cheated and got away with it. And how many footballers over the years have set out to deliberately break an opponent's leg, in some cases end the career of their fellow professionals and walk away with nothing more than a three-match ban and a small fine? How many footballers have cheated and got away with it and what makes them so different to other athletes?

We will never do away with cheating in sport, it won't happen, no matter how many words are written how many voices are raised. We will never have that level playing field that sports fans across the world crave and we will never be in a situation where the scientists and sports doctors or the British Olympic Association come up with a foolproof system of illegal drug detection because for every five scientists working on a way to improve the system of detection there are ten scientists, tricksters or rule-benders looking to beat it.

There is a saying that prostitution is the oldest profession in the world.

It isn't. Cheating is, if the cheat is making money or earning a living.

Although prostitution is well documented in the Bible, even older documentary evidence also shows that Solon founded the first of his Athens' brothels in the 6th century BC, to fund amongst other things religious temples. I would still bet my bottom dollar that those early prostitutes of Greek, Chinese, Egyptian or Biblical origin, prior to the said sexual act taking place, used every method at their disposal to gain an unfair advantage over their fellow professionals in attracting the cash-rich, aroused individual with a pocketful of gold coins and an overwhelming desire to go forth and procreate.

The line between gamesmanship and cheating is a thin one, the risk and reward great. This book does not attempt to decipher exactly where that line is, I simply ask you to keep an open mind. The purpose of this book is not to differentiate between various sports nor do I attempt to offer a solution to the problem. Neither do I subscribe to the theory that we allow athletes to use any concoction or cocktail of drugs under the sun and let them get on with it. They need to be protected from themselves and the crooks and con men only too happy to make a quick buck at the expense of someone else's body. We need a fair and just punishment system in place and the athletes need to be aware of the punishments should they choose to flout the rules, but sadly I don't have the answers.

The purpose of this book is to explore what drives the sportsman to break the rules. What is it that makes the sportsman and woman cheat? What separates the gamesman from the cheat and why do we differentiate so much in our punishments of individuals and their particular sport.

The official's conversation was brief and to the point. He introduced himself first of all then continued with the formalities.

"Is that Mr Chambers?"

"Yes, that's me."

"Mr Chambers, I have some bad news for you, I'm afraid."

Dwain Chambers had been reading a book. Now the pages started to shake as if a mini earthquake had just occurred in the hotel bedroom.

"Yes."

"Your recent urine sample taken in Saarbrucken on August 1st 2003 has tested positive for a newly discovered steroid."

Dwain was, for once, speechless as he struggled to hang onto the phone. The official asked him if he understood. He simply answered yes.

"Your drug test has come back positive, Mr Chambers," the official repeated.

Dwain Chambers' stomach lurched and just for a split second he wondered if this was some sick joke. But then, why should it be some sick joke? It was only a matter of time before the truth came out. His whole world started to crumble around him and yet an enormous feeling of relief welled up inside him.

"A report will be sent to the UK Athletics Board," continued the official, "and you will have to attend a disciplinary hearing."

Dwain didn't hear the official's last few words. He replaced the receiver and began to pack his suitcase. It was over at last. His eighteen months of drugs hell was now officially at an end.

BORN TO RUN

I was born in Islington, London, April 5th, 1978 and issued with my Government name, Dwain Anthony Watson (Watson being my mother's surname). My birth took place in the Royal Northern Hospital. I lived with my two sisters, Loraine and Marie. When my mum was carrying me, my real father (Robert Chambers) left the family home. He showed up on the odd occasion afterwards but I can't ever recall him living at our house. My older sister Christine, who currently lives in Derby, experienced the same treatment as I did by my father: it was a case of here today, gone tomorrow. I also have a brother named Robert who I've never met; he lives in Derby as well. Sad to say, Christine and I never met until I was around fifteen. I thought the meeting a bit crazy really. My father had never bothered with me or my other sisters for years and all of a sudden he wanted us to meet. I think it was a bit of a guilt trip or something like that. Surprise, surprise, the happy family syndrome did not last and my real father and I are as distant as ever again.

Thankfully though, the relationship with Christine blossomed and we are still close today.

My stepfather came onto the scene almost as soon as I could remember. Your memories are very vague as a small child but as far as I can recall he has always been around. He is called Lascell Golding. As far as I was concerned he provided for me and he was my dad in the same way as other boys on my estate had a dad. That said, there were an awful lot of single parents, boys without a dad at all. Sometimes I looked upon myself as fortunate, other times I wondered just what it was I had done to make my dad walk out on my mum as I arrived on the scene. These are the thoughts that young boys have when Dad does a runner. Dads that do runners, please take note!

I wouldn't say I had a happy childhood growing up in the same house as Loraine and Marie, Mum and Lascell. Although Lascell was good to me and Mum and my sisters from a financial point of view, my stepfather and I never really got on when I was young. I think it had to something to do with my stepfather and my real father not seeing eye to eye. I remember a few very strained meetings in the house when Lascell and my real dad were in the same room. As a kid, no matter what your real father has said or done to you he is still your father and there is still a bond there. I must have given Lascell a bit of a hard time and, as young as I was, I was determined that he would never really replace my biological father. I realise now it was all very unfair on Lascell. It wasn't until I became an adult that I found it in my heart to call him Dad. We now have a very strong and close relationship and I am proud to call him Dad.

He didn't help his case with his strict upbringing. Man, he was tough. We were hardly ever allowed to play outside as my mother was afraid we would cause trouble. I don't know where that came from. At the beginning she had no reason to keep me inside the house. The London streets were a lot safer then; no such thing as the knife crime and black on black gang fighting that there is now. I remember being cooped up in my bedroom being told to play with a few games while, from my window, I watched the other kids tear up and down the street.

To be honest, the most fun I ever had was on a Monday when I went with my friends Michael and Anthony Facey and James Davis to the local cubs for a few hours. Red and green tie, grey shorts, knee-high socks and worn-down black plimsolls. Man, what a sight we must have looked. But those two hours were like a breath of fresh air. I enjoyed the supervised activities and mixing with lads of the same age. Mum and Lascell were glad too because they were fairly certain I wouldn't get into any trouble.

You might think I'm being a little harsh but things were quite difficult for us as kids. Our stepfather was very vocal and spoke his mind. Because of his overpowering presence we never answered back to him; this included my mother. It was the norm in a black family unit at that time. Fathers were in charge, fathers were king of the castle. So for years we would have to keep our mouths shut. This was so frustrating as we were never given the chance to express ourselves. This knocked my confidence for years. I moaned and moaned at my mum to let me out and, if Lascell was out working, occasionally she would let me. Man, what a mistake. Every time I was allowed out of the house I would end up in trouble. I never intended to get in trouble, I was just like a dog off a leash. I went bloody crazy. If only they'd let me out a bit more often.

Anyone who has traditional God-fearing, Christian black parents will understand. They don't spare the rod. All those bible sayings would come out as I got positively battered for the trouble I brought to their door. At times I would hate my parents for not allowing me and my sisters a chance to be kids and have fun and I would curse them quietly as they doled out the beatings. I understand it now. While I certainly don't agree with the level and ferocity of some of the beatings, I understand that at the time it was considered normal to batter the shit out of a child. Thankfully most of society seems to have moved on.

As I've grown older and become a parent myself I can now understand the stresses and sacrifices both Mum and Dad (Lascell) went through in order to put a roof over our heads. My stepfather worked late and my mother, a nurse, literally had to run from her shift at work to pick me and my sisters up from school. She'd come home, cook, clean, wash and dress us, and put us to bed with a full stomach. For some reason she would always try and get us up to bed before Dad came home. Lascell worked long hours. By all accounts he would return home tired and miserable. Looking back on it, I suppose up in our bedrooms was probably the best place to be. Mum would do all this for us and always seem to be in either a state of panic or stressed to hell. It was a fine balancing act and at the end of each evening she would breathe a sigh of relief. When her alarm clock went off at six the next morning she would start all over again.

Mum and Dad, I take back all the hatred I once directed at you both. I never told you enough but I love you so much. At times I hated our childhood but realise in your own minds there was a method in your madness. It's finally beginning to make a little sense. I've learned a lot from Mum especially. She tried to instil values into us: stick it at school, learn to love books, and respect those around you. Above all, believe in yourself and stand firm in what you think is right.

My mum and Lascell decided to get married. I must have been eight or nine years old at the time. My sister Loraine took my stepfather's name as he played a better role in Loraine's life than her real dad did but, even though I can't really say my real dad did anything for me, I decided to keep my paternal surname Dwain Anthony Chambers. Even at that young age I knew what I wanted and although there were some heated discussions (and a regular hiding or two) Mum allowed me to keep the name Chambers. At the time Lascell didn't seem bothered either way, but deep down it must have pained him. Here he was bringing up another man's boy, working all the hours God sends and that's how I thanked him. Sorry, Dad.

It was around this time that I discovered I could run. Running fast is a gift, something you are born with. No matter how hard you train or whether you have the greatest coach and back-up in the world, if you aren't made to run fast it isn't ever going to happen. Even as an eight or nine-year-old growing up in Partington Close, Islington, running the streets with my friends, I was aware that I had something special. At that point in my life I hadn't even been near an athletics club let alone seen a coach. And yet, getting involved in the skirmishes and scrapes that all boys of that age do, I was acutely aware that not only could I outrun boys of my own age but also the ten- and eleven-year-olds couldn't get near me either. For fun I would race my mates on their BMX bikes and beat them comfortably. We would laugh about it at the time and my mates would call me a freak. I didn't care, eight-year-olds, ten-year-old boys on bikes, I simply loved beating them.

And when I ran, whether in a play race or running from the boys from a nearby estate, I was at peace with the world; content, confident in my own ability, simply amazed at how quickly I could pump my little arms and legs when I wanted to. It's difficult to describe but it was as if I was in another world. The wind rushing past my face, every muscle in my body, every sinew stretched and taut and pushed to the limit. Trees, bus shelters, indistinguishable shapes flying past my face. And that oh so special adrenalin surge when victory was assured, victory in a play race or victory in managing to outsprint the aggressors, the bullies intent on causing me harm.

And as a ten-year-old, in 1988 I remember watching replays of arguably the greatest assembled field for the 100 metre Olympic final. I watched the fastest men in the world in a race against each other. Little did I realise at the time but I was about to watch the most controversial race of all time.

They were all there: Carl Lewis, Ben Johnson, Williams, Mitchell, Calvin Smith, Da Silva and of course our very own Linford Christie. Being the Brit, Linford was of course the man I wanted to win. Little did I know as I watched my hero limber up he would become my agent many years later and during my junior days a newspaper would christen me 'Little Linford'.

In the minutes preceding the start I couldn't help being drawn like a magnet to an almost trance-like Canadian sprinter, a man at the top of his game. Ben Johnson was focused, he had tunnel vision of his lane only. His personal tunnel ended 100 metres away in the shimmering Korean haze. Nothing else mattered. He was on his own; the thousands of people in the stadium, the race officials, the other runners were simply not there.

As the gun fired Ben Johnson's head jerked up and he got one of the best starts of his career. He thundered down the track like a thoroughbred racehorse in a five-furlong sprint. Lewis and Co tried to catch him but were left trailing in his wake and he was never headed as he powered towards the gold medal and a place in history with a new world record time of 9.79. He was even afforded the luxury of slowing slightly as he crossed the finish line and raised his right arm in a victory salute while almost casually flicking a glance towards his great, now defeated rival, Lewis.

My mum Adlith, my stepfather Lascell and I watched in astonishment from the front room of our small terraced house in Islington as Ben Johnson pulled away almost effortlessly from the field. Neither Linford Christie nor Carl Lewis were at the races, so to speak. As I say, the memories are sketchy but I'm told by my mother that we all cheered as Linford Christie breasted past the finish line in third place.

He had won an Olympic medal. The fact that it was bronze didn't matter. The man, *our man*, had won a medal at the Olympics; he was now recognized as one of the quickest men on the planet. The memory of that race will stay with me forever. I still watch it to this day on video. And for a few short days Ben Johnson replaced Linford Christie as my hero.

As the Canadian flag fluttered in the late afternoon Seoul breeze, the national anthem 'O Canada' rang out round the stadium and a shiver ran the length of my spine. Oh, how I wished God Save the Queen had been playing. Oh, how I wished it was me standing on that podium. I was ten years of age and I discovered I now had an ambition, a goal and a focus in life. While my friends wanted to become footballers, cricketers and astronauts, I had just one wish in life... to stand on *that* podium with a gold medal hanging from my neck and the Union Jack being hoisted aloft. I wanted to be the fastest man in the world.

Then everything changed.

I remember the announcement on the BBC news. I heard words I had never heard before. Drugs – stanozolol – steroids. Johnson was a drugs cheat and a fraud. I listened in horror as it was announced my hero had been stripped of his medal and his world record. I shook my head in confusion as my father tried to explain. Carl Lewis was promoted to the gold medal position, and Linford Christie awarded the silver. Oh well, at least that's good for

Linford, isn't it? Suddenly it was Linford Christie who I looked up to.

But then events took another turn for the worse. It turned out that Christie's urine sample also showed suspect readings. What was going on? I was as confused as a ten-year-old could be and even my dad couldn't explain it in terms that a small boy would understand. What were drugs and steroids anyway and why were they so bad?

Later Christie was cleared when it became apparent that his readings were as a result of drinking ginseng tea. No further action was taken against him and he was allowed to retain the silver medal from the 1988 Olympics.

The reverberations from that race lasted many years with many fingers being pointed. As recently as 2004 Ben Johnson accused the American sports authorities of protecting American athletes at the expense of foreign ones. Let me just say that that's a very interesting analogy.

To this day Johnson claims a 'Mystery Man' who he names as one André Jackson was the man who put the stanozolol in his food. Good call, Ben, but a few years later you admitted you'd cheated. During a comeback period in 1993 in Montreal he was found guilty of doping again, this time for excess testosterone.

Even as far back as 1988 Ben Johnson (and other athletes) insisted that they used drugs in order to remain on a par with the other athletes on drugs who they were competing against. It bears some weight. Four of the top five finishers of that 100 metre final at the 1988 Olympics have tested positive for banned drugs at some point in their careers. Somewhat unfairly, some may say, that out of these four athletes only Johnson was forced to give up his medal.

I still look back on that race today. No one can take away from Ben Johnson that he was the fastest man around at the time; no one can take away that elation he felt as he crossed the line in front. Many years later he would say:

"I did something good in my life. My mom and dad saw me run faster than any human, and that's it. Better than a gold medal."

I can relate to that, I can understand what drives a man to the ultimate sacrifice. I can understand that drive, the need to run faster and I can understand the temptation Ben Johnson succumbed to. I can understand it because I too relented under that pressure.

But now, just like me, he is 'the cheat'. He has never recovered; he will always be 'the cheat', not the fastest man in the world… 'the cheat'.

Like me Ben Johnson had his prize money taken away from him and he was stripped of medals he had won. The only difference between Ben Johnson and me is that he made the mistake over and over again. I've learned from my past mistakes. Now I run clean. I feel better for it both in body and mind and my conscience is clear.

I was brought up to believe in the Christian Church and its teachings and philosophies; no matter who has wronged me, spoken out against me, ridiculed me on television or in the newspapers I will always give them a second chance. I will always forgive them.

I remember a passage from Matthew; it goes something along the lines of:

Then Peter came to Jesus and asked, 'Lord, how many times shall I forgive my brother when he sins against me? Up to seven times?' Jesus answered, 'I tell you, not seven times, but seventy-seven times.'

There we have it. I'm not perfect by any stretch of the imagination but I have made just one mistake during my long athletics career. Furthermore I have served my sentence. My mistake has brought my family to the brink of financial ruin and I must live with that forever. Leonie, my partner, has supported me both financially and with unquestioned loyalty. She has backed me every inch of the way. She has forgiven me and I'm sure the Lord has too. What I can't understand is why others haven't got it in their hearts to do likewise. I am further disappointed that prominent members of the church haven't joined in the debate. They have been conspicuous by their absence.

In this book I must explain to you, the reader, why I succumbed to that temptation. I don't expect you to understand but if my explanation and subsequent conclusions make just one young athlete change their opinion about performance-enhancing drugs then this book has been worth writing.

If I'm totally honest with myself the next eight years were not pleasant ones in the small house in Partington Close. I felt caged and restricted and my relationship with Lascell deteriorated, affecting my relationship with Mum. Poor Mum, what she must have gone through...

Like most youngsters placed in a similar situation I found a release: running and athletics. By now my speed on the streets and the track was beginning to get noticed and I progressed through the various school and minor athletics channels catching the eye of the local coaches.

It was my primary school teacher Dave May who first encouraged me to run in supervised structured races. I wasn't the world's greatest scholar and was always getting into trouble with him. My first event was a cross-country race though I don't recall where. I simply remember how much I hated it. The whole event was too long and there seemed little point. I dare say the boy that came first had a totally different take on the race but, to me, running through mud and shit across the fields and tracks of North London seemed just about the craziest waste of time and effort available. My chest burned, my calf muscles ached and, halfway through the race, I feigned injury on the root of a tree that jutted out above the ground.

I remember sitting by the side of the track thinking *shit, what's all this about.* Nevertheless I got my breath back, got a second wind so to speak and finished the gruelling three-mile circuit swearing I would never run again.

In 1991 I was introduced to my first real coach, a guy called Selwyn Philbert; he would become my coach for a number of years. Boy, was he mad! He had me doing all sorts of crazy shit. As a sprinter I had no idea what training was about so when he said run I ran, as simple as that. He was an eccentric, of that there was no doubt, and if you don't believe me ask any athlete at New River Sports Centre in Haringey about him. But Selwyn Philbert modelled me into a sprinter and believed one hundred per cent in my ability. Selwyn said some nice things about me:

"I think Dwain is going to be one of the best 100 metre sprinters Britain has ever seen."[2]

Although Selwyn was one crazy son of a bitch I can honestly say he focused me and set me on the straight and narrow. It was during my time with Selwyn that I made my mind up as to which career I would follow. I have an unenviable record when it comes to dumping coaches and people who are trying to look after me. I haven't always made the right decisions and I know I've upset a lot of people along the way. Again, I think this stems from my insecurity; my father walking out of my life didn't help. You try to think you are big and tough and that it hasn't affected you but deep down inside you know that it has.

At age sixteen my athletics career hit the big time and I became English Schools Intermediates Champion at 100m. I was nearly remembered for something far more embarrassing. I remember that during these championships I had arrived at the competition with the wrong kind of underwear. Normally I would wear boxer shorts but have thigh-length tights over them. The uniform they provided me was simply vest and shorts and I was expected to wear them. I never wear shorts! I slipped my boxer shorts underneath but there was no place for the tights. I started with a few stretches, then a fifty-metre run prior to the race beginning. I was in full flight and something caught my eye! Guess what? I was hanging out! I was so embarrassed. I had to do a quick fix with a few safety pins and half a minute later I became the English Schools Champion with my dignity intact. Phew!

It was tough remaining focused as a teenager. Believe me, I was sorely tempted to drink alcohol and run around with the girls like my friends. But I had discipline, I had a goal in sight and I was prepared to give up whatever was necessary in order to achieve it. I took some stick from my friends: no late nights, boozing, clubbing, etc. They were huge sacrifices but I wanted that goal so much. I can totally understand how Michael Jackson must have felt growing up as a child. Both our lives consisted of all work and very little play. Without realising it we were both valuable products with great potential and we had to be kept on the right path, otherwise we would fail. During my youth I can recall times when I wanted to go out with my friends and my coach would be at my door waiting for me to get ready for training. Situations like that would piss me off so badly I would end up training like a madman. But, for what it's worth, it gave me that fire an athlete needs in order to become a champion.

A few short months later I was offered a sports scholarship to Harvard University which I politely declined. Yes, dear reader, you read it right... I turned down a scholarship to Harvard University in America. The University of Presidents, entrepreneurs, industrialists, scientists, great authors and, of course, the world's greatest sportsmen. Seventy-five Nobel Prizewinners are affiliated with the university. Since 1974, nineteen Nobel Prizewinners and fifteen winners of the Pulitzer

Prize have attended Harvard. The names of the famous simply trip off the tongue: T S Eliot, Theodore Roosevelt, Franklin Roosevelt, John F Kennedy, George W Bush and Vice-President Al Gore graduated from Harvard College. The man of the moment, Barack Obama, graduated from the Harvard Law School.

So why did I turn down the scholarship?

I had heard of Harvard, of course I had, but I didn't know what the university was all about. I remember receiving a phone call from an American guy very early one morning. I was half asleep and wasn't really concentrating. I asked him what it meant and he rambled on about a scholarship and an allowance and free accommodation and it began to sound quite good. I liked the idea of America and Massachusetts. It sounded exciting... different. What I didn't realise at the time was what an opportunity I'd been given.

I'd talk it over with someone, see just what sort of university this 'Harvard' was. A couple of days later I woke up and went downstairs determined to discuss it. Mum was at work and Lascell was ready to leave for work. Within five minutes he'd gone through the door and I never had a chance to discuss it with him. I thought about someone... anyone... to talk this over with. This was a big decision. (I didn't know just how big.)

In the end I talked it over with a couple of my friends. I'll spare them the embarrassment and not name them. Friend number one had never heard of Harvard and didn't even know it was in America and friend number two told me I was beating the American top sprinters so why the hell did I need to go there anyway? I would have to start studying again too. That was the only advice I received from anyone relating to Harvard and it was good enough for me. A few days later I received an official-looking letter from Harvard University confirming the offer in writing. I threw it in the bin and two weeks later I received another call from the same guy. I told him no and I never heard from them again.

The decision to reject a scholarship for Harvard University is probably just as crazy as the decision I made to go down the illegal drugs route. Knowing what I know now about Harvard University I just can't believe I didn't investigate the offer further. It was my decision and mine alone and I know I can't blame my friend or anyone else. But again... looking back on that period of my life and the opportunities that arose, it would have been nice if I'd had someone to talk it over with.

A year later I was selected for the 100m and the sprint relay at the European Junior Championships. This was my first major title shot! I was a bundle of nerves when it came to the final but I remember thinking this was the big time. I loved everything about it: the atmosphere, the crowd and the attention of the press. The race went down to the wire. I was involved in one hell of a battle with a Welsh athlete by the name of Jamie Henthorn. I'd always remembered him as being a giant in comparison to me and the other athletes, a huge boy. As we both dipped towards the finish line there was nothing between us. We both crossed in a very respectable time of 10.41 seconds. Incredibly I was given the verdict over Henthorn. Maybe I had the bigger chest, I didn't care.

I had won a gold medal. A little later I took my second gold medal of the championships in the sprint relay. I was a happy man, two gold medals.

The same championships a year later would be a different kettle of fish altogether. I was a year older and more experienced. I had more races under my belt and probably came into the race as favourite. Perhaps my over-confidence affected my performance, I just don't know. I ran an abysmal race. I finished in fifth place with Jamie Henthorn just ahead of me in fourth place. Sprinting is won and lost in your head. The mind is so important and perhaps contributes to eighty or ninety per cent of your performance. Oh well, I thought, at least we still have the 4 x 100m relay to look forward to. I spoke too soon. We cocked the race up, almost dropping the baton. I won Jack Shit and returned home dejected and wondering what the hell it was all about. I did however swear to myself I would never again go into another race as cocky. I also wondered if my performance on the track had been adversely affected by life at home. Things were not going well. I'd managed to bite my tongue in our house until I was eighteen years of age. By this time there were simply too many adults living under one roof and, in particular, two adult males vying for the position of top dog. I'm not getting at my stepfather; I was probably as much to blame as he was. The simple truth of the matter was that we didn't get on living in the same house. It's the law of the jungle and two dominant alpha males do not mix. That's not the way I saw it at the time of course; I disliked him immensely. Everything was Lascell's fault, I was completely blameless. Yeah right.

Then it happened. There was one almighty blazing row and Lascell and I stood nose to nose cursing each other. I was eighteen, an athlete and very, very fit. Lascell didn't lift his hands to me. I'd registered a small victory but it was time to go; at that point I'd decided to move out.

I had no money or place to live. My mother was devastated. I think Lascell deep down was relieved. Me? I wanted to be free. I'd been cooped up there for far too long. I wanted to go out with my friends, have nights out, be allowed to stay over at someone's house without it being a crime of the century, all that fun stuff. But above all I wanted to mix more with girls. I'd felt stifled in that house, felt restricted in my pursuit of the fairer sex.

Once out of the house I had to grow up real fast. I needed a place to live. I was told by a friend in athletics to call someone who may be able to help me with a place to stay. He gave me his phone number. I made contact with Sir Eddie Kulukundis OBE. Sir Eddie is a member of a Greek shipping family. He once said, "My luck is that my parents were very wealthy." That may be so but he is also a very generous man with his money. Sir Eddie Kulukundis has given more than £2 million to British athletes over the last twenty-five years including some prominent names: Steve Ovett, Linford Christie, Sally Gunnell, Roger Black and Denise Lewis to name a few. It has been estimated that Sir Eddie has financially supported sixty to seventy athletes in a similar way to me as well as supporting other projects. He is also married to the actress Susan Hampshire. Some of my fellow athletes who told me about him said he was a great guy and that he helped talented athletes such as myself. I can't remember that first meeting or indeed the first phone call; all I knew was that I was not going back to live under the same roof as Lascell. I was determined and if I'd had to make a phone call to Jack the Ripper for a roof over my head then I would have done so.

Sir Eddie agreed to help me. I found a small one-bedroom flat in Finsbury Park and Sir Eddie paid my rent for a year. This helped me big time. I was able to train and attend college.

Sir Eddie, I would like to say thanks for all your help over the years. Without your support during that crucial time in my life I would never be the athlete I am today.

FAME, FORTUNE AND RECOGNITION

Life really started to change once I had left home at the tender age of eighteen. It seemed as if I had gone from being a normal kid to a mini superstar overnight. It was somewhat surreal. I never noticed a gradual progression, it just sort of happened. I noticed the way people looked at me in the street. There were other times when I would wake up, get out of bed, turn on the television and I would see my face on the box. How crazy is that! The same thing would happen with the newspapers. On one such occasion I'd gone into the corner shop and picked up the Daily Mirror, turned to the sport pages, as all sports fanatics do, and there I was in all my glory splashed over the centre pages of the section. My mouth just dropped open there and then and I became aware of fumbling clumsily in my pocket for some change. An uncontrollable grin fell across my face... Dwain Chambers, sprinter, colour photo too.

I walked up to the counter to pay for the paper desperately trying to look cool and unaffected, desperately trying to wipe the grin from my face. It was no good, it just wasn't going to happen. The shop owner looked at me then looked at the newspaper. Foolishly I'd left it open at the page. He explained he'd been reading it earlier and thought it was the young black kid that was often in his shop. He asked me, "What's it like to see yourself in the newspaper?" I was honest, I didn't try to act all matter-of-fact. I told him that it was an amazing feeling. It still is. I'm thirty years old now and each time I open a newspaper and see an image of myself I still get that buzz I once felt as a teenager. I can never understand the celebrity set that get upset with the media coverage and start lashing out at the paparazzi. After all, in the beginning that's what they wanted. Now they are up there it's not as if they can just flick off a switch. Even that ill-fated day outside the court when the press were like a pack of wild dogs I knew they had a job to do and even after the verdict they would somehow help me to pick up the pieces of my life.

As my times improved and I won more titles, the press coverage increased and I even started giving television and radio interviews. I started to notice a slight change in the way people treated me. Most of it was good but occasionally I got into an odd scrape, normally a drunk or a gang of boys wanting to take me down a peg or two. I'd never really noticed that normal service in a clothes shop or restaurant was just that... normal. I stood in the queues like the next man, suffered from an occasional bad-tempered assistant and the usual delays. Sometimes I would have to wait forever to get any sort of service. Now it was different. I was being plastered all over the BBC, Sky and local television. It seemed like every other day my picture would be in at least one or two of the national newspapers. And those same shop assistants and waiters now had a bizarre fixation to attend to me in double-quick time. I was now being attended to as 'Mr Chambers, how can I be of service, sir?' Now that blew my mind. Being spoken to like that made me feel like I was a member of the royal family. I was eighteen years of age and in my mind I'd done nothing. At first I didn't let it get to me, I felt a little stupid, self-conscious and even apologetic to the person next to me who should have been served before me. Incredibly they didn't seem to mind; it was as if they were privileged to be queue-jumped by Dwain Chambers. No, it didn't get to me at first but then I actually began to believe I was something special.

I'm ashamed to say it now but, as an eighteen-year-old kid, this had an adverse effect on my ego. Lo and behold my head grew ever larger. I was always told by my mother to love and respect your elders, and at no point should you ever act as though you're bigger or better than anybody else. I stuck to those rules as long as I could but where I could use what fame I had to get a discount on meals or get me and the boys into a club for free, boy, I played that card. I played it long and I played it hard and, boy, did it work. My fall from grace after getting caught probably brought me back down to earth and I can relate to those journalists who occasionally labelled me arrogant. On reflection I probably was, but at the time I didn't see it that way.

Occasionally the athletics got in the way of my life but I seemed to cope quite well. In 1997 I took Gold in the 100m and sprint relay at the European Juniors. I won the 100m in 10.06, a world junior record then, the first by a British sprinter since Peter Radford in 1958. Following my success in the European Championships I had run fast enough to compete in the up-and-coming World Championships which were being held in Athens. For some strange reason I was denied the opportunity to run as I was too young and inexperienced, but yet I had just run one of the fastest times in the world. I was offered a place in the heat of the 4x100m relay where we went on to achieve a bronze medal. In 1998, aged twenty, I took a silver medal in the European Senior Championship behind Darren Campbell in a time of 10.10 and was third in the World Cup in a time of 10.03.

The money was rolling in by now and for a couple of years I had a ball. I'd just turned nineteen years old when I bought my first house and my favorite car, the BMW E36 M3. To begin with, I found all the house business hard work but was determined to get things right as I realised even back then that it represented my future and that of my family. An athlete's career doesn't last forever and I was determined to make the most of it. I was getting to grips with paying bills and mortgage payments. I was never one to squander my money on unnecessary things. I made sure I paid everything on time. I paid my taxes, put some money away for a rainy day, paid my agents, and looked after my mother. However, as was to be expected, on the odd occasion I would have mad nights out with the boys. This is when all the trouble started; this is when I discovered the pleasures of the flesh.

During my off-season break which only lasted three to four

weeks I went absolutely crazy. It was as if I'd been chained up like a dog for too long. I'd been throwing myself into training and never put anything into my body that I thought would affect my performances in any way. I made sure I was in bed early and up early for training. But during those three to four weeks' break… man, I was off the leash. I would go out with the boys for a few drinks and then hit the clubs. This typically would happen three to four nights each week and if the boys didn't have the money to go out I'd see them alright. We would be getting in at six or seven the next morning; it was a good thing I lived by myself. I would never get away with that if I was living under my mother's roof. Man, she would have gone crazy.

Before we hit the clubs we would place a bet between us on who could get the most girls' numbers. At first that was all it was and we had a great giggle. On average I had the least amount of numbers as I was very particular. The other guys were sniffing around like dogs, collecting telephone numbers like confetti. From there we moved on and actually began contacting them and dating them a few days later. It became kind of addictive to me. I'd heard the expression 'addicted to sex' but before that didn't know such a condition even existed. I thought it was something invented by the media. As time went on I became more and more greedy. Girls seemed only too happy to jump into bed with me at the drop of a hat. At any one time I had at least two or three girls on the go. At times it was fun having that many women, (if not a little exhausting!!), but come Christmas and Valentine's Day or a birthday, it got really sticky. Because of all the lies I was telling these girls, it became hard for me to be in more than two places at once. It was not unusual for me to climb from one girl's bed late afternoon and be in a different bed by early evening. I would often lie to them and tell them I couldn't see them on a particular weekend because I was heading to Paris, Birmingham or Munich to run. They'd want to tag along but I told them my coach had a strictly no-girlfriend policy. In reality I was at another girl's house just a few miles away.

The more I became a familiar face the more interested girls seemed to become and the easier they were. Now this was great for my ego at the time but I also saw how devious some girls could be and how cheap they were. Most of the women I came into contact with were only interested in me because of who I was. Some, I think, genuinely liked me though at that time I just couldn't tell. I remember one girl from a bar in Covent Garden who made it clear what she wanted to do to me around the back of the bar. Let's just say it involved her mouth and a certain part of my anatomy. I didn't particularly like the girl and resisted the temptation. Nevertheless it didn't matter one bit. Within a few days one of my friends overheard her bragging to her friends about the act she had performed on the famous athlete. The ones who really stood out were the ones who wanted to sleep with me behind their boyfriend's back. I never knew any of the boyfriends but knew the girls were in relationships. Some I resisted, some I didn't, and after three or four passionate encounters they were back with their men acting as if nothing had happened. Why? I don't know; you would have to ask them. I remember being particularly taken with one girl from a nice part of Belsize Park. We made love several times in her apartment and it dawned on me I was beginning to fall for her in a big way. Then all of a sudden she went off the scene; her mobile phone seemed to be turned off constantly. Two weeks later she introduced me to her fiancé in a London club as if nothing had happened. I was gobsmacked, totally dumbfounded as she stood there and lied to her fiancé saying we'd known each other for years and were just good friends. I'm not scared to admit that she stole a little bit of my heart but at the same time taught me a valuable lesson.

I would occasionally be faced with girls who knew I had slept with their friends and they too wanted to sleep with me as they wanted a piece of the pie, so to speak. Again you would need to ask them what their reason was. Me? I was just an unmarried twenty-year-old having the time of his life.

Being a celebrity comes with a price. If you think it's all fun and games, forget it. One of our favourite places to go for a night out was a city approximately one hundred miles away from London, and noted for its nightlife, and it was there that I witnessed the other side of fame and fortune: jealousy, first-hand. One of my great pals at that time was fellow sprinter Christian Malcolm, a Welshman and already a bit of a celebrity on the scene. I loved the city, loved the people, the Welsh accent, the pretty girls who seemed to wear next to nothing even in the depths of winter and the all-round feel of a very friendly city. The people out and about in the city centre on a weekend are genuine hard-working people who definitely know how to party and have a good time. Christian had called and told us he could get us into a club not far from the city centre. I called Joel and my other friends Mark Finlay, Gerald Rackara and Emmanuel Southard and they were all up for it. We booked a few hotel rooms for the next Saturday night and off we went. Christian was true to his word and we breezed into the club for free. I can't remember Christian being there for some reason, but you'll find out why in a minute. This was the plain crazy part of being a celebrity with money; even in London we'd head for the clubs and they would allow us to walk to the front of the queue and let us in without paying. It was stupid as, once we were in, the owners just knew we would rack up a bar bill ten or twenty times the usual client. They probably put the entrance fee on the tab anyway! But... we fell for it every time. Mugged off, always. As we were escorted to the front of the queue by the doorman one or two of them seemed a little bit pissed. I thought perhaps there had been a little trouble earlier on and just shrugged it off.

And that night, did we go to town. It was a fantastic club, certainly more girls than guys and we positively revelled in the ambience of the place. We were surrounded by beautiful Welsh girls, each one of them drinking the best champagne on our tab! At one particular point I needed to visit the toilet. When I came back to the table I couldn't believe what was going down. Joel, Emmanuel, Mark and Gerald were being absolutely battered by the doorman with the odd local putting the boot in too. The girls we were with were screaming and crying; the picture resembled a Wild West scene. I ran over to intervene. Big mistake. Before I knew it I had been grabbed by four doormen and I was wrestled to the ground. Two of them held me by the shoulders and one of them tried to headbutt me as I lay on the floor.

"What the fuck are you doing?" I shouted. "I ain't doing anything." One of them smacked me in the mouth, told me to shut up. They took cheap shots at me as they held me on the ground, one of them told me to shut my rich black mouth up.

That's what it was all about.

I lay pinned to the floor as I watched at least twenty bouncers beat four of my best pals to a pulp and then it was over. The guys lay on the floor. Emmanuel looked in a bad way; he's the type of guy who would fight ten men if necessary to protect his pals but never ever looked for a fight. I was raging as they let me up. I was the only one standing. I found out later it was an orchestrated well-planned attack by a bunch of jealous or racist thugs, perhaps both. Joel explained they'd come over when I was in the toilet and accused us of emptying the place of champagne. Can you believe it? One of the doormen then accused Joel of smoking dope. A local kid was making his mouth run, calling us flashy selfish bastards, then he'd thrown a punch at Emmanuel. His fist glanced off Emmanuel's chin. Emmanuel had then hit him with a return punch that knocked the aggressor to the floor. By all accounts the doormen piled in from all angles but not at the guy who'd thrown the first punch.

I was furious and called the police from my mobile phone. The guys were actually all okay and the police arrived within a few minutes. We knew we were onto a loser as the police walked into the club and the doormen were relaying their side of the story before they even reached the table. They searched all of us there and then for drugs and, surprise, surprise, they found nothing. The doormen looked a little uncomfortable as the police looked at our injuries. The doormen were almost unmarked but they managed to wheel one of their members in front of the police with a rather bloody nose. The bastards.

I was shooting my mouth off calling them racist thugs and demanding they were locked up. The only people escorted into waiting police cars were me, Joel, Mark, Emmanuel and Gerald. I noticed one of the policemen shaking the hand of the head doorman as we were taken to the cars, flashing blue lights and all.

We were told we were being taken back to the hotel and we could file a complaint but it was not likely to go anywhere as there were more witnesses on their side than there were on ours. The police were simply out for an easy life. I wasn't having any of it, I wanted some action and I made this known in the hotel lobby. A young white policewoman, slightly built, aged around thirty, was particularly nice and tried to calm me down. She took me by the arm and I asked her if I was under arrest. She just smiled and shook her head.

"No, Dwain," she answered, "I just want to get this sorted out."

She took my arm and steered me away from the rest of the crowd, explaining that it could all be sorted out without going to the station. If I wanted to file an official complaint we could do it in the morning.

"I want to do it now," I responded.

"Fine," she said, pulling out her notebook. "What room are you in? We can do it there; no point in driving twelve miles to take a few notes."

I stood with my hands on my hips. "Great," I said, "let's do it now" and I located my room key and stomped off towards the lifts. We hardly said a word in the lift and as the door opened I made my way along the corridor to the room.

What happened next took my breath away and left a sour taste in my mouth. As we got in the room she closed the door behind me and took off her jacket. I asked her what she was doing. She replied she was now officially off-duty and this could wait until the morning.

"You're coming back in the morning?" I asked in all innocence. She loosened off her police regulation tie and wandered over to the minibar. She bent down and, opening the fridge door, located a half-sized chilled bottle of wine.

"I'm going nowhere, Mr Chambers," she replied with a smile on her face.

My mouth dropped open, any alcohol I had in my system left me right there and then. An attractive Welsh policewoman was laying it on a plate. Now, any other time I wouldn't have hesitated to pull back the sheets and get it on with the girl but tonight was different. Tonight I felt abused, battered and bruised and now, at this precise moment, I felt I was being propositioned quite simply for who I was and so that this girl could brag about her conquest in the station the next day. She didn't give a shit how we'd been treated in her home city, why we'd been beaten up for no reason at all. She wasn't interested in justice, or her duty and responsibility as a member of the police. She was a disgrace to her profession and I told her so. She left in tears. I felt good that I'd actually had an effect on her. She didn't deserve to be in the force.

We went to the station the next morning and made some statements. However it went no further.

It is common for celebrities mixing the same scene to be thrown together in relationships. I was never fortunate enough to date another celebrity, but I did stumble across another personality who was in the public eye. She so happened to be the sister of the world's most famous footballer David Beckham. Back in those days Joanne Beckham was on fire, I mean absolutely stunning. It seemed every man in London was on her case asking to date her. I was one of those men and I wanted her badly. This chase took some time, but it finally paid off. We first exchanged words and numbers in the legendary Eros nightclub which is located in Enfield, just off the A10. I remember the occasion clearly: the dance was called Sweet Harmony. (Good choice, huh?) I had Joanne's number in my pocket for a few days before I plucked up the courage to speak to her. I kept telling myself that there must have been a truckload of men trying to get through to her and by delaying the call I'd blown it. Our conversation was short but ever so sweet. Normally when you agree to go out on a date with a woman you go to a restaurant or to a bar. But this was a bit different. Between us we knew that being seen together would be bad news for both parties. At the time the paparazzi drifted in and out of our lives fleetingly. Being snapped by the paps would make headline news and they would never be off our case. We both agreed to give the restaurants and clubs a miss and meet at my house first; we'd see how the relationship went. Our relationship never went beyond casual, we were both happy with that. It lasted about five months and there would be periods where we would go two or three weeks without speaking to one another, then once again our paths would cross and we would pick up where we left off. I must admit to having special feelings for Joanne but I never ever told her. She never mentioned her feelings about me. Joanne, please forgive me if any of this gets you into trouble but I found our relationship fascinating. I had the opportunity to go to Joanne's parents' house. It was late at night and I remember driving down her street while talking to her on the phone. I had to creep up the street with my car lights off so as to not draw any attention to myself. I finally sneaked into her yard and she let me in through the front door. We kissed and cuddled for a few minutes and she led me into the hallway.

The first thing I noticed was a huge pile of papers that must have been at least three foot high by three foot wide. "What's with all the papers?" I asked her. She told me that her dad had kept every single press cutting of David since he first started playing football. I was seeing Joanne when I was around twenty-one, I'm thirty years old now and I still remember that moment. God knows how high that pile must be now! I was truly amazed at the sight of all those papers. It told me a lot about Joanne's father. I would give almost anything to have my father support and follow me with such persistence. David is a tremendous footballer and not only a national icon but recognized and loved all over the world. Apart from the odd minor indiscretion he has kept his feet well and truly on the ground. I would like to think that has a lot to do with his father's support and indeed the rest of his family. Things pretty much remained the same between Joanne and me, on and off for a while. Then we both went our separate ways.

As well as fast cars this was a period in my life when I began to take an interest in motorcycles. There is nothing more exhilarating than taking a fast bike out onto the open road. The only trouble in London is that there isn't any open road! It was in April of 2001 that I took my latest bike, a Honda CBR 900 Fireblade, down my front street. There was no need for a helmet as I was only going down to the bottom of the street, turning around and then accelerating back up towards my friends. Everything went according to plan until I came to stop. I hammered on the brakes attempting to bring the bike to a screeching halt inches from my front gate. I braked too hard and the patch of oil in the street didn't help either. I remember nothing about the accident. My friend Christian witnessed the whole incident. As the front wheel hit the oil patch it locked briefly and then connected with a dry section in the road. This had an effect not unlike a catapult as the front wheel gripped the road again. The forward momentum of the bike combined with my weight flung me over the handlebars like a stone in a catapult's pouch. Christian says I flew through the air one way as the bike somersaulted like a rocket in the other direction heading straight for my other pride and joy, my BMW 5 Series parked outside my yard. The bike smashed into the car with a sickening thud. It buried itself in the back bumper like a hatchet as every window in the car exploded. At this point I was beginning my downward spiral heading for the tarmac with my face out in front ready to break my fall. How I didn't break my neck I just don't know. Christian swore I'd killed myself as my face took the full impact and my body buckled. I slid twenty yards along the road. When the boys got to me I was unconscious and my lip was hanging off flapping around like a piece of raw steak. I was only just regaining consciousness twenty minutes later when the ambulance arrived. I spent three days in hospital with every doctor and nurse telling me it was a miracle I'd survived. Incredibly I didn't have as much as a bruise on my very valuable legs though I'd fractured my cheekbone, dislocated both shoulders as well as breaking several ribs and numerous fingers into the bargain.

I decided there and then that I wouldn't be replacing my written off Fireblade motorbike. The BMW was also a write-off and as I surveyed the damage caused by the bike I reflected on just what might have happened to me if the bike and I hadn't parted company as we flew through the air.

Kelly Holmes was another girl who crossed my path, someone I had always felt attracted to. During the summer of 2000 we had started speaking to one another. Nothing intimate, just the odd hi and bye, a few words here and there, an occasional smile. As time went on we started to converse a little more. I decided to be brave and ask her out on a date. To my surprise she said yes. We both agreed to meet halfway at a location in between Ilford and where she lived in Kent. Now, call me the ultimate romantic or call me stupid but I suggested a Pizza Hut that was fairly noticeable on a main thoroughfare through Dartford. I can hear what you are thinking… Pizza Hut for the first date, stringy cheese and french fries, the inferno with extra chillies. Not exactly the ultimate venue? Well, say what you want because the atmosphere was just perfect. The mood was nice, not too full on and not too intimate. When I come to think of it, it wasn't intimate at all but it suited us nevertheless. We got to know each other quite well. I told her about my background, my friends, my Jamaican roots, and we laughed a lot. She told me where she lived, that she lived with another female flatmate and a couple of dogs. Nothing heavier, I kind of knew that it wasn't going to go anywhere despite how much I was attracted to her. Our date lasted a couple of hours, we parted with a kiss on the cheek and that was that. Although we didn't set another date we knew we would be thrown together towards the middle of the summer, this time when we were on the Grand Prix Circuit. I still held a brief hope that we would get it on but somehow I knew she wasn't interested. I followed her career for years and always counted her as a friend, cheered her on in more races than I care to recall. When she made those personal comments about me when I was fighting my corner a little bit of me died.

A quiet roof over my head helped and in 1997 again at the European Junior Championships the topsy-turvy world of a top sprinter continued. That year I took the gold medal quite comfortably. To top it off we also won the gold medal in the sprint relay. This was my last championship as a junior and it was nice to go out on a high. But now things would get more difficult.

In 1998 I took a silver medal in the European Championship and was third in the World Cup. By this time I had joined the Nuff Respect Camp, Linford Christie's Sports Management Company. I was enjoying my running so much and, looking back on each race, the thing I remember so vividly is how consistent I was. I never seemed to be bothered with any major injuries either. Apart from an odd twinge here and there I was pretty much completely clear of injury.

The Nuff Respect camp was run professionally and clearly a company heading in the right direction. However there was one major problem. I was in the same stable as Darren Campbell. To say it was a little difficult would be an understatement. Two world-class sprinters in one camp is a recipe for disaster. Although Darren and I spoke we were never fond of each other; how could we be? We were both fighting for the same gold medal. Darren was without a doubt my greatest rival and I respected him enormously but the truth of the matter was it wouldn't work being in the same stable. Look at all the great sporting rivalries over the years. Seb Coe – Ovett, not exactly bosom buddies were they? McEnroe – Borg, Prost v Senna. "Metaphorically," Prost once said, "Senna wanted to destroy me." That was how I felt about Darren, not in a nasty way but in a sporting way. It would be the same as Ali fighting Joe Frazier and vice versa. I dare say underneath they had enormous respect for each other but in the ring they wanted to knock the living daylights out of each other.

They fought three times with two of the brawls considered among the greatest fights in history. Many say their first fight at Madison Square Garden in 1971 was one of the greatest fights in history. When they met for the third time in 1975 'The Thriller in Manila' Ali verbally assaulted Frazier to such a degree in the months leading up to the fight that Frazier remains psychologically damaged to this day.

I am still convinced it was a big mistake to bring us together.

As I started to gain a better understanding of how agents and athletes work I started to realize that my time at Nuff Respect would be short-lived. At times I felt, wrongly no doubt, that Darren got preferential treatment over me. This was only an assumption as I had no proof but things just never felt right. Despite my insecurity I choose to channel that energy into my running. Putting all those emotions aside, I must admit I did enjoy myself at Nuff Respect. I often asked Linford question after question as I was fascinated by the fact that I was sitting next to my hero! Linford was always very patient and took time to answer everything. I remain on very friendly terms with him to this day.

At the time I was being coached by Mike McFarlane and Darren Campbell was being coached by Linford. Don't get me wrong, it was the best feeling ever being a part of my hero's team but when it came down to business on the track I wanted to beat Mr Campbell! At the 1998 AAA Championships in Birmingham on July 26, the result of the 100 metres was as follows: 1st Darren Campbell 10.22 2nd Dwain Chambers 10.23. As you can see there was nothing in it. A year later I reversed the placings and beat him but was touched off for the gold medal by Jason Gardener. In the 2000 championships I had my revenge getting the gold medal in a time of 10.11. Darren came second in a time of 10.12.

Darren took the gold medal in Budapest in the European Championships while we were both with Nuff Respect. He took the gold medal in 10.04 seconds just edging me out. To some, a silver would be okay; to me it was failure. I was twenty years old but I acted like a schoolboy venting my frustration by storming through the changing area, throwing my bag and spikes around. I was so angry and must have looked so intimidating. I found out afterwards I made one of the young kit-carriers cry. At the time I never even noticed the poor boy such was my tunnel-visioned anger. I was now getting seriously pissed at being unable to transfer my junior talent to senior level. A sign of things to come perhaps? I ended the season with 10.03 in the World Cup, to me that was better than the silver medal I obtained at the European Championships. Darren may just disagree.

1999 was a better year and I was third to Bruny Surin in Nuremberg in 9.99 seconds. I was pleased with the time as I was only the second European sprinter to break the ten-second barrier after Linford Christie. This was a great feeling as I really wanted to establish myself in track and field. To run sub-ten seconds at this stage of my career was great for me especially going into the World Championships. Some quarters of the British press were making me favourite for a gold medal. That was just plain stupid as Maurice Greene and Bruny Surin were once again in the final. I often wonder if certain elements of the British press build you up

Me as a baby with Mum and godfather, Joel Edwards

Me and my childminder

Me on my 10th birthday

Christmas celebrations with the family

Yours truly and my sisters Loraine and Marie

A young me with my dad, Robert Chambers

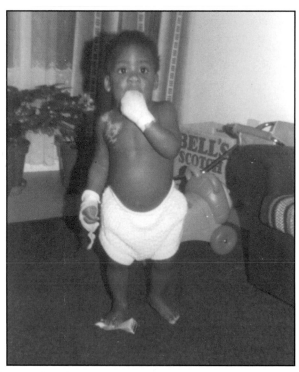

A few weeks after my argument with a kettle. Mum told me I screamed all the way to the hospital

Caught with my pants down again

in order to knock you down. That theory was proved correct when I read the papers when I got home and they were branding me a failure.

For me the form worked out correctly as I took the bronze behind Maurice (Gold) and Bruny (Silver) but I was improving as I set a new personal best time of 9.97 seconds in securing the bronze. I was now being labelled as the next Linford Christie. To me this was a dream come true and yet something niggled inside me just how far I was behind Maurice as he crossed the finish line. I had a chance for revenge in the 4x100 metre relay even though they were talking the American team up. Their line-up was legendary. First leg Drummond, then Montgomery, Lewis and Maurice Greene on the anchor. I would run the anchor for Great Britain against the world's fastest man as they were calling him. It came down to a straight fight between me and the fastest man in the world. There was nothing in it as we were both handed the baton within a hundredth of a second of each other. We were neck and neck as we both set off down the home straight and I felt good as I focused on the finish. I kicked on and became aware of that glorious feeling of leaving Maurice trailing in my wake at thirty to forty metres. I was beating the world's fastest man, I was going to take the gold medal for the Great Britain team and get my revenge. We were on the verge of becoming world champions in the space of a few seconds.

It was not to be.

Something happened that simply blew me away. At sixty-five metres I was still a metre ahead and focusing on the finish line which was tantalizingly close. On my right shoulder I became aware of Maurice breathing down my neck and at seventy-five metres he was past me. Don't ask me how he did it as I certainly wasn't slowing down. By the time he hit the line he was a metre and a half to the good and won quite comfortably. I felt I'd failed even though we as a team secured a silver medal.

Throughout my career I always believed in patience and in a belief that the times would improve as I trained harder and grew older. Looking back on that race in the relay against the Americans I started to doubt my theory just a little. Nevertheless I tried to take comfort in my times and the fact I had walked away with two medals from the World Championships against the fastest men in the world. Next year was Olympic year and just a little improvement would stand me in good stead. I tried to focus on the fact I had beaten Maurice up to seventy metres. All I needed to do was work on my stamina and the back end of the race and the gold medal would be mine.

As much as I love Australia I think I'm jinxed by that country. I finished fifth in the World Juniors in 1996, in the championships that were held in Sydney. So coming to the Olympic final in the same city I had hoped to exorcise those demons. I had suffered a little with cramp in the semi-final which didn't help but nevertheless I had managed to secure a place in the final. This was my first taste of the Olympics and I loved it. I loved the atmosphere of the Olympic village and the way the athletes are treated almost godlike. I loved the appreciation of the crowd, the opening, closing and winning ceremonies and the village as it settled down at the end of each day. This time I would have my day with Maurice Greene. He had had an unconvincing season, way below par and surely beyond his best. And as I settled into the blocks my mind drifted back to that relay race when he breezed past me at the seventy-five metre mark. I had succumbed to the sprinter's temptation of daring to think of defeat, fearing the opposition. An Olympic final is where personal bests and world records are run, where the mind must focus and propel the body beyond its limitations. But not when the game of the mind has been lost.

I didn't run well: 10.08, a dreadfully disappointing time for an Olympic final. Maurice Greene took gold yet again and I was even edged out of the bronze medal position.

As I trudged back through the village it didn't look so good, didn't feel quite as special. I vowed that the next time I came to an Olympic games I would have my head sorted out.

I was quietly optimistic as the World Championships in Edmonton loomed on the horizon in Canada in 2001. It was nearly a year since I'd just missed out on a medal at the Olympics in Sydney. The Olympics in Sydney gave me a whole new focus. I loved it, it was where I wanted to be and I was focusing all my attention on Athens 2004. Not only was I determined to get there, I was determined to get on that podium this time, bring a medal back for my country. I had geared up my training to a new level since Sydney; I was training harder and yet smarter than I ever had before. I was confident. I was even running my mouth off in the press. I can steal Olympic champion Maurice Greene's world

100m crown, I suggested. I will win the war of nerves in Sunday's final.

Two years previously in Seville I'd taken the bronze medal when Greene won gold for the second time. I thought I had what it took to destroy the fastest man the world had ever seen. "Every dog has its day," I said in a BBC interview. "Maurice has been at the top for four years, but I believe I can beat him." I rambled on; some would say I was arrogant, I didn't listen to them. "You have to have it upstairs to beat Maurice," I said. "Ninety per cent is in the mind. If the body is willing but the mind is weak then you aren't going anywhere. His whole aura can have an effect on your mental focus." I started getting personal as the interview progressed. I started saying he strutted around, played the mind games. "I will focus on myself," I said. "I've been up against him time and time again and it's worn thin. I'm not conscious of him any more. I can read him like a book. I know he's going to strut around with his tongue hanging out." I even recall being in the call room during the World Championships in Seville, minutes before we were scheduled to walk out to the track for the men's 100 metre final. I sat down on a chair as far away as possible from the rest of the other competitors. Maurice was doing his normal thing, strutting and pacing up and down. I took no notice of him. Then I noticed that each time he paced up and down he would come closer and closer to me. I decided to move to another part of the room. To my surprise Maurice still insisted on making his presence known. At this point I was on edge. I had no other alternative but to hold my ground and remain seated. Finally we were given the call to walk to the track; I was the last to leave the room with Maurice just ahead of me. I was given the perfect lane draw. I was in lane 4 and Maurice was in lane 5, but my nightmare only got worse. Maurice had purposely put his track bag in my lane and decided to prepare for his race by running in his own lane. Like a mug I politely moved his bag back into his lane, then focused my attention on the race at hand. Based on that experience I felt I had a newfound confidence. It took me a while to realise what Maurice was actually doing to me. He saw me as a threat and wanted to distract me, my concentration. Throughout the summer of 1999 I was being taught how to block out negative vibes. I carried that mental approach with me to every major championship and it seemed to be getting better and better. So you can imagine as I started to improve in races around the circuit my confidence grew; it's only natural. In hindsight I should have kept my mouth shut, but I was young. I remained confident in Sydney and failed to medal. So in Edmonton I carried the same mental approach.

Sprinting is all about confidence; it's one big mind game. I'd prepared well. Now it was time to let my body and mind take over. I went through my familiar preparation and routine as I settled into the blocks. I focused on an object one hundred metres away then looked down at the track as I took a deep breath. The familiar sound of the gun as I burst from the blocks. A sprinter knows whether they have got a good start or not, perhaps one out of three races that dream start happens. I can't explain how, but it just happens you have to let your subconscious mind take over. Everything just clicks into place. It's the greatest feeling in the world as the body seems to synchronize and a surge of confidence sweeps over you.

I'd got that great start.

But this time the confidence evaporated in the heat of the Edmonton day. By the time I'd run the first twenty metres I was done! What was happening? Within those first twenty metres the Americans Maurice Greene and Tim Montgomery had taken yards out of the field. This can't be happening, I thought to myself. I'd trained so hard and yet with only a fifth of the race run it was all over for me. If you're not in the mix within the first twenty metres it's all over.

What were the Americans doing that I wasn't? I went through the formalities forcing my body to respond but in truth I'd lost the race in my head. There is no more demoralizing feeling in a hundred metre sprint than knowing the race is lost in two or three seconds. Your legs turn to jelly, your arms feel heavy and you start to run stiff. At this point you just want to quit. All of this happens in less than a few seconds. Now, of course you don't want to quit, so you fight against your body, you fight against your mind and try and override the obvious that all the training, all the sacrifice has been wasted in a few short seconds.

I can't describe it. I've talked with premiership footballers who compare it to missing a penalty or rugby players who slice the ball wide from the middle of the pitch when attempting a drop goal from twenty yards. It isn't the same! The footballer and the rugby player have the whole game to make amends, turn the game and their own performance around. A 100 metre sprinter does not have that luxury. A 100 metre sprinter's game lasts just ten seconds and if, in that first few crucial seconds, he or she finds that they've missed that break then there is no way back.

Maurice Greene crossed the line to take the gold medal in a time of 9.82 seconds. A good time, I shouldn't have been so disappointed. But wait. As he crossed the line he broke down from a knee injury he'd been carrying most of the season.

The man ran 9.82 whilst injured? It beggared belief. What was happening? Maurice Greene has never been found guilty of using performance-enhancing drugs and I am happy to think that I was beaten by a supreme athlete who was 'un-controversial' at the time. Sadly even Maurice, although never tested positive, has not escaped untarnished. In April 2008, the New York Times reported that Greene had paid a Mexican discus thrower, Angel Guillermo Heredia, $10,000 which Heredia claimed was in payment for performance-enhancing drugs. Greene admitted meeting Heredia and making the payment, but claimed it was common for him to pay for 'stuff' for other members of his training group, and reiterated that he had never used banned drugs. He has dismissed all Heredia's accusations and continues to insist he ran clean. I hope Maurice continues to check out exactly what sort of 'stuff' it is he is supplying to his group as he commands enormous respect in the sport. I find that a staggering admission and in many ways worse than taking performance-enhancing drugs yourself. Coaches and peers and World and Olympic champions perhaps do not realize the influence and respect they command of young athletes. It's one of my major complaints that coaches, extremely influential figures, who have admitted taking and supplying drugs, were freely allowed to attend the 2008 Olympics and given the all-clear and approval by the British Olympic Association (BOA) which totally flouts the BOA's own byelaw. Don't get me wrong, I believe in my heart they should be given a second chance and they have. But why can't the BOA find that same forgiveness for me? It seems to me that the BOA enforces the rules when it suits them. On the one hand they are happy to give the benefit of the doubt to forgetful athletes who have missed three drugs tests, and at the same time they openly employ coaches who have supplied drugs in the past and praise them to the hilt when the gold medals start rolling in. The BOA have also allowed Andrew Davies to step forward and coach Michaela Breeze, the sole GB weightlifter at Beijing. Apparently we only have one weightlifter good enough to go to Beijing. Davies was one of three British athletes to make an early exit from the Barcelona Olympics after testing positive for the stimulant Clenbuterol in an out-of-competition test conducted by the Sports Council. At the Barcelona Olympics Clenbuterol, known to promote muscle growth, was not on the IOC list of banned drugs but it is now. Davies claimed he had taken the substance to relieve a tight chest. But if it wasn't a banned substance back then, why was he sent home in disgrace? It's certainly a grey area; was he or was he not a drugs cheat? The BOA have come out and defended Davies saying he was never found guilty of a doping offence. Yet he was sent home for testing positive to a drug that wasn't on the banned list at the time. Confused? Yeah, me too, and it all stinks of double standards once again.

Tim Montgomery finished second in that race and, as we all know, was found guilty of using performance-enhancing drugs, eventually being stripped of the medal. Worse still, he was even accused of supplying heroin and money laundering. He later served forty-six months in prison. Bernard Williams finished third that day and thankfully for the sport of athletics Bernard has steered clear of any drugs controversy and holds his head high as one of the clean guys and someone who hasn't succumbed to temptation. Bernard Williams won a gold medal in the 4x100 metre relay at the Olympics in Sydney and another gold at the World Championships three years later. Testimony indeed that you can run clean and still win.

Greene, Montgomery, Williams; at the time I was thinking, just what was it that the Americans had that the rest of the world didn't? Drive, determination, facilities, money? Who knows? I smiled as the BBC cameras focused in on me, but deep down I was in turmoil, emotionally wrecked. I'd given heart and soul to my sport and hadn't come anywhere near a medal position. Something wasn't right. I could have sat back, accepted that I just wasn't up there in the top bracket. It was tough, I'd trained every day of my life since I was a small boy; I wanted to be up there with the best. I needed a different coach, new training methods; someone who could improve my technique, I just wasn't progressing. I was desperate. Perhaps at this time the devil was slowly sowing the seeds for my conversion to the dark side, the dark side of athletics, a world of deceit and lying, a world where the athlete wriggles and squirms in an attempt to evade the testers, a world of double standards, of potions and pills and chemically manufactured substances... a world of drugs and a world of hell.

I sat alone in my hotel room and watched the replays of the race and the American 123 over and over again on CNN. The American network were lording it up; they constantly mentioned the 123 and the dominance of their sprinters. The more I watched the more depressed I felt. One thing I try not to do nowadays is to make rash decisions when you are in an emotional state. I was fuming. In 1999 Tim Montgomery had finished way down in sixth place. Okay in 2000 he was a part of the men's 4x100 metre relay team which went on to win gold, but Tim never took part in the individual 100 metres so I didn't consider him a threat. Then in 2001 this guy turns up for the race looking as if he'd put on a few pounds and then kicked my ass. Tim was good but there was no way in the space of two years that he could make such a dramatic improvement. Something had happened in those two years; it was as if he had discovered a strange and secret formula.

Tim and I had raced one another on numerous occasions and had been more or less running side by side. I'd win one, he'd win one, but always by the smallest margin, that's how it went. It was difficult to separate us by more than a couple of inches. I hadn't done anything wrong. I'd been happy with my efforts in training. I'd steered clear of injury and always took careful note of what I was eating and stayed away from recreational drugs and alcohol. Now Tim Montgomery was taking three metres out of me.

How? I needed some answers.

The next day I got in touch with my agent, Ayo Falola. Ayo travelled with the athletes that were a part of the Stellar Management group.

A part of me was even thinking about quitting the sport altogether though I hid that from him. "I need a new coach," I said to him in no uncertain terms. I was with Mike McFarlane at the time who'd looked after me well but I just felt I needed something more. "A change is as good as a rest," he replied cheerfully. I was convinced the likes of Tim and Co had discovered a secret formula. At that time it never crossed my mind that it was performance-enhancing substances. No. In my naivety I really believed they were on some sort of scientific training programme and diet. I never once thought about actually taking any drugs in order to beat them. I believed that I could do it naturally. I just wanted to be able to run as fast as they were. I needed to know what that secret formula was.

"One other thing," I said as he agreed to start looking for a new coach for me that week.

"Yeah, Dwain man, what is it?"

"Make sure my new coach is training the Americans."

It was a rash request with no real grounds or logic but something told me that was where I needed to go. Ayo kept his promise and booked me on a flight to Miami in January 2002. I was off to meet my new coach, ironically a Ukrainian, Remi Korchemny, with an impressive pedigree working with Kelli White, Chryste Gaines, Chris Phillips and Alvin Harrison. With a newborn optimism I boarded the flight at Gatwick. Little did I know at the time it was to be the biggest mistake I would ever make.

AMERICA

I took my friend and training partner Jonathan Barbour for the simple reason I didn't want to go alone. We touched down at Miami International Airport and, despite the warnings about US immigration procedures, we were ushered through within minutes. Little did I know at the time that the United States Anti-Doping Agency (USADA) and the Feds were watching proceedings from a blackened-out window high up in the terminal building. They were investigating a certain company called BALCO, the Bar Area Laboratory Co-operative and its founder and president Victor Conte. They were particularly interested in a certain Dwain Anthony Chambers who'd stepped off the flight from London Gatwick only twenty minutes prior. I was walking into the lion's den.

They were aware that Tim Montgomery was parting company with Victor and BALCO and it just so happened that a certain Mr Chambers was the perfect choice to fill his shoes. Little did I know that the coach of Justin Gatlin, Trevor Graham, had sent a syringe of the designer steroid THG to the USADA. You may be wondering why Trevor Graham had THG and what possessed him to then hand it into USADA. Right, where do I start? Before I had even mentioned to Ayo that I wanted to find a new coach, Trevor Graham, Victor Conte, Tim Montgomery, C J Hunter and Marion Jones were in business together. Allegedly, Victor had been supplying Trevor's group since 2000. Marion Jones dominated the Sydney Olympics and the group believed it was all down to 'pharmacology'. I figure with the right training and right mental attitude the extremely talented Marion Jones would have achieved this regardless of the drugs she was pumping into her system. Victor had explained to me the constant battles between rival coaches and athletes. Egos were flying all around the track, the coaches argued the case for their particular athletes, boasted when their athlete outperformed a rival. Trevor Graham was out to get one over on John Smith's group. They were winning everything with ease at the time. I could relate to Trevor. I too was mad at losing races against people who had no history of running fast. Tim too had become frustrated at losing and wanted to get even. Trevor and Victor had put their heads together previously and come up with a title for what they were hoping to achieve.

It was called Project World Record. The relationship was short-lived. A financial matter or a non-payment of some sort resulted in a break-up in the relationship between Victor and Trevor Graham's group. Perhaps Victor should have laid low then, knowing what he knew and, more importantly, knowing how much Trevor knew!

Trevor walked and took Tim Montgomery, one of his stars, with him. Victor still wanted to achieve his goal; Victor set out to find another athlete who could beat Tim Montgomery. There was only one man in the world who could do this and Victor couldn't believe his luck when a certain Ayo Falola was making enquiries on behalf of an athlete called Dwain Chambers.

As a result, the BALCO laboratory in California, owned by Victor Conte, would eventually be raided by agents and San Mateo County Narcotics Task Force.

We settled into a nice apartment I'd booked in downtown Miami. After taking a day or two to get over the jet lag we made our way by taxi to the stadium of the Miami Dolphins on a bright but cool January morning. It was hugely impressive as we entered the arena and, as we presented ourselves to the main office, we were handed our access all-areas pass cards and given a quick tour of the stadium by a pretty nineteen-year-old black girl with a permanent bright white toothy grin etched into her face.

As we entered the arena I recognized Korchemny no more than twenty yards away. He was standing with Kelli White and Chryste Gaines. I was in awe of this woman. She was an athlete I'd admired and respected for so long; Olympic gold medal winner in Atlanta and two World Championship golds as well. Korchemny gave a kind of staged, couldn't be bothered either way, type of wave. It was as if he couldn't really care whether he wanted to coach me or not. Who could blame him with so many stars around? At this stage I felt like a teenager wanting to make the school team. I wanted him to respect me, I wanted him to look at me the same way he looked at Kelli and Chryste.

Kelli and Chryste were more pleasant and seemed genuinely pleased to meet up with Jonathan and me.

The warm-up and light training session with Remi was fairly standard stuff. I knew he wouldn't change my technique overnight but I guess I expected a little more dynamism and at least one or two pearls of wisdom during that first encounter. We met nearly every day in that first week and got to know Kelli and Chryste quite well. Well, actually I got to know Kelli very well indeed but more of that later. Looking back on that first week I knew something just wasn't quite right. It was difficult to describe but a kind of atmosphere hung over the training session. Not an unpleasant atmosphere, don't get me wrong, but something told me I just didn't belong there. I was conscious of finger pointing and whispering. Sometimes groups of other athletes would suddenly stop speaking as I approached them. What were they talking about? I just didn't know, though now I have a bloody good idea. I discussed the training with Jonathan Barbour each night in the peaceful surroundings of our apartment. We both agreed Remi handled the sessions well and he commanded a certain respect from the athletes involved but it was hardly ground-breaking stuff. I wondered what the hell I was doing there.

It was towards the end of that week when I noticed a shift in attitude towards me. Remi appeared to take more interest in me, discussing my technique and telling me on more than one occasion that he could turn me into an Olympic champion. He told me I had a natural ability and the other athletes seemed that little bit warmer, more eager to strike up a conversation.

The real drama (though I didn't know it at the time) would take place as we left the stadium that evening.

Jonathan and I had showered and changed, shared a drink with Kelli and Chryste, then made our way back down into the stadium, out onto the grass and over to the main exit area on the far side. I was aware of a stocky bespectacled man with a thin moustache leaning against a wall. He was carrying a brown paper bag. (I kid you not!)

"Hi," he boomed in an overconfident heavy American voice. "I'm Victor Conte and I know just what you need to progress your career, Dwain."

Hindsight is a wonderful thing and I know the cynics reading this book will be saying I should have turned and walked the other way, but why? At this point I was a guest of the Americans; why shouldn't I speak to someone who was quite clearly a part of the set-up. I didn't know this Victor Conte, no one had ever mentioned him, I'd never set eyes on him and I certainly didn't know he was president of BALCO. I hadn't even heard of BALCO! I was aware of Remi standing close by.

Of course I wish I had walked the other way because something was telling me this was a little too convenient. Who was Victor Conte and what was in that brown paper bag? More importantly, how did he know I was here, how did he know my name? It must have been Remi. My coach had set up this 'accidental' meeting; how could I walk away? I looked at Remi. He said nothing but gave a barely recognizable nod. I should have walked. I wish I had because something just didn't feel quite right. I turned to Jonathan, he shrugged his shoulders. I walked over to Victor Conte and he held out a hand. We shook hands and he said he wanted to talk to me about improving my performance.

"I'm all ears, Mr Conte," I replied, "I'm all ears." I made sure I spoke loud enough that Remi would hear.

Victor Conte was in your face, Victor Conte didn't beat about the bush, Victor Conte was direct and told it how it was. He was an impressive, confident man and, sad to say, I warmed to him. I trusted him. I fell for his convincing sales pitch. Some people will find this hard to believe but even to this day I still speak with Victor Conte. Victor played a very important role in my life at the time. I was twenty-two years old. Nothing was too much trouble, no phone call inconvenient or too late at night. Victor was... still is... a nice man. In a strange way Victor acted as a father figure and I trusted him and looked upon him in that way.

Between Victor and Remi I learned so much about myself, learned about the hypocrisy in life and more so in sport and what makes the world go round. In a word, money. Having Victor around was great; he was a friend and someone who I shared everything with.

In time I became fully aware of Victor's role and his purpose in recruiting the best athletes in the world. Victor was a pharmacologist with a living to make. I suppose Victor is of the opinion that athletes should be allowed to take these banned substances in order to compete on a level playing field as long as the steroids and drugs are carefully controlled and supervised. I don't subscribe to that theory but I can understand why men like Victor and others do. Where the danger lies, claimed Victor, is when unqualified coaches and backstreet gyms start dishing out all manner of shit to young kids eager to progress.

"You need pharmacology, Dwain."

"Pharma..what?"

I wanted to know more about pharmacology, I wanted to know what would make me fly (Victor's words, not mine) and I wanted to know whether these substances were legal. I was clean, always had been, and I wanted to stay that way and yet deep down I wanted the respect of my coach, and medals. I asked Victor a dozen questions that night as the sun went down over a now cold Dolphin stadium. He didn't give any answers; he was so matter-of-fact, so cool and so relaxed. He kept telling me to talk to the other athletes, talk to my coach Remi, Chryste Gains and Kelli, Alvin Harrison to name a few. I told him I would. I was there for a month so would catch up with him again. We shook hands and he slapped me on the shoulder as I left. Strangely enough he hardly looked at Jonathan and certainly didn't approach him. Daft as it may seem, this reassured me a little. Whatever this pharmacology thing was, he wouldn't just give it to anyone. I reassured myself that he wasn't in it for the money and convinced myself it was some sort of legal vitamin supplement programme and I also believed he would only give these supplements to the best athletes under the sun. After all it was apparent he had a stableful of thoroughbreds.

It was clear this Conte fellow had respect but more importantly the respect of my coach. Not once did Remi Korchemny ever advise me against any meeting with Victor Conte. It was as clear as day: Victor was part of the team. Remi's team.

I'd sleep on it, discover a little more about pharmacology, maybe talk to Chryste and Kelli the next day. In fact, I confess to thinking about Kelli White quite a lot. I'd seen her compete on TV and felt a certain attraction towards her as she gave post-race interviews. And, yeah, I would talk to Chryste the following day as I respected the Olympic gold medallist that little bit more.

I needed to talk to someone. I rang John Regis just as soon as I got back to the apartment. John was my agent for Stellar Management, the sports management company I'd signed up to. John Regis was a 10.15 100m sprinter in his day and a man whom, at the time, I respected enormously. I took him through my day and the strange meeting with Mr Conte. I explained the pharmacology and the meeting with Chryste and Kelli. I must have sounded excited as John kept telling me to calm down. His last words were very poignant, he almost whispered them and at the time I hardly heard them, barely took any notice. But now I wish I had.

"Be careful," he said as I thought about tomorrow and what lay ahead.

"Be very careful," he repeated.

I met with Chryste the following day. I'd planned my questions carefully. What do you take? Is it illegal, harmful to the body, etc, etc. There were a hundred questions I wanted to ask but in the end

I asked just one.

"What's the deal with Victor Conte, Chryste?" I asked as she went through a series of stretches over by the advertising boards.

"He's cool," she replied. "He is a very educated man who knows what he's doing."

Chryste Gains. Olympic gold medal winner in Atlanta, two golds and a silver at the World Championships and an unblemished athletics career for nearly ten years and she thinks Conte is cool. What the hell did that mean? I should have probed, should have asked more, but no. Dwain Chambers, the man eager to progress, eager to please his newly appointed coach was happy with an answer that meant Jack Shit. But it was just the sort of answer I wanted to hear. It was good enough for me.

I'm sure other people have been in similar situations, happy with half answers, not wanting to probe further in case you hear an answer you don't want to hear. Maybe a mother not wanting to ask her teenage daughter whether she is having sex with her boyfriend or a parent not wanting to raise the subject of drugs with their children, just in case they get an honest answer that will tear their life apart. That's what it was like for me. I didn't take it any further because I didn't want anyone to answer me honestly, tell me I would be cheating.

Later that day I telephoned Victor and said I wanted to talk further. The line seemed strange, a sort of clicking noise every now and again. Victor apologised, said he would get the engineers to take a look at it. The engineers had already taken a close look at Victor's phones, only these engineers weren't working for the

United States Telecommunications Authority.

I was nervous before the meeting with Victor in his plush apartment. Again I had the list of questions ready as I had had with Chryste. I wanted some answers, my head was full of doubts. Victor talked. He was mellow and composed, and spoke in a soft voice and put me at ease. However this time I was ready to ask the questions that were tearing me apart.

He explained at that second meeting the benefits of a new designer steroid called tetrahydrogestrinone (THG). He used the word steroid openly. I should have got up and walked, I almost did. But again, ever the salesman, he calmed me down. He explained that these steroids simply aid recovery. He explained that this new drug allowed the athlete to train more often and harder. He called it The Clear and The Cream.

"Is The Clear and The Cream illegal?" I asked.

"It's undetectable."

"Is it banned?"

"The Clear is not on the prohibited list and neither will cause a positive test."

A warning bell triggered in the distant reaches of my brain. "What do you mean by that?"

"It isn't on the list of banned substances, it's a recovery agent."

That word again.

I sat in silence for a second or two.

"Isn't that cheating, Victor? I've been clean all my life."

Victor leaned back in his fat leather chair. He seemed to take a second or two to compose himself before delivering his answer.

"They're cheating you, Dwain." He smiled. "You're a very talented athlete but you are not competing on a level playing field, my friend. Most of the top sprinters are on steroids; every time you race against them, you are at a disadvantage."

I thought the penny had finally dropped. It all started to make sense: these athletes running so fast and remaining so consistent throughout the season. I knew that the vast majority of athletes were on something to help them train harder. I just never knew what or how they were doing it.

I thought back to that race in Edmonton and I thought of Chryste and Kelli. Were they on it too? Was I being stupid? I thought about the times I had trained for hours on end, how I'd pushed myself so hard I just wanted to curl up in a ball and die. Then to come back the following day after I'd just pushed my body to its limit and be faced with an intense gym session, that's the last thing I wanted to do. It was natural; the body needs a recovery period. Rest. These steroids counteracted that feeling, helped the man or the woman that wanted to progress, to train even harder to do just that.

This man in front of me, this pharmological expert, is telling me it's undetectable and it isn't even on the banned list.

"How could this be possible?" I asked. "I know how often I get tested, it would be impossible to cheat the system."

"Well, Dwain," Victor replied with a knowing grin, "the system allows people to cheat."

"How?" I asked.

"People in sport have been cheating the system since before you were even born. It's a business and the authorities know it.

Sponsors will only be attracted to athletes that are showing good potential, such as yourself and athletes that are winning. Dwain, you're a smart man and you've not had the best of races over the past few summers. You're losing to people who are taking performance-enhancing substances. You know how hard it is to race at the top level week in and week out. Recovery is the key. A normal athlete who is clean and training very intensely leading up to a weekend's meet will have to wait a week to ten days in order to recover and come back fighting."

Victor stood up and took a slow deliberate walk around the room before speaking again. I sat back mesmerised.

"An athlete that is using drugs will recover within two to three days. While you are resting, Dwain, the other athletes on drugs are racing and winning medals and making money for themselves." He smiled at me. "And their earning capacity is increasing every time they run."

I sat there listening with my mouth wide open. I couldn't believe what I was being told. Victor went on to tell me that people have the wrong impression about steroids. Many think steroids make you run faster while on the drugs, but they tend to cause muscle tightness and sprinters actually only run freely once the steroids have worn off, which takes ten days to two weeks. Steroids simply allow you to recover a lot quicker. Sure they help to build muscle, but here's the real truth: STEROIDS ENHANCE RECOVERY, WHICH ENABLES A DEEPER TRAINING LOAD AND THAT IS WHAT MAKES AN ATHLETE RUN FASTER. Whilst I will never take anything like that again, there seems to be a misconception that athletes using drugs are on an easy route to a gold medal in the Olympics. They are not. It still takes a tremendous amount of work.

Victor explained that THG would allow an athlete to train more often and with more intensity, which would ultimately make me run faster during competition.

"Athletes realise the potential of using drugs, Dwain," he said. "They are aware of the punishments that will be enforced upon them should they get caught, but it has been made so easy for athletes to cheat the system almost anyone can do it. The authorities administer most of their tests when they know the athletes won't be taking anything. There are over two hundred countries that compete under the IAAF rules yet only about twenty-five of those have independent drug testing federations. Now you tell me how many athletes are cheating, Dwain."

The conversation had taken a bizarre new twist. We weren't discussing the merits of cheating or the benefits of performance-enhancing drugs or the damage they could do to a young athlete and I wasn't asking the questions I had wanted to ask. Here was Victor Conte letting me in on his theory that the authorities knew exactly what was going on and actually making it possible, even easy to play the system. I was dumbfounded as Victor continued.

"The system allows those athletes that are not from one of those twenty-five countries to blatantly use drugs and they are allowed to compete at the same events as you are. As a British athlete, Dwain, you are probably at a greater disadvantage than any other country in the world." He laughed. "You must provide your federation with your whereabouts, and a drug tester will turn up unannounced and test you any time of the day or night."

Experience told me that Victor was right.

"And yet countries such as Jamaica haven't even got a drug testing programme," he announced shrugging his shoulders. "Even in countries where they test regularly there are ways to easily get around the system."

He explained the duck and dive system where an athlete must provide a mobile telephone number where they can be contacted twenty-four hours a day. A tester will call the athlete and notify them of their intention to test them. If the athlete suspects a trace of a banned substance is still in their body then he or she fills up their voicemail to capacity. The tester can't then leave any messages advising the athlete that they are to be tested. I had heard about this dodge before but because I'd never contemplated taking drugs I didn't realise how easy it was.

"Only the stupid athletes get caught."

His words would become prophetic in eighteen months' time. Victor spoke for at least half an hour on how flawed the dope-testing regime was and how it was flawed deliberately to enable people to cheat. This was jaw-dropping stuff and I took it all in.

I wanted to know why he had chosen me. I plucked up the courage and asked him.

"Why me?"

His answer was simple: there were no other athletes out there who he believed were better. Victor said I had the potential to be an Olympic gold medallist. He could make me the fastest man in the world.

"Dwain, this is your calling," he said. "It's time to step up. We want you."

I admit I was flattered and yet this THG thing still bugged me.

"How can it not be on the banned list?"

"Dwain," Victor replied, "it's very simple. We are now in the twenty-first century; science has progressed by leaps and bounds. The anti-doping agencies have a database with most of the drugs known to be used in sport. As a scientist, I understand how things work within the world of drug testing and this has enabled me to develop undetectable drug programmes. Chemist Patrick Arnold was the creator of The Clear or THG. He created THG by using a combination of the steroids trenbolone and gestrinone, which resulted in tetrahydrogestrinone or THG. It is kind of like the way they graft a lemon tree with a lime tree and get a lemon/lime tree. All anabolic steroids are simply modified testosterone molecules. THG is a new anabolic steroid that is not on the prohibited substance list. When Patrick provided me with the first batch of THG, I determined that it was too strong and may possibly cause side effects including muscle tightness, so I diluted it by fifty per cent. Now you can understand how this type of anabolic substance would go undetected as it is not known to the relevant anti-doping agencies. It is also important to understand that there is a rather large list of performance-enhancing drugs that are undetectable by the testers."

"What do you mean, undetectable?"

"The dopers will likely always be one step ahead of the testers,

Dwain. The testers can only ban what they find to be an illegal performance-enhancing substance and THG is a newly created anabolic agent that they do not even know exists at this time. Each of the approximately thirty known anabolic steroids tested for have what is called a mass spectrogram fragmentation pattern similar to a fingerprint. If they don't find an exact match, then they do not report a positive drug test. And I'll tell you something else, if the scientists working for the testers discover THG tomorrow, it will not be long before rogue chemists have discovered a new steroid and athletes taking THG will simply switch to another new one that is not on the banned list."

I sat in silence for at least two minutes. Victor said nothing. He just let me think about what he had said. He had explained things so simply. What was I thinking? I'll tell you what I was thinking. I was thinking that I had been conned and cheated; I felt as if I'd been mugged off since I'd started competing as a junior. At that point in the proceedings I was seething and I was thinking how many medals and championships I'd been cheated out of because the men who I was running against had been able to train harder, longer and smarter than me, thanks to the help of THG and other undetectable substances.

What was the problem? I thought back to that stupid advert where the young man fails his exams and is speaking to Maureen Lipman, his aunt, on the phone. He tells her he has a qualification in sociology. In the 'it's good to talk' advert for BT, Maureen Lipman declares her nephew has an 'ology'. If he has an 'ology' he is a scientist, she says. Almost comically I was thinking because

Victor Conte had an 'ology' he was a scientist. I looked over his shoulder at the wall behind him, his wonder wall with his certificates and diplomas. This man is a scientist, I thought. I now respected the man sitting in front of me and I was seriously considering going onto his programme. At that particular moment a wave of nausea swept over me. I thought back to my recent races, to the races where I'd been pipped at the post or certain races where I'd been beaten out of sight. Victor finished by reeling off an impressive list of clients in baseball and American football too.

I told him I'd sleep on it. But yes, I admit it, at that moment in time I knew my decision boiled down to running clean or cheating, whatever it was Victor was saying about recovery agents and undetected substances. I was considering putting something extra into my body, I justified even thinking about it, convincing my mind that it was not going to give me an edge but it would simply level the game.

I'd crossed the line, the point of no return; I was actually contemplating cheating. And I was justifying my decision to even think about cheating because everyone was telling me it was the others cheating me. The thought of being caught for drugs played on my mind for days, and as much as I tried to convince myself that I'd never need drugs to win, the fear of being left behind whilst all the other athletes continued winning played a huge part in my decision to take drugs. From the moment I stepped foot in America my one and only focus was to work on my technical aspects and a better training regime as I believed that to be the weak link in my chain.

Victor had opened my eyes. The quest to improve my technique had gone out of the window; he'd convinced me that my technique wasn't the issue.

It is worth noting that at the time of going to publication, five thousand Olympic dope tests have been recalled amid rumours that a new designer steroid has been discovered. Nearly half the countries that participated in the Beijing Olympics failed to tell organizers where their athletes were so they could be drug tested outside of competition. A report issued by independent observers for the World Anti-Doping Agency said 102 of 205 countries represented did not provide Olympic officials with information about their athletes' whereabouts. It is each country's responsibility to notify testers of its athletes' whereabouts during the Games. The countries were not reprimanded during the Games but were to receive written notification afterwards.

My mother used to say to me, "The grass isn't always greener on the other side." I never really understood what that meant until the day I got that dreaded phone call saying I had failed a drug test. Despite all the negative thoughts that were going through my head, the one defining factor that continued to rewind and play again was the words that came out of Victor's mouth. He smiled as he said it, placed a hand on my shoulder and squeezed gently.

"You will be able to run to your full potential; you will go from being number five in the world to number one."

The thought of being number one in the world surpassed

everything. The thought of being caught seemed insignificant and anyway Victor had reassured me it wouldn't happen. I couldn't help but think about all the glory, how happy my country would be, my friends and family, to see my mother's happy face, knowing that her son was the fastest man in the world. I would be able to earn enough money so I would be able to look after my mother. It's only right that I return the favour. She had been looking after me and my sisters all her life. Now it would be me in the driving seat. I just wanted to make my mother proud.

I think it was at that meeting that I caved in. I can't ever justify my decision to cheat, and I won't ever try to. I'd been an honest athlete all my life up to then but, during that month in America where I succumbed to temptation, my whole life had been turned upside down. Everyone, and I mean everyone, was telling me the stories of some of the top guys in the world and how they'd been on the gear at some point or another. They told me how they would fill up their mobile phone voicemail box and that some drugs such as EPO disappeared from the body within ten hours. And, to top it all, here was Victor telling me the substance he was prescribing wasn't even on the banned list.

I came out of the meeting a lot wiser than when I'd gone in, but my head was even more messed up than ever. I also took it upon myself to ask other athletes about drug use within sport and they insinuated that a vast majority of athletes, especially those who were consistently successful, were on some form of undetectable substances, substances that had not made their way onto the banned list as yet.

The apartment I'd rented for a month had internet access. I spent that night surfing the net and, in particular, Wikipedia. I checked out my great rivals and their achievements and their personal bests. I found a link similar to this one there:

http://en.wikipedia.org/wiki/List_of_sportspeople_sanctioned_f or_doping_offences

It contains a list of sportspeople who have been involved in doping offences: either those who have been found, or have admitted to, taking illegal performance-enhancing drugs or prohibited recreational drugs, or have been suspended by a sporting body for failure to submit to mandatory drug testing. I scrolled down the list and to my astonishment it contained nearly seven hundred and fifty names. Mr Conte and his clients were right: this was bloody huge and these were only the athletes who had got caught!

I called Jonathan over. We sat with open mouths as I took him through the names in alphabetical order. Little did I realise the name Dwain Chambers would soon be added to that list. I searched further. At the Summer Olympics eighty-three athletes had been found guilty of taking illegal performance-enhancing substances and, where appropriate, had had their medals taken away.

Although two American athletes were found taking illegal substances at the Barcelona Olympics in 1992 not one American athlete has tested positive at any Olympic Games since. Well done

America; it certainly looks as if whatever the Americans have been doing since 1992 to 'clean' their athletes up has certainly worked. Yeah right! Again, Victor's bold statement about the drug being undetectable carried a lot of weight.

I went to sleep with those comforting thoughts. I was in America, land of the free; Chryste thinks Conte is cool and not one American had tested positive in an Olympic Games since Barcelona.

The following day the training resumed and I had more contact with my fellow athletes. Remi was always there; even if he wasn't getting involved in the training and coaching he was always there, as if he didn't want to let his athletes out of his sight. Despite his conviction and subsequent ban I'll go on record as saying that Remi was a good coach. In many ways he was like another father figure to me. In the cold light of day I now know that in a way Remi and Victor were kind of 'grooming' me and part of me is angry with them, but at the time it didn't seem like that at all.

More so now than before, I wished I'd been a lot smarter with my decision-making, but you have to understand I had no one outside of my athletics circle to talk to. Those in my circle, my peers, were already on performance-enhancing substances and I had already got in too deep just by entertaining the thought of taking them. I had no real opinions on the rights and wrongs of taking drugs; up until then I hadn't even thought about it and it certainly wasn't ever discussed in the changing rooms and stadiums around the UK among the top athletes.

The only people I could talk to were the same people who were encouraging me to take drugs. I have no idea what or where I would be if I hadn't taken drugs. I may well have retired through frustration at losing who knows what. I had to make a decision and I had to make it fast! Everyone I spoke to in America who was in the know was totally convinced that THG was untraceable and one hundred per cent sure that the majority of athletes in the top performing countries were on it too. On more than a dozen occasions it was put to me that we were merely redressing the balance.

My head was in turmoil: I wanted someone to talk to, someone to understand what I was going through but I had no one. I don't want to bleat on and I'm not going for the sympathy vote here but there's something I must get off my chest. There are times in your life when you need a father to talk to, a father to be there for you. A father is a very important role model to a son and someone whose advice I would think carries a lot of weight. My father left me when I was still in nappies and although my stepfather Lascell filled his shoes he was not my father.

I envied one thing about Sebastian Coe and that was the relationship he had with his father Peter. (Sadly Peter passed away during the Beijing Olympics.)

Peter Coe was a true father and Seb's full-time coach. He guided Seb through every stage of his athletics career offering advice on training, diet, tactics, everything. He was at Seb's side every step of the way at every race and not once did Coe ever think of replacing him. Had Seb Coe been in my shoes in America his father Peter would have been there for him. Seb Coe documents well that if anyone had even mentioned drugs in front of him, his father would have seriously hurt them.

I had no one, no father, and my family thousands of miles away on the other side of the Atlantic Ocean, as was my agent. Sure I could have talked to Jonathan but he was not my father and I never found it in my heart to burden him with that sort of pressure.

Part of me wanted to walk away, get on the next plane to London and be done with them. But part of me wanted to win, win at all costs. I had two gremlins on my shoulder and the one shouting the loudest was shouting 'get even'.

One incident in America unnerved me and looking back on it I should have seen the danger signals. I was training with Remi and ended up on the far side of the track as I slowed down. Tim Montgomery was there looking none too pleased.

He snarled at me, "Yo, Dwain! You with that nigger Conte?"

Now at this point let me explain to you, my readers, that the word nigger is used freely in some parts of the States. A nigger can be black or white, good sometimes, occasionally bad. On this occasion Victor Conte was not in Montgomery's good books.

"Don't go anyway near that cocksucker Conte. Let me tell you, Chambers, he's bad news."

I didn't know it at the time but there was one hell of a row brewing between Montgomery and Conte. Tim's partner Marion Jones was involved too and of course Trevor Graham, Montgomery's coach. The row was over money (surprise, surprise). I don't want to get involved in any accusations and I've touched on it earlier. There are plenty of theories flying around cyberspace, just Google Trevor Graham, Victor Conte and you can read about it till the cows come home. I don't know who owed who and how much it was but the disagreement was so big and had festered for so long that Trevor Graham wanted to bring Conte and BALCO into the open. There was also another theory flying around but one I'm not so sure I believe. Like I say get Googling and read all about it.

Some people including Victor alleged it was Graham who prompted the BALCO inquiry when he sent an anonymous sample of THG to the United States Anti-Doping Agency. Who knows what Graham was thinking and how much he wanted to protect his own athletes and indeed his own income. Some say Smith and Graham decided to turn in the THG sample as a noble deed. Others say it was purely as a result of competitive rivalry. Only Trevor Graham can answer that question; you, the reader, can make your own mind up.

At the time Tim Montgomery didn't elaborate on why I should stay away from Conte. Perhaps he knew that the syringe had been sent. He had probably taken a fairly well-educated guess that I was clean and maybe didn't want me dragged down with the rest of them. I don't know. I just wish Tim Montgomery had elaborated more. I wish he'd been a bit more constructive and persuasive instead of simply hurling obscenities in the direction of Victor. I wish Tim Montgomery had said, "Piss off out of here, Dwain, because you are about to be dragged into the biggest drug scandal in sport in living memory." He didn't and the rest, as they say, is history.

The brief conversation with Tim unnerved me as I lay wide awake that night. Obviously I didn't know that Graham had sent in the syringe but now, looking back on it, I'm fairly certain Montgomery and certain others did. My opinion only. I'd like to think that Tim Montgomery was trying to give me a warning. One thing is for certain though: THG at the time was undetectable and unless Graham had not sent in that sample thousands of athletes would still be running today under the influence of the steroid. (Many still are.) It took the USADA time to discover the chemical make-up of the drug and to find a way to test for it. Therefore we can safely say that the steroid at the time was undetectable and used by the masses. As soon as it was announced that the drug was detectable, the majority of athletes ran to the dump to get rid of the evidence. But who's to say there isn't another steroid out there right at this very moment, similar in chemical make-up, undetectable and with the same performance-enhancing qualities. It makes you think, doesn't it?

Montgomery was the first person I'd heard during my time in America really bad-mouthing Victor. He had to have a reason. I tried to focus on more pleasant thoughts as I drifted off to sleep. The image of Kelli White filled my head.

I had admired Kelli White from way back in early 2001. Until I met her I'd only seen images of her on television. I had a very strong attraction to her, of that there was no doubt. When I had the opportunity to go and train in America I never realized that I would be working alongside her, training with her every day. She was even prettier in the flesh. The first time we touched base with one another was when I arrived in Miami during the month of January 2002. I met Kelli one day, then Victor and Remi the next. We never spoke much during that period, just the odd hello and goodbye. I confess to being a little shy and overawed. I wanted to talk to Kelli badly, in order to let her know how I felt about her and just at the point I thought I'd summoned up the courage, I was told she was already in a relationship. I left America without declaring my feelings for Kelli and kept telling myself she was strictly off limits.

I returned to San Francisco towards the latter part of February. This is when I was introduced to my full athletics and supplement programme. I detail the programme fully in the next chapter. I was also given a brief insight as to who else was involved, i.e. my training partners Kelli White, Chryste Gaines and Alvin Harrison. As time went on, I became more and more familiar with associating certain athletes with certain drugs. Victor would encourage me to talk to the other athletes on the programme. He suggested that I talk to the others about how they coped with all the physical and mental stresses of the programme. I made Kelli White my main confidante and the attraction grew by the day. One morning we had to all meet up at the golf course down in Oakland in order for us to do our hill sessions. This involved simply sprinting up inclines two hundred metres long. It was tough work and nobody, but nobody, enjoyed this part of the training. Midway through the session I asked Kelli, "What do you think about Victor?" It was meant as an icebreaker, a general chat about the man I'd grown to trust and like. The response was vicious: "Don't mention that motherfucker's name to me!"

Kelli turned her back on the group. What had happened to change her opinion of Victor? Up until that point she always seemed to have a certain respect for him.

An embarrassing silence ensued, I expected someone to back him up, defend him a little, but one by one they walked off in different directions. I remained where I was, I was conscious of my wide open mouth. I was shocked by her outburst and had never heard her swear before. What the hell was all that about, was the thought that first came to mind. I shook my head in disbelief, asked her to explain, but she just mumbled and walked off.

Later that afternoon I went to see Victor about some things and to also ask him about his relationship with Kelli White. I went into detail with Victor about what Kelli had said and how she was acting. Victor just shrugged his shoulders and explained that there was a little tension between Kelli White and Chryste Gaines. He called it healthy competition. Although Kelli and Chryste were training partners, they were also rivals. I knew what he was talking about as I'd experienced the same thing with Darren Campbell at Nuff Respect. They both worked with Victor under the coaching instruction of Remi. When confronted with any questions relating to Victor in front of other people they would react with fierce denials. Everybody knew that nearly all the athletes with Remi were on the programme with Victor too and yet it seemed that Kelli and Chryste didn't want to be associated with him. (In public that is.)

Kelli and I became closer; we found ourselves thrown together on many occasions, at times it seemed to be fated. We were comfortable in each other's company and I had heard from a 'source' of mine she was no longer dating. She had had a bust-up with her boyfriend. We chatted for hours about something or nothing just glad of a shoulder to lean on. Inevitably we got onto the subject of drugs. We were sworn to secrecy so talking about it with someone else on the programme took the hugest weight off both our shoulders. During our summer training which lasted from March until May of 2002 Kelli White and I became very close friends and we began dating. We kept this secret from the rest of the group particularly because Kelli's ex was well known to the group being an athlete himself. Most of our dates took place at her apartment or in my hotel room and although we went out together for dinner or a drink downtown we never displayed any public shows of affection for each other. At last the ice was broken and we spoke about our feelings for one another. It was all very healthy and as athletes I think it did us both good: we were motivating each other on and off the field. Talking and training alongside Kelli helped improve my mental approach during my time in America and it also helped me deal with this new regime that I was so unsure of. Later, as I opened up to her about the torment of injecting myself with EPO, HGH and insulin as well as suffering with cramps, I thought that I was the only athlete that felt saddened by what I had lowered myself to doing. We both agreed that we hated having to cheat to win but we realized that our competitors were doing the same thing. Walking away from the sport we both love was never an option. However our support for one another helped pull us through the constant nightmare of this dark, dark world of drugs.

Our close relationship would last throughout the winter of 2002 and the entire 2003 season. Although fun at times we had some major bust-ups. Being on drugs made me and maybe Kelli and other athletes who were on the programme quite snappy. At times we became hot-tempered and very aggressive towards one another, especially when things became more and more competitive within the group. It was during this period I noticed a change in myself, Kelli and the other individuals. At times we would argue with one another for no particular reason; then the next day things were fine again. I never liked to admit it at the time, but it was as if we had been cursed with a Doctor Jekyll and Mr Hyde personality.

PLANET PHARMACOLOGY

I've been asked many times when I finally took the decision to take THG, Tetrahydrogestrinone. It was towards the end of that first visit to America. As the time for the flight back home drew nearer I had it in my mind that I was missing an opportunity. Victor had talked the talk but was not putting me under any pressure. He made it clear that he could assist me in my performances but also made it abundantly clear that the decision was down to me. My only criticism of our discussions is that he didn't once say we were cheating the sport. He always made it clear that we were simply getting even, competing on a level playing field. Victor did not call me every day or put me under any pressure whatsoever as has been suggested in some quarters of the press. This was a far cry from the days where the East German coaches and secret police coerced young athletes into the murky world of anabolic steroids or the Russian and Chinese governments took talented small children away from their parents in the middle of the night to attend secret gymnastic camps in the middle of nowhere. This was a pharmacologist talking to a responsible adult (some may question that!) and allowing him to make up his own mind. It was a week to go before my flight left for London. I was twenty-four years of age and had a decision to make. The 'get even' gremlin was shouting ever louder. I read about arguably the most influential US athlete of all time, Carl Lewis. He too had been caught up in a drugs controversy, a cover-up, some may say. In 2003, Dr Wade Exum, the United States Olympic Committee's Director of Drug Control Administration from 1991 to 2000, supplied pamphlets of documents to *Sports Illustrated*. They revealed that no less than one hundred American athletes who had previously failed drug tests should have been prevented from competing in the Olympics at   Seoul in 1988. They were cleared to compete by the United States Olympic Committee. Among those athletes was Carl Lewis.

Carl had tested positive three times before the 1988 Olympics for illegal substances and had been banned from the Seoul Olympics and from competition for six months. The US Olympic Committee incredibly found in his favour and overturned the decision. The positive results allegedly occurred at the Olympic trials in July 1988 where athletes were required to declare on the drug-testing forms over-the-counter medication, prescription drugs and any other substances they had taken by mouth, injection or suppository. It was claimed Carl did nothing wrong. There was never any intent, it was claimed; Carl Lewis had inadvertently taken the banned stimulants in an over-the-counter herbal remedy.

The World Anti-Doping Agency's chairman, Dick Pound, dismissed Lewis's defence of no intent as a joke. Former athletes and officials came out against the USOC cover-up and there was a national yet controlled uproar.

Carl Lewis won two golds and a silver in Seoul in 1988. The medals have not been rescinded and stand to this day.

I had one final check to make, one last thing that would tip the balance: I needed to check out THG and the famous 'banned list' that I was hearing so much about. Some of you readers may be forgiven for thinking that we athletes have an awareness of what to avoid and a distinct knowledge of the 'banned list'. We haven't. In fact it's more worrying than that. I'll go on record and state here and now that, prior to meeting up with Victor, I'd never even set eyes on the 'banned list' from the World Anti-Doping Authority (WADA) let alone studied it in detail. Why should I? I was clean and under the impression that normal foods and drinks on the standard supermarket shelves were clean too. I thought that food and drink would be regulated, checked and double-checked by some organisation before they found their way into the shops. I even had a train of thought that these regulating authorities might get some sort of directive from sporting bodies such as UK Athletics.

Don't you believe it.

It boils down to the lone athlete checking it out. It's up to the athlete to check every ingredient on a can of coke, a bottle of lemonade or a cold cure drink or a pick-me-up. The responsibility lies with the athlete and ignorance is no defence. It's simple enough, I suppose; just check the ingredients against substances on the banned list and if they match up don't take whatever it is you are considering taking.

So as I sat in the hotel reception on the internet, I keyed in WADA. I searched through the site and, sure enough, the 'banned list' was there in black and white. *No excuses*, I thought as I waited for the page to load. If THG was on there I was out of America on the very next flight and Victor Conte was history! The internet connection was slow but eventually it began to load. I remember wondering how many substances were actually on there; thirty, forty perhaps? More? Maybe I could memorise them and then every time I picked up something in a shop or was given a new drink by someone I could simply check the label and recall the banned substances in my head. Yeah... that was it.

The WADA 'banned list' page loaded.

Reproduced below is a copy of the 2008 banned list from WADA; the 2002 version was similar except that THG was **not** present on that list.

As part of my determination and resolve to remember the substances I began writing them down.

Androstendiol
androstendione
bolandiol
bolasterone
boldenone

boldione (androsta,)

calusterone

clostebol

danazol, (hydroxyandrost, isoxazole)

dehydrochlormethy

testosterone (desoxymethyltestosterone)

drostanolone

ethylestrenol

fluoxymesterone

formebolone

furazabol

gestrinone

hydroxytestosterone

mestanolone

mesterolone

metenolone

methandienone

methandriol

methasterone

methyldienolone (methyl-1-testosterone)

methylnortestosterone

methyltrienolone

methyltestosterone

mibolerone

nandrolone

norandrostenedione

norboletone

norclostebol

norethandrolone

oxabolone

oxandrolone

oxymesterone

oxymetholone

prostanozol

quinbolone

stanozolol

stenbolone

tetrahydrogestrinone* (not on 2002 list)

Clenbuterol

selective androgen receptor modulators (SARMs)

tibolone

zeranol

zilpaterol

Forty-eight 'banned' performance-enhancing substances. I wondered whether it was physically possible to remember these names especially when some of them seemed so similar. I was about to get a shock as I scrolled down further. There were more substances and drugs on the list and a 'get out of jail card' for the testers that seemed to be saying that even if a drug WASN'T on the list an athlete could still be banned if the drug was said to have a similar biological effect. It read:

Trenbolone and other substances with a similar chemical

structure or similar biological effect.

It then listed more drugs:

endogenous AAS
androstenediol
androstenedione (androst-4-ene-3,17-dione)
dihydrotestosterone
prasterone (dehydroepiandrosterone, DHEA)
testosterone
androstane-5a
androstane-3a,17-diol
5a-androstane-17a-diol
5a-androstane-3ß,17ß-diol
androst-4-ene-3a,17a-diol
androst-diol
androst-4-ene
androst-5-ene-androst-5-ene androst-5-ene-androstenediol
androstenedione (androst-5-ene-3,17-dione)
epi-dihydrotestosterone
hydroxy-androstan-17-one
hydroxyl, androstan-17-one
19-norandrosterone
19-noretiocholanolone

At this point I laid my pen down and stopped writing.

WADA gives detailed explanations which suggest that even if a certain substance isn't on the 'list' it may be considered to be 'on the list' if it closely resembles something which is on the list. At least I think that's what the paragraph below is explaining... I think...

Where an anabolic androgenic steroid is capable of being produced endogenously, a Sample will be deemed to contain such Prohibited Substance and an Adverse Analytical Finding will be reported where the concentration of such Prohibited Substance or its metabolites or markers and/or any other relevant ratio(s) in the Athlete's Sample so deviates from the range of values normally found in humans that it is unlikely to be consistent with normal endogenous production. A Sample shall not be deemed to contain a Prohibited Substance in any such case where an Athlete proves that the concentration of the Prohibited Substance or its metabolites or markers and/or the relevant ratio(s) in the Athlete's Sample is attributable to a physiological or pathological condition.

In all cases, and at any concentration, the Athlete's Sample will be deemed to contain a Prohibited Substance and the laboratory will report an Adverse Analytical Finding if, based on any reliable analytical method (e.g. IRMS), the laboratory can show that the Prohibited Substance is of exogenous origin. In such case, no further investigation is necessary.

When a value does not so deviate from the range of values

normally found in humans and any reliable analytical method (e.g. IRMS) has not determined the exogenous origin of the substance, but if there are indications, such as a comparison to endogenous reference steroid profiles, of a possible Use of a Prohibited Substance, or when a laboratory has reported a T/E ratio greater than four (4) to one (1) and any reliable analytical method (e.g. IRMS) has not determined the exogenous origin of the substance, further investigation shall be conducted by the relevant Anti-Doping Organization by reviewing the results of any previous test(s) or by conducting subsequent test(s).

When such further investigation is required the result shall be reported by the laboratory as atypical and not as adverse. If a laboratory reports, using an additional reliable analytical method (e.g. IRMS), that the Prohibited Substance is of exogenous origin, no further investigation is necessary, and the Sample will be deemed to contain such Prohibited Substance. When an additional reliable analytical method (e.g. IRMS) has not been applied, and the minimum of three previous test results are not available, a longitudinal profile of the Athlete shall be established by performing three no-advance notice tests in a period of three months by the relevant Anti-Doping Organization. The result that triggered this longitudinal study shall be reported as atypical. If the longitudinal profile of the Athlete established by the subsequent tests is not physiologically normal, the result shall then be reported as an Adverse Analytical Finding.

In extremely rare individual cases, boldenone of endogenous origin can be consistently found at very low nanograms per milliliter (ng/mL) levels in urine. When such a very low concentration of boldenone is reported by a laboratory and the application of any reliable analytical method (e.g. IRMS) has not determined the exogenous origin of the substance, further investigation may be conducted by subsequent test(s).

For 19-norandrosterone, an Adverse Analytical Finding reported by a laboratory is considered to be scientific and valid proof of exogenous origin of the Prohibited Substance. In such case, no further investigation is necessary.

Should an Athlete fail to cooperate in the investigations, the Athlete's Sample shall be deemed to contain a prohibited Substance.

So that's quite clear, isn't it?

And as I scrolled onto page two even more substances on the banned list:

The following substances and their releasing factors are also prohibited:

Erythropoietin (EPO)

Growth Hormone (HGH), Insulin-like Growth Factors (e.g. IGF-1)

Mechano Growth Factors (MGFs)

Gonadotrophins (e.g. LH, hCG), prohibited in males only

Insulins

Corticotrophins

and other substances with similar chemical structure or similar biological effect(s).

Look at that last line again. It comes up quite often.

All beta-2 agonists including their D and L-isomers are prohibited.

As an exception, formoterol, salbutamol, salmeterol and terbutaline when administered by inhalation, require an abbreviated Therapeutic Use Exemption.

The following classes of HORMONE ANTAGONISTS AND MODULATORS are prohibited:

Aromatase inhibitors including, but not limited to:
Anastrozole
letrozole
aminoglutethimide
exemestane
Formestane
testolactone
Selective estrogen receptor modulators (SERMs) including, but not limited to:
Raloxifene

tamoxifen

toremifene

Other anti-estrogenic substances including, but not limited to:

Clomiphene

Cyclofenil

fulvestrant

Agents modifying myostatin function(s) including but not limited to:

myostatin inhibitors

Masking agents are prohibited. They include:

Diuretics*

Epitestosterone

Probenecid

alpha-reductase inhibitors (e.g. finasteride, dutasteride)

plasma expanders (e.g. albumin, dextran, hydroxyethyl starch) and other substances with similar biological effect(s)

*Diuretics include:

Acetazolamide

amiloride

bumetanide

canrenone

chlorthalidone

etacrynic acid

furosemide

indapamide

metolazone

spironolactone

thiazides (e.g. bendroflumethiazide, chlorothiazide, hydro-chlorothiazide),triamterene, and other substances with a similar chemical structure or similar biological effect(s) (except for drosperinone, which is not prohibited).

S6. STIMULANTS

All stimulants (including both their (D- & L-) optical isomers where relevant) are prohibited, except imidazole derivatives for topical use.

Stimulants include:

Adrafinil

adrenaline

amfepramone

amiphenazole

amphetamine

amphetaminil

benzphetamine

benzylpiperazine

bromantan

cathine

clobenzorex

cocaine

cropropamide

crotetamide

cyclazodone

dimethylamphetamine

ephedrine

etamivan

etilamphetamine

etilefrine

famprofazone

fenbutrazate

fencamfamin

fencamine

fenetylline

fenfluramine

fenproporex

furfenorex

heptaminol

isometheptene

levmethamfetamine

meclofenoxate

mefenorex

mephentermine

mesocarb

methamphetamine (D-)

methylenedioxyamphetamine

methylenedioxymethamphetamine

p-methylamphetamine

methylephedrine

methylphenidate

modafinil

nikethamide

norfenefrine

norfenfluramine

octopamine

ortetamine

oxilofrine

parahydroxyamphetamine

pemoline

pentetrazol

phendimetrazine

phenmetrazine

phenpromethamine

phentermine

4-phenylpiracetam (carphedon)

Prolintane

Propylhexedrine

Selegiline

Sibutramine

Strychnine

tuaminoheptane and other substances with a similar chemical structure or similar biological effect(s).

The following narcotics are prohibited:

Buprenorphine

Dextromoramide

diamorphine (heroin)

fentanyl and its derivatives

hydromorphone

methadone morphine

oxycodone

oxymorphone

pentazocine

pethidine

Cannabinoids (e.g. hashish, marijuana) are also prohibited.

I threw my pen in the bin.

Just to make things even more complicated WADA then goes on to explain that in certain sports such as Billiards, Bobsleigh, Boules, Bridge, Curling, Gymnastics and Motorcycling beta blockers are also prohibited. The beta blockers include:

Acebutolol

Alprenolol

Atenolol

Betaxolol

Bisoprolol

Bunolol

Carteolol

Carvedilol

Celiprolol

Esmolol

Labetalol

Levobunolol

Metipranolol

Metoprolol

Nadolol

Oxprenolol

pindolol

propranolol

sotalol

timolol

All inhaled Beta-2 Agonists, except salbutamol (free plus glucuronide) greater than 1000 ng/mL and clenbuterol (listed under S1.2: Other Anabolic Agents)

Alpha-reductase inhibitors

probenecid

Cathine

cropropamide

crotetamide

ephedrine

etamivan

famprofazone

heptaminol

isometheptene

levmethamfetamine

meclofenoxate

p-methylamphetamine

methylephedrine

nikethamide

norfenefrine

octopamine

ortetamine

oxilofrine

phenpromethamine

propylhexedrine

selegiline

sibutramine

tuaminoheptane

and any other stimulant not expressly listed under section S6 for which the Athlete establishes that it fulfils the conditions described in section S6;

Cannabinoids

All Glucocorticosteroids

Alcohol

All Beta Blockers

I closed the internet connection feeling dismayed and annoyed. The banned list isn't a banned list, it's a bloody farce. Even if by some miracle an athlete could remember all of the ingredients on the list and manage to steer clear of them all, they could still fall foul of WADA and the authorities because of the warnings that appear time and time again interspersing the list. Statements such as *including, but not limited to...*

And *other substances with a similar chemical structure or similar biological effect(s).*

It was at that point that I realised just how difficult it is to steer a straight course through an athletics career and wondered just how many 'clean' athletes have been labelled a cheat because they have unwittingly and/or accidentally taken a substance that appears on the banned list, or worse, been accused of taking something which is not on the banned list but may have a similar chemical make-up to something that is!

The banned list is never talked about in the UK as I firmly believe the vast majority of UK athletes do not ever consider taking anything remotely illegal. But then again, how would they know? How is it possible to carry around a list with nearly three hundred named substances that are said to be illegal? How practical is it to pull out the banned list in a supermarket and check it against the ingredients on everything you put into your trolley? And even if they do, what about the WADA warning that states even if something is NOT on the list it will be deemed to be on the list if it resembles something that is on the list? How is an athlete supposed to know if the experts and chemists and pharmacologists don't even know? In a recent conversation with a famous athlete he said an athlete these days needs to be a bloody chemist too!

I printed the list off. It ran to nearly eight pages. I went over it three times and found no reference at all to THG. Victor was right: it wasn't on the banned list.

As I picked the telephone up and dialled Victor's number I reassured myself that the gremlin was right. In my own mind I wasn't cheating; I was getting even. I felt it had been the other athletes cheating me. But more than that I was annoyed with the authorities and their 'banned list' that no one could ever hope to keep to. I screwed up the eight pages of A4 paper and threw them into a bin. A useless, worthless waste of part of a rainforest.

"Victor. It's Dwain."

Victor exchanged some pleasantries and rambled on a bit about the weather and his busy day ahead. I didn't take much notice.

"Victor... I'm ready to go onto your programme."

As I replaced the receiver I felt as if a weight had been lifted from my shoulders. I'd lived with making this decision for nearly three weeks. Every night it was the last thing on my mind as I went to sleep and it was with me first thing every morning as I woke up.

But now that I had made the decision, strangely I felt relaxed. I was also looking forward to seeing just how good I really was at my chosen career as a sprinter now that I would be competing evenly. At this point I can hear my critics screaming at me, telling me I'm wrong, that the sprinting world is predominantly clean, that the fastest men on the planet can compete without resorting to injections and creams. If they want to believe that, fair enough. However I'm a realist; at the time I was a realist and everyone in America was telling me I was the only top sprinter in the world not playing the system. The subsequent positive tests of the likes of Ben Johnson and Tim Montgomery and Justin Gatlin make me think that those voices were telling the truth. And yet, as comfortable as I was with my decision at the time, I couldn't help remembering that WADA warning that appeared again and again.

I now realise how wrong that decision was way back in January 2002. The drug I was about to pump into my system wasn't on the banned list and I took comfort from that and it helped sway my decision. I want to do my bit for the sport and stop other young men and women like me from making the same mistake. I want to tell them that drugs are not the answer but the athletics authorities must get real and not bury their heads in the sand. The WADA banned list is a joke as I'm sure I have demonstrated in this chapter.

Athletes will always be tempted to cheat especially if drugs are not on a list that the authorities and WADA have compiled. It was a combination of that and the fact that I firmly believed that I was the only sprinter in the world not cheating. You may think that's a rather dramatic statement but, believe me, at the time that is exactly how I was feeling. Imagine going into a school exam with twenty-nine classmates and just before you are asked to pick up your pen and get on with the exam, the teacher comes in with a sheet of paper and announces that she has the answers to the questions on your examination paper. She then places the sheet of paper on her desk and invites anyone who wants to, to take a look at the answers. She then leaves the room.

Imagine... she has invited the class to look at the answers. How many of you reading this would be tempted to get off their chairs and take a sneaky look. Two or three perhaps... maybe more?

Those that wouldn't look, hats off to you and your moral standing. However, let's take it a step further. Let's imagine you are sitting there and you have opened the paper and have begun looking at the questions. Oh dear... there are some toughies in there. You look up and one by one your classmates begin to wander to the front of the class. Shock horror, they are reading the answers, they are cheating! And you watch as every one of your classmates, one by one, take it in turns to look at the answers to the questions. They return to their seats with huge smiles on their faces.

You are now sitting there knowing full well that your classmates will get better grades than you unless you join them and take a sneaky peek at those answers. Everyone has cheated; you simply need to get even.

The teacher is still out of the classroom. How many people put in that situation would still turn around and say, "I wouldn't take a look."

Rightly or wrongly, that was the way I was feeling at the end of my third week in America.

Victor came round to my apartment later that evening. Thankfully Jonathan had taken off downtown. Victor took me through the programme and showed me how to take THG. He placed drops under my tongue explaining this was the easiest and quickest way to get the drug into the bloodstream. He also made me apply a lotion or a cream to the forearms. He gave me a diary of when and when not to take it. He gave me the programme for February and March.

I was to take the designer steroid Tetrahydrogestrinone (THG) in the form of a liquid and by cream. Once undetectable, this is the designer steroid, nicknamed 'The Clear', that I tested positive for in 2003. It is worth remembering that this drug was not on the banned list when I was taking it.

I was tempted into the use of THG as it improves the body's capacity to train and compete at the highest level by reducing fatigue associated with training and the time required to recover after physical exertion. Quite simply it is a recovery agent. It allows the athlete to train harder and longer. It is also associated with reducing recovery time following injuries.

February 02

Sun	Mon	Tues	Wed	Thur	Fri	Sat
					1	2
3	4	5	6	7	8	9
10	11 THG liquid 30 units	12 THG cream 2 spoons	13 THG liquid 30 units	14 THG cream 2 spoons	15	16
17	18 liquid 30 units	19 cream 2 spoons	20 liquid 30 units	21 cream 2 spoons	22	23
24	25 liquid 30 units	26 cream 2 spoons	27 liquid 30 units	28 cream 2 spoons		

Possible side effects of THG use include jaundice and liver damage, acne, heart problems, depression, paranoia and aggression. I confess my limited use of THG did not cause me any of these problems but I do admit looking back that I did sometimes suffer from uncontrollable and quite frightening mood swings.

Effects specific to males include the development of breast tissue, infertility and baldness. What! Nobody mentioned that to me. Again thankfully, to the best of my knowledge, my limited time on THG has not affected my fertility, nor am I going bald or growing man breasts. I wish to remind you, the reader, again that THG was the first drug I took. I took the road to hell in convincing myself that this drug would simply make me or allow me to train harder.

Victor was quick to point out that THG would not benefit me unless I stepped up my weight sessions in the gym. Time and time again he said that THG was simply a recovery agent allowing me to train harder and for longer. As you would expect this was music to my ears. I was thinking, perhaps reassuring myself, that it wasn't really cheating in the real sense of the word and of course it wasn't on the banned list. As you can see it was all very straightforward stuff, methodically planned and detailed in writing.

Victor gave me enough supplies of THG to last until I came back to America on my next pre-arranged trip at the end of February 2002. He also gave me an idea of the cost of a year's programme. Expensive at nearly $30,000. It wasn't a problem. I was earning big money at the time. I had a few more training sessions with Remi prior to leaving for home. I took THG from the middle of January until I left for England. I expected to feel a little different and was perhaps a little disappointed that I felt exactly the same as I did before. The only physical difference was that I'd begun to experience the first signs of stomach cramp each evening. It was fairly mild at first and Victor had warned me that this was an unfortunate side effect. Over the coming months they would get a lot worse.

I was in the check-in section of Miami International Airport when I noticed that a young couple in front of me were having their entire hand luggage searched with a fine tooth comb. Shit! What if they search my bag? I had enough drugs in my bag to kill an elephant and the awful truth dawned on me at that moment in time that I didn't have a clue whether they were legal or not. Here I was sitting in an airport lounge about to board a flight to the UK with a shed load of drugs in my suitcase. Nervous? You bet I was nervous. Nervous and terrified. I think Jonathan noticed it too, asking me several times if I was okay. I gave him some bullshit excuse about my fear of flying and he seemed to accept my explanation. We stood almost silently as we got nearer and nearer to the British Airways check-in desk. I had tubes of The Clear and The Cream as well has a few bottles of EPO and HGH which were encased in ice packs as they needed to be kept cool. I had all of these items in my luggage that was about to go into the hold and a couple of tubes in my hand luggage. They were labelled up 'flaxseed oil and joint cream'. I had been told by Victor that if I was ever asked about the tubes this was to be my explanation. What the fuck was flaxseed oil, I thought to myself and how on earth am I going to give a detailed plausible explanation if asked what it was used for.

America after 9/11 is one of the most security conscious places in the world to fly in and out of. The thoughts were flying around my head: drug dealer, terrorist. Victor's words reverberated around my head. *The drug is untraceable*. What did that actually mean? I wondered whether THG had been invented by BALCO and could not be identified by the airport authorities. Perhaps they had some sort of machine that detected all the harmless stuff and at the same time flagged up a warning when the dodgy or unknown stuff went through the system. I was now thinking jail and was convinced the eagle-eyed officials would spot the nervous man sweating profusely and trembling visibly. How do they do it? I thought to myself, how do the drug dealers and mules and carriers walk through these airport terminals like they do? How can anyone climb aboard a plane with a bomb in their shoe without showing any signs of distress?   It beats the hell out of me because here I was showing the distress signs over a drug that I didn't know was illegal or otherwise. For all I knew it could have been purchased quite legally over the counter of any pharmacy in America. But that was it... I didn't know. Surely Victor would have advised me not to carry it on an aeroplane if it was classified as illegal.

"Good day, sir."

The pretty girl in a smart uniform brought me back to the present. She rambled on I heard very little until....

"Could anyone have given you anything to carry in your bags?"

Oh fuck.

"Well, sir?"

Yes, I wanted to reply, *it was Conte, Victor Conte, he made me do it. I'm innocent, can't you see, I'm innocent, I don't want to go to jail.*

Instead I just shook my head and grinned like the idiot that I was.

More toothy whiter than white all American smiles. "And could anyone have interfered with your bags, sir?"

"No."

"Thank you, sir, have a nice day."

I was in the clear; I convinced myself I had been as cool as a cucumber. Nothing to worry about, Dwain, you're being stupid.

My persona changed as soon as I reached the hand luggage inspection team and my leather flight bag disappeared into the airport X-ray machine. My watch, belt, mobile phone and loose change were dropped into a white plastic tray and I was directed to the electronic arch metal scanner. Two burly American cops armed with sub-machine guns eyed me cautiously as the airport security guard beckoned me forward and frisked me. I looked to my left and noticed my flight bag passing through the rubber flaps and onto a conveyor belt. The two officials monitoring the screen were talking. Were they talking about my bag? Was I imagining it? One of them stood, he nodded at a different official standing outside a small cubicle twenty-five yards from the security scanning machine just as the security area led out into the duty-free shopping mall. I picked up my bag and Jonathan said something. It didn't register. I needed to get past *that* man standing outside *that* cubicle.

I tried to look confident as we approached him. I talked to Jonathan, made a comment about getting a beer.

"You don't drink beer," he said.

The strap of my flight bag felt wet and clammy. The man took a step forward.

"Could I have a word, sir?"

I looked around. The two cops had followed, no one else was in the vicinity; he was talking to me.

"Sure," I said with a false smile. "What about?"

He didn't answer my question. Jonathan looked puzzled. I shrugged my shoulders as if to say this won't take a minute. The official asked me to take a step inside his room and I made my way through the door he was holding open for me. I smiled, he didn't. This was it, I was heading for the slammer.

We were joined by another official and he took my bag from me. He knew exactly what he was looking for as he reached inside for the tubes of THG. He fingered them and then scrutinised the BALCO labels.

"Would you care to tell me what this is?"

"Flaxseed oil," I replied.

"And what's it used for?"

"It's a muscle rub... I'm an athlete, it aids recovery."

"We know who you are, Mr Chambers," the other official replied. It unnerved me and if those officials had asked me one or two more questions I would have cracked and blurted out everything I knew right there and then. I'm the world's worst liar, they knew it and I knew it and any official with two weeks' experience sitting in front of me there and then knew that I was lying. They knew from my reactions, my stuttering and my nervousness not to mention my sweat-drenched brow in the perfect air-conditioned building known as Miami International Airport.

"It must be good," the other one countered. "You have enough of it on you."

I nodded my head and grinned at him. Any minute now the cops would burst in.

Only they didn't.

The older more experienced gentleman handed me back the tube and bid me farewell; told me it was just a routine enquiry. I have my own theory on what happened that day at Miami International Airport. I figured that because Trevor Graham had already sent in the anonymous sample to the authorities that a full investigation was already underway. The police, FBI or whoever it was who were heading the inquiry needed more time to conclude their investigation. To drag me into the mire there and then would have meant that the cat would have been let out of the bag. They would get me soon enough; they would already have the information that I was flying back into the United States at the end of February. They would let me go for now. They would give me enough rope to hang myself.

I left the cubicle and met up with Jonathan and cursed myself for being so stupid and paranoid. Of course it was just routine. I had just been one of the one in ten, unlucky enough to be pulled in. The flaxseed oil explanation had worked a treat. I began to feel that Victor had thought of everything. No way was I going to get caught.

I was invincible.

MY COCKTAIL OF DRUGS

In late February I arrived back in America. By this time I had taken a complete cycle of THG and I was about to start the March programme. I was racked with severe stomach cramps sometimes for up to an hour at a time. I was like a heroine addict going through cold turkey. I prayed it would never happen in public and thankfully it never did. Otherwise I'd have been carted off to the nearest hospital and I would have been able to do nothing about it.

Now, a little education. It is worth bearing in mind that I researched these benefits and side effects fully, only **after** I had been on the programme for nearly a year. What I found out horrified me. More of that later. I do not know what damage I have done to my body. I can only thank the Lord that I was caught when I did. I dread to think what damage the young Eastern bloc athletes have suffered over the years with their ongoing consumption of steroids and potions, and once again I ask the coaches and so-called doctors who encouraged and supplied them to examine their consciences.

The following diary pages and the previous one for February

were supplied by Victor Conte of the Bay Area Laboratory Co-operative (BALCO). I detail in this chapter the particular benefits and side effects in layman's terms. Some of them look positively wondrous and you may be forgiven for asking the question, "Why are they banned?" I asked myself the same question when making the decision to go onto the 'programme' while I was in America. Most of the drugs at the time seemed simply to be replacing substances that the body produced anyway. Others I was persuaded were no worse than coffee.

As you can see from the diary, I was also introduced to EPO on the 24th March. Victor explained simply that this was all part of the 'programme'. Not once did I hesitate to take anything prescribed to me. I secretly hoped that it may even lessen the stomach cramps and I had full confidence in Victor and his team.

Erythropoietin (EPO): Boosts the production of oxygen-carrying red blood cells. EPO is released naturally from the kidneys and acts on the bone marrow to stimulate red blood cell production. An increase in red blood cells improves the amount of oxygen the blood can carry to the body's muscles. It may also increase the body's capacity to buffer lactic acid. Lactic acid is bad news for athletes as it collects in the joints causing swelling, stiffness, inflammation and, in some cases, severe pain. Those unfortunate people who suffer from gout know all about lactic acid.

EPO specifically helps to improve endurance performance or to improve recovery from anaerobic exercise. When taking EPO it can cause the blood to thicken excessively. The heart has to work harder to pump the thicker blood and the blood is more prone to clotting. Consequently, prolonged EPO use can increase the risk of heart attack, stroke and clots in the lungs. The risk is exacerbated by dehydration which of course usually occurs during exercise.

March 02

Sun	Mon	Tues	Wed	Thur	Fri	Sat
					1	2
3	4	5	6	7	8	9
10	11 THG liquid 30 units	12 THG cream 2 spoons	13 THG liquid 30 units	14 THG cream 2 spoons	15	16
17	18 liquid 30 units	19 cream 2 spoons	20 liquid 30 units	21 cream 2 spoons	22	23
24 E=2x50	25 liquid 30 units	26 E=2x50 cream 2 spoons	27 liquid 30 units	28 E=2x375 cream 2 spoons	29	30 E=2x375
31						

It is worth pointing out at this stage that I was being routinely tested for performance-enhancing substances by an independent tester. I think these tests were carried out to reassure the athletes. Not once during the year of 2002 did I test positive. Check the diary: I was practically a walking junkie and yet nothing showed up on any BALCO tests. This was the calendar for THG, EPO and the Growth Hormone only. The Insulin, Loithryonine was not listed here. I had a separate sheet for each and didn't take those quite so frequently.

I was on the lot and the sophisticated modern-day tests detected nothing. I thought I was invincible and, as you can see, barely four months into my programme I was on drugs nearly every day. The real proof of the pudding however would come when I was tested by WADA and the authorities. I trusted Victor and I clung to his every word, but there was always a nagging suspicion that perhaps the authorities' tests were carried out more rigorously and more professionally.

As you will see in the table for April, the time had come for me to get my blood drawn. This couldn't have come at a better time. I was going through a phase of overheating which contributed to a lot of my cramping. Being in such a hot climate did not help me either. My fluid intake was poor, and on average I was only taking on board one and a half, maybe two litres a day. I told Victor about my hot flushes and he suggested that I should increase my fluid intake to four litres. Two litres during training and two litres after training. Electrolyte sachets became a factor, to help reduce the chances of cramping. The increased fluid intake would help keep my body temperature down and, as a secondary back-up, Victor suggested I walk around with a tub of Tums. Tums contain a number of ingredients. Calcium and sodium were the ones that would play a vital role in the prevention of my ongoing cramps. When these elements are depleted in the human body, normally during exercise with heavy amounts of sweating, cramping can occur. As we all now know, being on EPO causes the blood to thicken. I was very aware of all of these side effects as Victor and I sat down for hours on end talking about the pros and cons of taking these types of 'enhancements'. The purpose for me was to improve my red blood cell count and this meant taking my base rate humadecrat level from 46 to 50. Now Victor had provided me with all the relevant supplements, i.e. iron, vitamin E, folic acid, selenium, vitamins C, B1, B2, B6 and B12 in order to counteract the possibilities of me clotting. Our hospital visit was arranged by Victor through a private hospital in the Bay area and I'd rather not name them. They were unaware of who I was, but yet I was still scared. Victor and I drove up to the hospital. He told me where to go, what to say and what to do when I arrived there, and he waited in the lobby while I walked towards the front desk. I signed in and waited for my name to be called. What scared me the most was the thought that the nurses might know I was up to something. How many other Balco athletes had been here before me? Were they able to tell if I was using something by just looking at my blood; did I look drug induced? Far too many thoughts were flying through my head.

"Mr Chambers," a young lady announced.

"Yes, ma'am."

I walked towards an open cubicle where a nurse was waiting happily for me. I entered the cubicle with one bottle of water in one hand and three files in the other hand. I sat on the bed; the nurse was very pleasant. While I was having my blood drawn I lost all thoughts of the nurse having any suspicions about me as we were sitting together talking about tattoos. One thing she did comment on was the size of the veins in my right arm. Having to think quickly I told her that I went to the gym on a regular basis.

"I can see that," she said.

Once my blood had been drawn I hopped off the bed, said goodbye to the nurse and walked briskly towards Victor. Victor and I continued to talk a little further about the other drugs I was taking. At this stage in my programme I was undergoing what Victor called a 'corrective phase'. The purpose of this was to figure out what the right dosages were. Victor would always say to me, "A chain is only as strong as its weakest link." And in my case my weak link was my low red blood cell count; this needed improving. The same corrective phase took place with THG or The Clear and The Cream as it's commonly known. Although I had a few sleepless nights over the episode, the next blood draw on the 17th of the same month was rather routine, performed by a young female doctor who barely uttered half a dozen words during the entire examination. It was towards the end of the month that I had my first session with my physiotherapist (come-psychiatrist!) Sarah Connors. Sarah has been my physio for over twelve years. I owe this woman and her family my life as she's had to put up with me and my juvenile behaviour for a long time now. I've always been upfront and honest with Sarah and as she went through the normal warm-up routine and stretching exercises with me she asked how America and the new training regime had gone. I told her everything was good and it broke my heart that for the first time in our professional relationship I'd lie to her. I would lie to her throughout the entire period I was on the programme.

I was on drugs and she believed that all my hard work had been achieved naturally.

I had now been on the programme nearly four months. How was I feeling?

In a word – confident.

Although slightly concerned at the ever-increasing cramping and the worries about blood clots, I was feeling fitter than I ever had in my life. No wonder, in the gym I was lifting weights like they were going out of fashion and of course I could get in there more often because of my now improved recovery period. My overall body weight shot up from 195lbs (88.63kg) to a staggering 217lbs (98.63kg). I had gone from a personal best in my squats of 180kg to an impressive 230kg and I jump squatted this weight for three repetitions. My bench press also improved from one repetition for 140kg to three reps at 165kg. All these improvements also had a huge effect on my diet. I was able to eat the American version of a full English breakfast plus four American-size pancakes with cream and strawberries on top and two glasses of orange juice; and that was my breakfast before a training session! Lunch, snacks and dinner were just as bad. No wonder my weight had increased. It had finally come to a point where I had to stop the amount of food I was taking on board as it made it very difficult for me to run. The first doubts were beginning to creep in. Victor and I re-examined the dosages of THG and he suggested that I take a lower dose. Within a week or so I was back down to my normal running weight of 195lbs. Although not one hundred per cent convinced that the programme and in particular THG would get round the testers it had been proven that it could and it was working. I was supremely confident and I looked forward to seeing the results on the track.

There were three meetings in April in America and I planned to run at them all. There was a meeting at Mt San Antonio College on Sunday 21st and one the following Saturday at Penn State. Because of the stomach cramps I missed all of them and watched on the sidelines as Kelli and Chryste both competed. The cramps were now beginning to concern me. They weren't happening too often but they were severe and prolonged and God knows how much they took out of me in terms of strength. The following morning after a particularly bad attack it was like the feeling after a dose of bad flu. Although the meetings I missed were insignificant, what if they hadn't been? I returned home to England feeling rather despondent. It took a day or two to get over the jet lag. It was on the last day of the month that I sat at home watching TV while I massaged The Cream into my arms. The Cream acts as a masking agent and it leaves a white residue on the arms which takes about an hour to disappear and smells a little like burnt almonds. It had barely worked its way in when the doorbell rang. I don't remember a feeling of panic as I calmly walked towards the door, the residue on my arms clearly visible as I was wearing a sleeveless vest top. I opened the door and an official-looking man spoke. Although I had never met him I knew exactly who he was and what he was there for.

"Mr Chambers, you have been selected for a random test."

His words chilled me to the bone. Look at the diary for April. In the month of April 2002 I pumped THG, EPO and growth hormone into my body seventeen times and here I was about to be tested for them. The thoughts running around my head were predictable. I was anxious to say the least, no matter how reassuring Victor's words were at the time, how comforting those 'clear' tests from BALCO seemed, I was positively shitting myself with fear. I remember walking the man into the lounge. The tube of THG lay on top of the television and the faint smell of almonds permeated the air. (Or was it just my imagination?)

He was a dour man, not too talkative and, as the rules state, he could not leave my side until I had peed into his canister. Of course I couldn't pee, could I. As much as I tried I just couldn't manage it. Something in my brain was telling my bladder not to function and I took the canister from him at least a dozen times over the next hour and a half but each time came out of the bathroom apologising. The official kept telling me not to worry. He explained it happened a lot and he wasn't going anywhere. Victor had warned me about this first test and I knew it was inevitable. I thought I had prepared for it, thought I could be cool. It wasn't the case. As I walked around the lounge sipping at a glass of water filled with ice I was sweating like a bull. The man must have noticed as well. The central heating had been turned down to a minimum; it was the end of April in the UK and it certainly wasn't warm.

Eventually I managed to satisfy his requirements. I remember handing it over to him and staring at the canister as if it was some kind of radioactive substance. He noticed my reaction and passed a comment. "Don't worry, son, it's only a little urine." He laughed. He proceeded with filling in the relevant paperwork. When undergoing an in or out of competition test you are required to fill in a section which gives you the opportunity to list all supplements which have been taken by mouth or injection within the previous seven days. I couldn't list THG, EPO, HGH or Insulin on my list so I wrote down that I was taking multivitamins.

To me it wasn't just a little urine: it was a cocktail of drugs that would bring my life tumbling down around me. When the man left I dashed into the kitchen, picked up my mobile phone and keyed down to Victor's name. I didn't even think about the time difference as the phone rang out. Victor answered; he sounded groggy, he was still in bed.

"I've been tested, Victor," I blurted into the phone. I was on the point of tears and Victor heard it in my voice. He simply told me to relax.

"But I was rubbing the cream in when he came to the door, it was on my fingers and could–"

Victor cut me off mid-sentence.

"Dwain – relax, stop being so silly. I've told you before, as far as the labs are concerned THG hasn't even been invented. How can they possibly test for it?"

"But the EPO, Victor, I've been taking EPO as well."

There was an uncomfortable silence at the other end. All of a sudden Victor didn't answer back immediately. A few seconds passed then he spoke.

"When did you last take EPO?"

I thought back; it only felt like a day or two and I knew EPO could hang around that long. This was it. Victor's silence confirmed my suspicions... I was fucked... the EPO was in my system and the man was on his way to the lab. I could hear Victor rustling some papers.

"Relax," he said again. "I have your calendar here and you should have taken EPO on the 23rd."

This time there was silence at my end as the news sank in.

"Dwain, you have been following the calendar day by day, haven't you?"

"Yes."

"Then you have nothing to worry about."

His words had a calming effect on me and I began breathing normally again. I apologised for waking him and said I'd call him in a few hours. He berated me for answering the door to the tester. I apologised and hung up. I looked out my calendar and, sure enough, it confirmed the last day I'd taken EPO. I thanked my lucky stars I'd followed the programme verbatim. Incredibly I was due to take EPO first thing the next morning and I thought once again about tipping the whole lot in the rubbish bin. What if the official had turned up a day later? It didn't bear thinking about. That's how risky taking drugs is: I'd taken EPO nine times in April and yet opened the door to someone I hadn't ever seen before. That was stupid.

However, there is an easy way around the system and one that is fairly foolproof.

Quite simply you hide. The testers have a record of your home address and whenever you go on holiday or even spend one day away you must notify them of the address you will be staying. After a couple of years on the circuit you do it automatically; you never ever forget. Fact. In the majority of dope-testing countries the authorities have the mobile number of the athlete and should you be away from your address they will call you and instruct you to be somewhere within a few hours. The theory is quite simple: the authorities should be able to perform a random dope test at any time of the year. But it doesn't work because the good old dope testers give you a get out. Bizarrely, and for reasons only known to them, the testers allow you two strikes; that is, they allow you two chances to hide. To miss three tests is seen as blatantly playing the system and a one-year competition ban is imposed as well as a lifetime Olympic ban imposed by the BOA. Therefore, if an athlete is on drugs and is within a period where the drug is still in his or her system, they will disappear off the face of the earth until any trace of the drug has gone from their body. How do you disappear? Simple, you don't answer your front door to anyone you don't know and you don't answer your mobile phone to a number you don't recognise. When you are in competition you are not taking anything and therefore if you are tested at the track there should not be anything in your system.

I have never missed a test in all my years of competition and have been asked on more than one occasion what I think of the three strikes and out rule. I have been asked my thoughts on Christine Ohuruogu too. She missed three out of competition tests, one in October 2005 and two in June 2006. She received a one-year ban for missing these tests. Our friends at the BOA also banned her from competing at future Olympic Games for Great Britain. She appealed to the Court of Arbitration for Sport but lost. She commented that she would probably leave Britain and compete in the Olympics for another country if her appeal was unsuccessful. An interesting decision, one that I don't think for one minute influenced the eventual decision to allow her to run at the Olympics.

I'll go on record and say that any athlete who misses three tests has to be plainly very naive and forgetful or has something to hide. Missing one test can be considered careless, missing two is almost unforgivable but missing three is the sign of an athlete with no focus at all or plainly someone trying to avoid the testers. Christine missed two tests in the same month knowing full well the consequences. I would think that having missed a test already in June 2006 alarm bells would have been ringing louder than Big Ben when the Mile End training venue was switched to the Olympic Medical Institute in Harrow. The first thing she should have done was to pick up the phone and notify them. That said, Christine was a little unfortunate. Testers waited for an hour at Mile End stadium, but she failed to appear after getting caught up in the London traffic. She was just unlucky and I'm glad the BOA had the good sense to overturn her ban and allow her to run for Team GB at the Olympics. I was one of the millions watching television who cheered her on to the gold medal that day in Beijing.

I shouldn't have opened the door. It was stupid and on that occasion I was very lucky that the official came on the day that he did. It was a close shave and I knew that time was running out. I wasn't devious enough and I wasn't cunning. I would open the door to a stranger and I wouldn't think to overload my voicemail box on my mobile so an official couldn't leave a message. It wasn't in my nature and it was only a matter of time before I'd be caught in the net.

You'll notice a pattern emerging in the month of April and, in particular, the days preceding a meet. That is, two or three days before each meeting I would take nothing. Everyone knew that during or after a race is the most likely time an athlete is likely to be tested. We also know that traces of a lot of performance-enhancing drugs leave the body within a few days. It isn't exactly rocket science that we don't take anything a few days prior to a meet. I was placing my trust in Victor, BALCO and the scientists telling me this but of course up until now the theory hadn't been proved to me. Now it was too late; the urine was about to be tested and all I could think of was the artificial shit I'd been putting into my body for four months. Surely, I thought to myself as I lay awake in bed that evening, something would show up.

It just so happened April was also the month I'd started on the Human Growth Hormone too. I injected this to aid recovery from heavy weight sessions. It is intimated that carefully administered doses of HGH can slow the aging process and that countless Americans over forty years of age take HGH as part of their normal daily routine. Growth hormones are powerful regulators and orchestrators of our bodies and behaviour. Levels of various hormones vary throughout our lifespan. HGH is one example. This very important hormone, produced by the pituitary gland in the brain, controls growth and development from infancy through adolescence and begins to decline around age twenty. There is yet another powerful argument (one that I heard a million times in America) that taking HGH was quite simply replacing a substance that is produced naturally in the body. In a discussion in a bar one evening, one of the American athletes likened it to vitamin supplements. It is worth bearing in mind however that, whichever way you look at it, HGH does improve muscle definition and reduces body fat and any athlete who takes HGH regularly has a very distinctive shape. I know, the same thing happened to me and I know who you are. Again HGH isn't the wonder drug we may think it is and there is a very worrying side effect in that it can increase the risk of diabetes. My advice to any young athlete tempted down the route of any supplement at all, legal or otherwise, is to go and research the side effects of everything. You have no excuse now that the internet carries so much information. You could have been forgiven for thinking yours truly had gained an 'ology' in pharmaceutical research during the period it took to write this book such is my in-depth knowledge of the subject. In reality the information is available to anyone with an internet connection.

Back to HGH. It may very well be that a certain steroid can give you a fraction of an advantage over a clean athlete at a particular time of the year and only then if you don't get hit with cramp halfway through a competition. But if you are increasing your risk of blood pressure, heart disease and diabetes to name a few and end up bald with man breasts and a smaller dysfunctional penis, I ask you... is it worth it?

April 02

Sun	Mon	Tues	Wed	Thur	Fri	Sat
	1 E=2x25	2	3 E=2x25	4 Blood draw	5 Birthday	6 Carbot meet
7	8 L +G E=4,000	9 C	10 OFF L+C E=400	11	12 OFF L=400	13
14 E=400	15	16 E=400	17 Blood draw	18	19	20
21 Meet MT SAC 100	22	23 E=400	24	25	26	27 Penn Meet relay
28 L+G	29 L	30 C				

May 2002. I waited for the phone call that never came. I awaited the stern voice of the official telling me I was up shit creek without a paddle. Nevertheless on Wednesday the first of May I still took EPO, THG and a growth hormone. The following day I applied The Cream to my forearms. As the first week in May turned into the second I knew I was in the clear. Victor had been right; he knew what he was doing and I looked forward to the meetings at the end of the month. I was tested yet again in May, the results were clear.

May 02

Sun	Mon	Tues	Wed	Thur	Fri	Sat
			1 E=400 L+G	2 C	3	4
5	6	7	8	9	10	11 L
12 E+C	13 L	14 C	15	16	17	18 Meet UK 4 x100 L
19 E+C	20	21	22	23	24	25
26 L Meet Portugal 100/200	27 C	28 L+E	29 C	30	31	

June 2002. Now it's getting really complicated and I need to look at the diary every day to make sure I'm on the right track. At times I forget whether I've taken something and on more than one occasion I know I've doubled a dose. I then resort to writing everything down. As you can see, I'm now taking drugs on the day of the meetings. This is something that really wrestled with my conscience, but by now I'm in too deep. I remembered the other athletes telling me that once I'm on the programme I must stick to it, otherwise it's curtains. They liken it to a course of antibiotics and more than one of them told me that if I stop in the middle there is more of a likelihood of being tested positive. Was it all worth it? The answer now is no but at Athens on the 10th June yours truly was in fine form and recorded a 200m personal best of 20.27.

June 02

Sun	Mon	Tues	Wed	Thur	Fri	Sat
						1 Meet Poland
2 E	3	4	5	6	7	8 Meet Seville
9 C	10 Athens	11 E+C	12	13	14	15 Meet UK L
16 C+E	17 L	18 L	19	20	21	22 Euro Cup L+S
23 Meet Spain C	24 Travel home E (important)	25	26	27	28 Oslo S	29
30 Meet Europa Cup L+C						

July 2002. I had been on the programme seven months and it was part of my daily life, my daily routine. I still had to be careful particularly when unexpected invites cropped up. On the 19th of July I was invited to a meeting in Portugal and needed to put an x against the 16th and 17th when I should have taken THG in liquid and cream form. I was now taking drugs in much the same way an elderly person administers his daily cocktail of heart pills, water tablets, and drugs to control blood pressure. But there are no pills to control the stomach cramps that were now beginning to concern me. For the first time I also asked the question, how long will I be on 'the programme'? I was twenty-five years of age and it is not unusual for a top sprinter to continue competing into his late thirties. My hero Linford achieved this and I remembered a conversation from way back when Linford explained just this and

July 02

Sun	Mon	Tues	Wed	Thur	Fri	Sat
	1 C	2 L	3 C	4	5 L+E	6 E+C
7	8	9	10	11	12	13
14 MEET (200) L	15 C	16 Lx	17 Cx	18	19 Meet Portugal	20 C
21 E	22	23	24	25	26 100m Commonwealth UK	27 L+C
28	29	30 4x100	31 4x400 After L+C			

told me that it was possible to compete at forty or more as long as the athlete looked after himself. And yet again, as I lay on a cold bathroom floor doubled up in pain, I realized that I wasn't looking after myself. How could I be? Someone who looks after himself, watches what he eats, doesn't smoke or drink, and yes... stays away from drugs. Not only was I plying myself with this shit but my body was rejecting them and yet still I continued to take them right up until I was caught. How crazy was that? Hindsight is a wonderful thing and I wish I'd thrown them all in the rubbish bin right there and then. But I didn't.

July 2002 was the XVII Commonwealth Games. They were held in Manchester from 25 July to 4 August 2002 and I was favourite to take gold in the 100 metres. It was all I was interested in and I'd convinced myself that to feel my best I needed to continue on the programme.

I was training harder than I ever had in my life with a determination that was at times frightening. I was focused on the last weekend of July 2002. I breezed through the heats. All of a sudden the doubts were dispelled and the cramps forgotten. I was feeling good and looking forward to the final. I would face Kim Collins from St Kitts and Nevis in the West Indies. Collins had only finished seventh in the 2000 summer Olympics. I was not unduly worried by him; he was fast but I was faster. I had to face fellow Brit Mark Lewis-Francis. Much slower than me on paper, I had beaten him seven times out of seven though he was getting closer and closer. In the field was the almost unheard of athlete Uchenna Emedolu from Nigeria and Canada's Pierre Browne. And, of course, Jason Gardiner was in there too. I remember surveying the field only seconds before the gun. I was worthy favourite, of that there was no doubt; there was no one in the field I couldn't beat. I just needed to remain focused, remember how I'd sweated blood in the gym and on the training track. That's what I told myself as I prepared to settle into the blocks. When they announced my name the 38,000 Manchester crowd gave me a huge cheer and a shiver ran the length of my spine. They were billing it as the greatest sprint race ever to take place in Britain. Tensions were high. Sometimes too much confidence can come back and bite you in the ass. In my mind I was ready for the big stage but really I wasn't. I had lost the fun aspect and changed my mental approach. I was now afraid of what I was about to do. It just didn't feel right. I started to sweat like mad, I had cotton mouth, that uncomfortable feeling when the saliva dries up and it feels as if you have a dozen cotton wool balls in your mouth. In the end I panicked and ended up running Kim Collins' race instead of running my own race.

Collins started off like an express train and immediately put me under pressure. I'd got a bad start; I felt a twinge in my thigh and remembered the 200 metres race in Birmingham earlier that month when I'd cramped up during the race. I still thought I might catch him as my best part of the race has always been in the last third. At fifty metres I got into my rhythm and felt myself winding up for the finish. At sixty metres I grimaced. I'd felt a twinge in my right thigh around the hamstring region. I gritted my teeth and decided I'd imagined it; mind over matter I told myself as I pushed myself to the limit. And then it happened. It was as if a sniper had been sitting in row Z of the Manchester Stadium with a telescopic sight trained on the back of my leg. Pop! Nothing. Just an excruciating pain and the overwhelming urge to throw myself to the ground. I stayed on my feet but pulled up. Incredibly Mark Lewis-Francis was clutching his hamstring too. What the hell was going on? Were there two snipers up there? By this time Kim Collins had powered to victory in a new national record of 9.98. I limped off the track clutching my right hamstring. Only I knew it wasn't a hamstring injury. It was the cramps again. Mike McFarlane asked me what was wrong as I moved over to the warm-up track and mercifully it started to ease a little. By this time the stretcher was out for Mark Lewis-Francis and he was punching the ground in frustration clutching at his hamstring. I was frustrated too, only I knew my hamstring was fine. I lied and told Mike I'd pulled a muscle, nothing serious I said. By the time I walked back to the changing rooms the cramps had almost gone. Physically I was fine… mentally I was in turmoil. Trust me, I was so pissed! I made my way to Manchester train station for the train back to London. I just wanted out of there and when I found out my bloody train was delayed by half an hour I paced the station like a madman. In the end I couldn't bear it any longer. I stormed along the platform and out to the taxi rank. I caught a cab from Manchester train station all the way to my house in Ilford. The taxi driver was so grateful for the fare but he never got a word out of me all the way. It was the most expensive cab ride I'd ever taken, costing me nearly three hundred pounds.

I remember watching the replays of the race on the TV that

evening and thinking for the first time since I started the programme of the serious damage I was doing to myself. I'd never had the cramps prior to going on the drugs, not even as a junior when my body was developing and growing. And now twice in one month the drugs I was taking had cost me two victories. I sincerely believed that in July.

August was another month and plenty of meets to prove to myself that what had happened the month before was a flash in the pan, something that could have happened anytime, anywhere. I was reassuring myself that I was still doing the right thing. If anything went wrong in August I was ready to pull the plug. Nothing went wrong in August, far from it. As you can see from the calendar, there were meets all around Europe and consequently the drug intake was drastically reduced in order to stay one step ahead of the testers. I was on the programme for only seven days in August 2002, as I was going through what's called a 'tapering phase'. I should have been tapering my programme two weeks before I was due to compete in the Commonwealth Games but Victor and I felt that winning the European Championships was more important. To be really honest with you, I was so glad that I had now started to reduce the amount of shit I was putting into my system, I had messed up my chances of winning a Commonwealth gold medal and I was afraid of messing up another chance of gold in the European Championships. I could now concentrate on running and not have to worry about following my drug programme. My body rewarded me in August 2002. The two big meetings were in Munich at the European Championships and in

Zurich. In Munich, for once, everything went well. The race went perfectly and I took the gold medal in a championship best of 9.96. I had another superb run in the relay helping to bring gold to the British team in a world-leading time of 38.19.

August 02

Sun	Mon	Tues	Wed	Thur	Fri	Sat
				1	2	3 Meet
4 Meet	5	6	7 Meet	8 Meet	9 Meet	10 Meet
11 Meet	12	13 C	14 L	15 C	16 Meet	17 Meet
18 Meet	19 L	20 C	21	22	23 Meet	24 Meet
25	26	27	28	29	30 Meet L (in evening)	31 C

I looked forward to the meeting in Zurich on the 16th with a new confidence. I hit a personal best in Zurich in the heats with 9.94, beating world record holder Maurice Greene into the bargain. Nothing was going to stop me in the final. It did. I ran disappointingly, finishing only third in a time of 10.05 against the wind. But it was my only slight setback in the month and on the whole I was pleased with my performances, totally different from the previous month. I couldn't help feeling that the improvement was down to the fact that my performance-enhancing substance abuse had been drastically reduced. What was I capable of if I came off drugs altogether? It is worth pointing out at this stage that I'd been dope tested no less than six times. I tested negative every time. If anyone at this stage thought that the dope testers were ahead of the game you now have your answer.

September 2002. I had a light drug intake in September too, only six days. I had no cramps. There was one major meeting that month: the Grand Prix Final in Paris on the weekend of the 22nd. I ran a great race. I was firing on all cylinders but just couldn't get past Tim Montgomery; he was in sparkling form. He charged through the finish in 9.78 to beat Maurice Greene's old world record of 9.79, set in Athens in 1999. The race was billed as a classic in the newspapers the following day. I'd pushed Montgomery all the way to the finish. One consolation was that I equalled Linford Christie's European record of 9.87.

The athletics season was all but over but still I pumped drugs into my body.

It was now the off season and the drug testers traditionally take a break. This is when the athletes that are on drugs play the system to the extreme as they know they are unlikely to get tested or even found as long as they keep their mobile voicemail box full. Dope testing is rare and of course, because there are no meets, an athlete can't be caught at the track.

In October my drug intake was stepped up. The table below shows I administered the substances twenty-one times.

October 02

Sun	Mon	Tues	Wed	Thur	Fri	Sat
		1	2	3	4	5 L
6 L	7 C+E	8 L	9 C+E	10 L	11 C+E	12 L+E
13 C	14 L	15 C	16 L	17 E	18 G	19
20 C	21	22 C	23	24 C	25	26
27	28	29	30	31		

As explained previously I wasn't just on The Clear (THG), EPO and a Growth Hormone. I was on Testosterone too. Testosterone is used in the winter to work alongside THG and is also rubbed into the forearms. I had a separate instruction leaflet telling me exactly where and when to apply it.

Testosterone cream can be purchased freely from the internet and across the counter in America and most European countries. It improves the quality of sleep and reduces cholesterol levels. In athletes it also gives relief from pain and stiffness in muscles and joints and increases bone density. It prevents excess lactic acid and other acid build-up in muscles and arguably prevents the risk of heart disease. Testosterone increases libido and regulates blood

Outside the High Court with my great friend and agent Simon Dent

Photograph by Ki Price

Photograph by Michael Freitag

World Bowl XV winners 2007
Josh Davis, Rich Parsons, Dwain Chambers, Coach Ron Hudson, Juan Wong,
Scott McCready, Justin Jenkins, Marcus Maxwell

**Victor's ZMA track team with Chryste Gaines and Kelli White. Kelli is lifting
her shirt, Chryste is on her right**

My teamates at Hamburg Sea Devils. That's me in the front row, number 18

Photograph by Olli Herdt

Photograph by Andrew Box

My debut at Castleford

Photograph by Colin Patterson

Storming to victory at Crystal Palace ahead of Maurice Green, 2002

sugar, blood pressure, and increases muscle mass and definition.

It is worth bearing in mind that after the age of twenty-five, the testosterone levels in men naturally begin to decline at an average of 1.25% per year resulting in fat deposits, sexual organ shrinkage, heart disease and loss of memory. There is a consensus of opinion in most athletes that testosterone supplements for athletes over the age of twenty-five should therefore be allowed. At this stage you are probably wondering why the hell everyone on the National Health isn't prescribed this 'wonder drug'. I have often wondered that myself.

Insulin was another drug I used during heavy winter training and sometimes used in conjunction with dextrose, whey protein and creatine. I injected three units into the lower part of my stomach after a heavy weightlifting session. I remember carrying out this procedure in the toilets of the changing room of the gym. Fairly stupid when I look back on it now and typical of your average junkie trying to mask his drug taking from the general public. Insulin is a hormone naturally released by the pancreas that helps glucose move out of the blood and into the cells in the body, where the glucose can be used as energy and nourishment. So far so good, but insulin is also a growth hormone responsible for building muscle. One danger with insulin is insulin overdose. Normal symptoms of an insulin overdose are very low blood sugar levels that will give way to headaches, irregular heartbeat, increased heart rate or pulse, sweating, tremor and nausea. There is also a disturbing link between insulin overdoses and suicide. In a nutshell, injecting insulin into the body of a non-diabetic is extremely dangerous. To the best of my knowledge, the dope testers do not test for excess insulin or the symptoms relating to potential overdose.

Then of course there are the stimulants taken just before each race.

Modafinil: Kelli White tried to get away with this stimulant as a treatment for narcolepsy. One tablet is taken an hour before competition. It is said to have the effect of a very strong espresso coffee or ten. In the United States, Modafinil is approved for the treatment of narcolepsy and shiftwork sleep disorder, again not unlike coffee, the world's most popular drug. Modafinil is a relatively new stimulant and there are not too many side effects as yet known though headaches and stomach disorders are quite common.

Liothyronine is the most potent form of thyroid hormone. It is used to accelerate the metabolic rate before races. I took two tablets one hour before competition. Possible side effects are heart palpitations, trembling, irregular heartbeat, heart oppression, agitation, shortness of breath, excretion of sugar through the urine, excessive perspiration, diarrhoea, weight loss, and certain psychic disorders as well as temporary hair loss. Nothing to worry about there then???

I took Modafinil and Liothyronine regularly; in fact I took them both before every race on the circuit in 2002. I was also tested on the track at least five times during the year and not once did I receive a negative result. November was almost identical as was December. Even on Christmas Day I had to take time out to take my dose of The Clear. I sat in the bathroom and drew out the amount of The Clear I needed when it dawned on me that I'd been taking these substances for a year. What had I achieved? Well, for one, I'd made it through ten dope tests and I'd won a gold medal in the European Championships in Germany. My European Gold medal which I won in the men's 100m went to a dear friend and his family. Ross Baillie, 21, was the Scottish senior record holder and finalist in the 1998 Commonwealth Games in the 110m hurdles. Ross, who was allergic to peanuts, had suffered a severe allergic reaction to a chicken sandwich which caused him to collapse and go into anaphylactic shock. Ross was taken to the Royal United Hospital in Bath where he passed away during the summer of 1999. He has a younger brother called Chris Baillie who aims to continue the legacy of his brother. Although my gold medal came three years after the death of Ross Baillie, winning a gold for him was always a top priority for me.

I'd also managed to equal my hero's European record of 9.87. So everything was rosy in the garden, wasn't it? Actually it wasn't. I thought back to the Commonwealth Games and the other races where the cramps had affected me. I thought back to the races I hadn't even got to and the races where I just knew that my body was fighting against me. I walked through to my bedroom and took out a copy of the doping calendar Victor had supplied to me, the very calendar you have read and studied in this chapter. And I counted up how many times I had rubbed a substance into my body, how many times I'd placed something under my tongue or popped a pill or injected a liquid into my stomach muscles. I counted the Cs and the Ls, the Es and the Gs. I went through them month by month and counted them. The lowest intake per month was six and the highest thirty-one. All in all, according to the calendar, I had taken performance-enhancing drugs in the form of THG, EPO and the growth hormone a staggering one hundred and eighty-seven times. I checked my own personal diary where I had noted the occasions I took stimulants before races and I made a note of when I'd taken insulin too. I stopped counting when I reached one hundred.

In the space of twelve months I'd taken drugs well over three hundred times.

I recalled the times I'd had to undergo blood draws just to make sure I wasn't heading towards a stroke or worse. I thought about the worry each time a race official approached me and yes, I thought about the athletes I'd beaten whilst cheating. But mostly I thought about what these drugs were doing to my body and how long I would have to take them for.

But above all I questioned the difference it had made. When I was clean my personal best had been 9.97 for the one hundred metres. And now, twelve months on after all the drugs I'd taken, after the sleepless nights, the anxiety, the pain of the cramps and my inconsistency during races and my disappointment at missing numerous events, I sat down with a PB of 9.87 and wondered… I wondered what the hell I'd been doing to myself and deep down in my heart I knew that, in the natural progression of a sprinter aged twenty-five, I probably would have equalled that time anyway and, who knows, may have even beaten it.

CAUGHT

I continued on the programme during November and December 2002. Don't ask me why, I knew why I had to continue on the programme but the constant pressure of hiding and lying started to worry me. There were so many negatives and yet the only positive was shaving a tenth of a second off my previous PB and even then I had a real belief that it would have happened naturally anyway. As I administered the first dose of The Clear under my tongue I could have shed a bucketful of tears. I wasn't hooked, these drugs were not addictive and yet I continued on the programme because I was afraid. I was afraid that if I stopped the programme something drastic would happen to my performance. I had a lucrative contract with Adidas which included a number of clauses. One was that I maintained a top three ranking in the world, otherwise my wages would be cut in half. Finishing the 2002 season as the second fastest sprinter in the world behind Tim Montgomery meant I had to repeat the same performance in 2003.

Once again I thought about the top sprinters who I knew were taking drugs, and were getting away with it and paying huge amounts of money for the privilege. "Why?" I asked myself again and again. Why were people paying thousands of pounds each year to laboratories such as Victor's all over the world? I thought about the East Germans and the Russians of the early seventies who chewed anabolic steroids like Smarties and I thought about their dominance in the strength-based sports of track and field and of weightlifting.

At the time I agreed to go onto the programme, I had some misguided theory that the drugs were temporary. It wasn't Victor's fault; he assumed I knew that I would be on the programme for as long as I was running.

Incredibly I never asked.

Looking back at those meetings with Victor, and again with the benefit of hindsight, there are so many questions I should have asked but didn't. Here I was, about to get into my second year on drugs and the awful realisation sank in that I would be on the programme another year and another and another...

They must work, I assured myself as I continued applying The Clear under my tongue and, as the drug worked its way into my system, like a junkie I lay back and relaxed and convinced myself I was doing the right thing. This would be the year, I told myself. 2003 would be the year that changed Dwain Chamber's life. I would be proved right, only it would not be in the way I dared.

As I started to get in to the swing of training, I needed to stock up on some more 'gear'. I called Victor, placed my order and waited for my supplements to arrive. Due to the nature of what was being delivered, Victor had them sent via FedEx, on an overnight shipment. Four days later and I was still waiting for the package to arrive. With every day that passed I called Victor and told him that the eagle hadn't landed. We both became nervous about the delay and wondered whether the package had been lost. Victor called the shipping department and tracked the package; he was told that it was in Customs, pending a departure date to my UK address. Finally, on the sixth day, the eagle finally landed. We have no proof of what the real delay was but I believe the Feds were monitoring our movements as well as examining what was inside my parcel.

The weather during November and December was a joke. It rained every day and quite frankly I couldn't be bothered to train. Throughout the two month period I was at home I continued to load up on EPO, Growth Hormone and THG. All in all I must have trained about three weeks over the two months. Christmas was on the horizon and I'd spent more time shopping when I should have been training. I should have known that things were about to turn sour as I had no interest in my athletic career and I started to lose focus. Christmas had come and gone and I was supposed to be travelling to Miami in January 2003 for pre-season training. I was all over the place, I never booked my flight on time so I had to pay for a more expensive ticket, and the same shit happened with booking my apartment. It cost me an arm and a leg. Once in Miami I began to feel at ease again. A week into my training when I was in the middle of a running session I felt a tearing sensation in my right hamstring. I've never been cursed with injuries but I felt this one was here to stay; it was serious. My pre-season training camp was cut short and I was advised to have a cortisone injection into the affected area so as to reduce any further swelling. I followed the advice of the doctor and had the injection. This kept the pain at bay for two or three days. I started training again but, with every step I took, the tear felt as though it was getting bigger and bigger. I was advised to get an ultrasound scan. The results showed the tear was an inch wide and three inches long. My 2003 season was in serious doubt. A tear of that size would take between four and six weeks to heal. This left me with only two options: I would have to draw my whole season to an end or I would have to recover from my injury then restart my winter work during the latter part of February into March. The occurrence of this injury never sat well with Victor and Remi as the dosages of THG, EPO and Growth Hormone were at the lower level of the scale so as to not cause any injury. Victor asked me what I'd done while at home in the UK. I had to swallow my pride and admit to him that I had continued taking THG, EPO and Growth Hormone but I never really trained. The light finally switched on. Victor yelled at me.

"Dwain, are you fucking crazy? You can't take this shit and just sit around on your ass. You need to work in order to get the full benefits. It's the equivalent of going to a high paid job, sitting around all day doing nothing and expecting money to go into your bank. If you don't work for your money you won't have any money to spend."

Red in the face, he continued, "Dwain, this protocol is highly certificated; you need to look after your body as these anabolic agents cause tightness in the muscles. This is why you've got this damned injury: poor application, man! It's inevitable you're going to get bloody injured."

I hung my head in shame. What could I say. I felt like a naughty schoolboy who had been called out in front of the entire school assembly. I still had a further three weeks left in Miami, so instead of going shopping I decided to continue training. I stayed in the gym a lot more as I couldn't run as much as I wanted. On the days I did run I had to work on running with short quick steps as running with a full-length stride caused me serious discomfort.

With no time to spare, I arrived back in the UK at the end of January and went to see my beloved physio Sarah Connors. She fixed me up yet again and I then had my eye on competing in the Indoors.

I was mouthing off Indoors too saying I would take the 60m world record. My form was poor and I even failed to get through the heats at the 2003 British Grand Prix. I finished fourth in a time of 6.68. The wheels were coming off big time and for the first time I began to miss days on the programme. There were days when The Clear and The Cream, Growth Hormone and EPO were deliberately forgotten. I tried to convince myself that my system had benefited from them during the previous year and I didn't need to be so meticulous about taking stuff every day.

I set my sights on the AAA trials. I needed to qualify for the IAAF World Indoor Championships. However, I suffered a defeat against Mark Lewis-Francis by a hundredth of a second and missed out on a spot at the Championships. I'll never forget that night. It was one of the low points. *Dwain Chambers, big mouth*, the papers were calling me, not even qualifying for the Championships I said I would win. Drastic action was needed if I was to regain my form and confidence. Incredibly, despite my misgivings and doubts about Remi and Victor and performance-enhancing substances, I chose to finish my coaching relationship with my trainer Mike McFarlane in favour of a permanent relationship with Remi. Yes, I'd convinced myself that was what I needed to do. I had to call it a day between Mike and I as it became difficult to have a relationship with two coaches. On the one hand Remi and Victor knew what was going on but on the other I couldn't let Mike in on the secret. This was a very difficult decision for me to make as it involved me lying to Mike about what was really going on. Since then I have seen the error in my ways and I have apologized to him about my actions.

The miracle I expected to happen did not materialise.

I knuckled down and focused on the 100 metres and trained even harder with a determination and aggressiveness that frightened me at times. I ran a couple of warm-ups in America. I finished third and fourth in competitions in California and Oregon. But I wasn't too concerned as I knew I had plenty more in the tank and surely the training and drug taking would pull me through.

I actually believed that I was going to win the 2003 World Championships in Paris. Whatever the critics say about me they can't condemn my positive mental attitude and my ability to bounce back time and time again. It's difficult to explain but it was as if my brain had split into two sections. Part of my head was convincing me that drugs were bad and my races that year were below average and yet I had the ability to somehow push that part of my thought system into a distant corner of my head. I forced the positive thinking section to the front and concentrated on keeping it there. I wouldn't let the negative side win and yet I knew it was still there.

I had spent more time in America with Victor and Remi. I'd seen Kelli too and we carried on where we'd left off. Our relationship was definitely more off than on but that is the nature of a long-distance casual acquaintance. As the day to leave for Paris drew closer I concentrated on keeping the negative vibes at bay. I concentrated on training and looked forward to catching up with Kelli and Remi again, spending a few days with my 'friends'.

Then Victor made it known to everyone that he would be turning up at the Championships in Paris. Victor normally took the laidback approach and let the athletes do the running and get the glory. This time it was to be different. Kelli White had been running well; in fact everybody that was on Victor's programme seemed to be doing well throughout the summer. Victor was proud of what he had created and he gave a series of press interviews. Suddenly, almost overnight, he had become a recognised face, a major part of the team. He told me that he was looking forward to Paris, watching his athletes running live in real competition. I got the distinct impression he was putting himself in the shop window.

My physio Sarah Connors was also in Paris. Once I'd committed to take drugs, letting others know what I was doing was out of the question. I told no one: not my family, not my friends, no one. I so wanted to tell Sarah what I was doing but it was out of the question and I had to fob her off with lies again and again.

Sarah had never met Victor before and their first encounter was in Paris. It didn't go down too well. Victor seemed very confident; he was telling everyone who would listen that I was going to become the new world champion. Sarah was one of the ones who listened but she looked unconvinced. Victor said I wasn't the same person Sarah had known, said that he'd changed me for the better. As we split up and went in different directions, Sarah and I made the briefest of brief eye contact and I knew from that moment that our relationship had changed. She knew and I knew that I was a liar and I'd kept the truth from the one person who had stood by me through thick and thin. I was a liar... again.

Typical of Sarah, she said nothing. Sarah never said much to me before the men's 100 metre final either but I was convinced she had guessed what I had been doing. Things suddenly started to feel wrong. I had lost all respect for myself, my world was starting to fall apart and there was nothing I could do about it. I arrived in the call room where athletes undergo kit and spike checks. I was a troubled man. Instead of staying relaxed, all I could think about was what were people thinking of me? If Sarah has suspicions, how many others have guessed too? These thoughts plagued my mind all the way to the start line. Mentally I had drained my body of any chance of being competitive. I could do no better than fourth place in the final.

Secretly I admired Kelli's determination and focus as she was able to keep her cool leading up to the World Championships in Paris. She went on to become double world champion in the 100 metres and the 200 metres. She was clearly stronger mentally than I was.

I found all the pressure too much to handle. My emotions were being twisted and turned inside out. Guilt, fear, anxiety; how on earth could I be expected to run my normal race? This is what drugs do to you.

I could almost compare it to the days when I was in secondary school and I had misbehaved. I knew my form tutor was in the process of sending a letter home to my parents; I was waiting for my punishment. On that start line I was so scared, I just couldn't perform. It's a shame that things had to end the way they did with Kelli and me; we were having so much fun. We parted ways after the Championships in Paris and we've never spoken since. It was strange... as if somehow we both knew that the shit was heading towards the fan.

After the World Championships in Paris, we were all at a Grand Prix meeting and as a group, (Victor's group), we were all encouraged to stick together. We weren't to mix with the other athletes. The atmosphere was strange... something was up. I wondered what all the fuss was about and why we couldn't act as we always had. I was annoyed with certain members of our group as they suggested I stay away from my GB teammates. I was determined that no one was going to tell me who I could and couldn't socialise with. I was in the hotel room about to arrange a night around town with two of my close GB teammates when my mobile rang. I was about to find out why Remi was so concerned. The caller was anonymous; she had an American accent and informed me that Victor had just been raided by the Feds. The Feds, I thought to myself... the Federal Bureau of Investigation. Why the hell would they be interested in Victor and BALCO? Surely this was a WADA problem or something that the IAAF would take issue with. I shrugged the phone call off as a crank and went to look for Kelli and the gang. By the time I had seen the other members of the group they too had received phone calls issuing the same news. This put immense pressure on all of us as a group. We would no longer be able to travel with our pre-race supplements or our EPO and THG. We were now all under suspicion as the news filtered around the world. We were all nervous and jumpy... we were living on borrowed time.

I remember lying awake that night and wondering about the urine sample I'd given at a pre-World Championship training camp in Saarbrucken, Germany in early August. I was conscious that I hadn't been sticking rigidly to Victor's programme and remembered, as I peed into the official's bottle, feeling slightly concerned as the urine hit the container. Normally you struggle to pee on command when the official appears, especially after strenuous exercise. This time I peed for England causing the official to make a comment as he watched me filling up the container. I'd heard nothing about that test, the last one I'd had. I swore to myself I was coming off the drugs for good. They hadn't done anything for me and I'd been taking them for over eighteen months. I couldn't handle the torment, the lies, the secrecy. Thank goodness that dope test was clear. At least I thought it was; it was well over a month now since the test. Surely I would have heard by now if there had been any problems?

Unknown to me, the IAAF, WADA, the US Doping Authority and the FBI at that time were working together on what was to be the biggest sports doping scandal in US history. It was rumoured they had discovered a new form of designer steroid called THG.

I was holidaying in the Bahamas at the Atlantis Hotel when I took the call that would turn my life upside down. I was with my then girlfriend Jeina, but the relationship was in its final days. Jeina and I hadn't seen each other for a while and we both knew the relationship was on rocky ground as the vibes began to get stale. We decided to try and pick things up and attempt to relight that fire, and why not. We were in paradise. If it couldn't work there it couldn't work anywhere. Three days in and we'd had a particularly nice morning together. We decided to walk back to our room from the beach. I was sitting upstairs in the room reading a book when my mobile rang. As always, my mobile was switched on and, of course, the mailbox was empty – as always. I'm a hopeless cheat. I'd notified UK Athletics of my whereabouts too. I didn't recognise the official's voice and at first I thought I was being called for a test. I wasn't. The official was brief and to the point. I remember he apologised and addressed me as Mr Chambers. He introduced himself first of all then continued with the formalities.

"Is that Mr Chambers?"

"Yes, that's me."

"Mr Chambers, I have some bad news for you, I'm afraid."

The pages on the book started to shake.

"Yes."

"Your recent urine sample taken in Saarbrucken on August 1st 2003 has tested positive for a newly discovered steroid."

I was speechless as I struggled to hang onto the phone. The official asked me if I understood what that meant. I simply answered yes.

As the conversation ended, I dropped the phone and sat in silence. Jeina asked me what had happened. I explained to her that I'd failed a drug test and we needed to go home right away. I took the lift down to the hotel lobby and told them to get me two tickets on the next flight to London. Our suitcases were packed and we were on a flight back to London later that evening. The return flight must have been a nightmare for Jeina as I hardly uttered a word during the seven-hour flight. When I got to Heathrow I turned on my mobile and made a few calls. I called Joel, my good friend and I called Mum just to let her know I was back home safe and sound. She asked me why I was back early and I blamed girlfriend trouble yet again.

I expected the news to be all over the front pages the next day. Mercifully it wasn't. I didn't know what to do and my so-called advisers were conspicuous by their absence. My agents at the time put me in touch with a solicitor by the name of Graham Shear. The news of my failed test hadn't hit the press yet, so I had to move quickly and provide Graham with all the information in order to defend myself. I was back and forth and in and out of different solicitors' offices in an attempt to try and give a valid explanation to the governing bodies as to why there was an adverse substance in my body. I thought taking drugs was stressful, but, boy, you have no idea the amount of stress I was now under. I was trying to defend myself knowing that I hadn't got a leg to stand on. As I sat in the office with a room full of expensive barristers, admin assistants and solicitors, I contemplated about how the hell I got myself into this mess and I remembered those prophetic words that Victor said to me as he handed over my first sample of THG:

"Dwain, don't come crying when the paparazzi come calling."

Now I know how Neo felt when Morpheus gave him the option of taking the red or the blue pill. On the one hand he wanted to know how deep the rabbit hole really went but on the other, when he found out, he didn't like it and wanted out, but by that time it was too late. I was in the same scenario.

The following week I received an invite to judge a Miss Jamaica contest in the Porchester Halls. I was reluctant at first but after a glass of wine and some encouragement from my friend Joel Campbell I thought what the hell; at least it would take my mind off things. It didn't... the pretty girls parading in their bikinis that evening did nothing for me. They might as well have not been there. However there was one girl who did take my mind off my troubles for a while. Her name was Leonie and she was sitting in the audience. As soon as I got talking to her something just clicked. At the end of the evening I asked Leonie if I could take her out. At first she declined politely. I now know she knew all about my reputation as a ladies' man and she wanted nothing to do with me. But on this night Dwain Chambers wasn't the cocky, arrogant, ladies' man she'd heard so much about. He had a troubled aura around him and perhaps Leonie sensed it. I'm a big believer in fate and the powers of God. I don't believe Leonie was there by accident that night: it was meant to be, she was meant to be there. Despite what was about to happen to Dwain Chambers, the good Lord was still looking after me. In the end I gave her my telephone number.

I slept better that night, in fact I slept like a baby. I was free of the secret I'd carried with me for so long. Any day now the news would be out there and I was almost looking forward to it. More importantly than that though was the fact that every performance-enhancing substance, every stimulant and growth hormone had been confined to the rubbish bin. For the first time in eighteen months I was clean and feeling so much better. And as an added bonus, the good Lord had sent me a guardian angel by way of a reward.

The day before the news was due to hit the papers, I was encouraged to leave town as the press would most definitely be outside my front door. At this point I called Christian Malcolm and asked him if it would be okay for me to spend a few days with him. He asked what the problem was and I told him I'd explain when I got there. Then I packed a bag, loaded up the car, and Casper, my Staffordshire bull terrier, and I made our way to Wales. On the way Leonie called me. I pulled the car over and talked with her for about ten minutes.

"You are about to hear something very bad about me," I told her.

Leonie listened as I explained everything and then told her I would understand if she never wanted to see me again. I was bad news, I said, and about to go through my own personal hell (though I didn't know at the time it would last as long as it has done). If she didn't want to come along on the roller coaster of a ride I was about to embark on she could simply walk away and I would respect her decision.

The next day Dwain Chambers was all over the newspapers and my neighbours informed me reporters were camped outside my door, just like rock fans queuing for tickets for the Rolling Stones last-ever gig. It would be three weeks before the press moved away from my house. I worried about returning home, facing my friends and family. On the whole they were very supportive and went out of their way to inform me when the press were hanging around outside my front door.

The headlines were scathing. It was the first time Chambers and 'cheat' had been linked but it certainly wouldn't be the last. The press were like a pack of hungry hyenas determined to get their teeth into me. Graham Shear issued the usual statement stating I'd never knowingly taken a banned substance. This was normal based on what I'd told him so far ; we were just buying a little time. Graham summoned me a few days later and said he wanted to know the truth.

I had tested positive for THG and nothing else and explained to Graham and anyone who would listen that THG wasn't on the banned list so how could I be found guilty for a drug that wasn't 'illegal' at the time I was alleged to have taken it? At that time the authorities knew nothing about the cocktail of drugs I was on.

I had a decision to take: fight or die.

At the time I was busted I knew that I had cheated and part of me wanted to hold my hands up and admit everything, take my punishment and get on with life. And yet a part of me also knew all about the shortcomings of the system and the establishment. I'd never even seen a 'banned list' let alone been educated on what and what not to avoid in over ten years of serious athletics. And here, I felt, were the same authorities who had neglected to inform and educate a young athlete only too happy to inform the press of his guilt. From that day on I was the bad bastard, Chambers the cheat.

But I had made my decision. I would take them on, do my research and fight. I was destined to lose, I knew that, and everyone I spoke to told me so, but I was determined to make a stand.

The first week in November 2003 the IAAF officially suspended me and my battle began. Suddenly my goal of going to the 2004 Olympics in Athens seemed a million miles away.

I spent over £60,000 on legal fees during the court case. It wasn't a court case to clear my name. I was guilty, of that there was no doubt, and I didn't spend £60,000 of my own money to defend the indefensible. I went into court knowing I would almost certainly lose but with a determination to bring to the public eye the difficulties an athlete goes through trying to avoid the pitfalls and temptations all too often placed in front of them. But more importantly I was taking on the authorities to expose the frailties of the system and their lack of support and information afforded to the average athlete.

My defence was based on THG not even being on the banned list so how could I be banned? We also argued that because so little research had been done into THG, because it had only just been 'discovered', how did the authorities know that it was performance-enhancing?

The case was heard by a panel. They asked the UKA/USADA whether they had carried out any studies on THG to find out whether it was in fact performance-enhancing. It was at this point they offered their only proof. They made it very clear they had never put aside enough time to do a human case study on THG. I believe the real concern lay in the fact that there were a total of some thirty athletes involved in this BALCO scandal. The time and money being pumped in seemed to be more concerned with ensuring that the authorities came out with a clean bill of health rather than helping the people that mattered, i.e. the athletes. They also claimed that, during tests, they had injected a baboon, not a human but a baboon with THG. It was all quite bizarre. The spokesman representing UKA/USADA claimed because the baboon's muscles increased in size that was sufficient evidence for them to say that it was performance-enhancing. This seemed to me to be just plain crazy. Everyone knows that in order to gain any muscle mass from taking any form of steroids you have to be on a cycle for at least four to six weeks and train in the gym lifting weights on a regular basis. So to see muscle growth in a few days looked to me like absolute madness. Whatever they injected into the baboon wasn't what I was taking, because I never got results that quickly. I was also quite disappointed that the baboon never turned up to give evidence on whether he noticed any improvement in his performance.

As expected I lost the case and awaited my fate but I had at least brought the matter to the attention of the world's press.

On the other side of the Atlantic the case against Victor Conte, Remi Korchemny and BALCO was building.

In the early part of 2004 my fate and that of BALCO became known. Remi and Victor were among four men indicted by a federal grand jury in America on charges of distributing illegal steroids. A week or so after, I was handed a two-year worldwide ban due to expire on November 7, 2005 and of course that now infamous lifetime suspension from the Olympics. I was strangely at peace but with a lot of decisions to make. By this time I was in a stable relationship with Leonie. The relationship blossomed and we set up home together. For the first time in my life I felt settled. Some of my friends told me that, despite being banned from the sport I loved, I was at peace with the world.

I talked things through with Leonie. Any decisions would need to be hers as much as mine and for the first time in my life I made it known to a woman that I wanted to start a family. Our family would need a stable home and an income; the father needs to provide for his family but, more importantly, the father needs to do what is right for the good of his sport and, of course, for the peace of mind the correct decisions bring.

It was then that we both set out our mission. I would be open and honest about what drugs I had taken and try to help UK and world athletics overcome the many obstacles placed in an athlete's way. I would tell them exactly how I evaded the testers and the precise times and dates I took the performance-enhancing substances. I would tell them just how easy it was to avoid the dopers and help them improve their effectiveness.

I started on my mission by asking Victor to prepare an open letter setting out the programme and detailing exactly what it was I was taking. Although a little reluctant at first, he nevertheless complied with my wishes. Victor's letter is copied below:

Dear Dwain,

Per your request, this letter is to confirm I am willing to assist you in providing UK Sport and others with information that will help them to improve the effectiveness of their anti-doping programs.

The specific details regarding how you were able to circumvent the British and IAAF anti-doping tests for an extended period of time are provided below.

Your performance-enhancing drug program included the following seven prohibited substances: THG, testosterone/epitestosterone cream, EPO (Procrit), HGH (Serostim), insulin (Humalog), modafinil (Provigil) and liothryonine, which is a synthetic form of the T3 thyroid hormone (Cytomel).

THG is a previously undetectable designer steroid nicknamed "the clear". It was primarily used in the off season and was taken two days per week, typically on Mondays and Wednesdays. Generally, these were the two most intense weight-training days of the week. The purpose was to accelerate healing and tissue repair. Thirty units (IU) of the liquid was placed under the tongue during the morning time-frame. THG was used in cycles of "three weeks on and one week off".

Testosterone/epitestosterone cream was also primarily used during the off season. It was rubbed into the skin on the front of the forearm two days per week, typically Tuesdays and Thursdays. The dosage was ½ gram which contained 50mg of testosterone and 2.5mg of epitestosterone (20 to 1 ratio). The purpose was to offset the suppression of endogenous testosterone caused by the use of the THG and to accelerate recovery. The testosterone/epitestosterone cream was also used in cycles of three weeks on and one week off.

EPO was used three days per week during the "corrective phase", which is the first two weeks of a cycle. Typically, it was on Mondays, Wednesdays and Fridays. It was only used once per week during the "maintenance phase" thereafter, typically this was every Wednesday. The dosage was 4,000 IU per injection. The purpose was to increase the red blood cell count and enhance oxygen uptake and utilization. This substance provides a big advantage to sprinters because it enables them to do more track repetitions and obtain a much deeper training load during the off season. EPO becomes undetectable about 72 hours after subcutaneous injection (stomach) and only 24 hours after intravenous injection.

HGH was used three nights per week, typically on Mondays, Wednesdays and Fridays. Each injection would contain 4.5 units of growth hormone. Once again, this substance was used primarily during the off season to help with recovery from very strenuous weight training sessions.

Insulin was used after strenuous weight training sessions during the off season. Three units of Humalog (fast-acting insulin) were injected immediately after the workout sessions together with a powdered drink that contained 30 grams of dextrose, 30 grams of whey protein isolates and 3 grams of creatine. The purpose was to quickly replenish glycogen, resynthesize ATP and promote protein synthesis and muscle growth. Insulin acts as a "shuttle system" in the transport of glucose and branch chain amino acids. There is no test available for insulin at this time.

Modafinil was used as a "wakefulness promoting" agent before competitions. The purpose was to decrease fatigue and enhance mental alertness and reaction time. A 200mg tablet was consumed one hour before competition.

Liothryonine was used to help accelerate the basic metabolic rate before competitions. The purpose was to reduce sluggishness and increase quickness. Two 25mg tablets were taken one hour before competition. There is no test available for liothryonine at this time.

In general terms, explosive strength athletes, such as sprinters, use anabolic steroids, growth hormone, insulin and EPO during the off season. They use these drugs in conjunction with an intense weight training program, which helps to develop a strength base that will serve them throughout the competitive season. Speed work is done just prior to the start of the competitive season.

It is important to understand it is not really necessary for athletes to have access to designer anabolic steroids such as THG. They can simply use fast-acting testosterone (oral as well as creams and gels) and still easily avoid the testers. For example, oral testosterone will clear the system in less than a week and testosterone creams and gels will clear even faster.

Many drug-tested athletes use what I call the "duck and dodge" technique. Several journalists in the UK have recently referred to it as the "duck and dive" technique. This is basically how it works.

First, the athlete repeatedly calls their own cell phone until the message capacity is full. This way the athlete can claim to the testers that they didn't get a message when they finally decide to make themselves available. Secondly, they provide incorrect information on their whereabouts form. They say they are going to one place and then go to another. Thereafter, they start using testosterone, growth hormone and other drugs for a short cycle of two to three weeks.

After the athlete discontinues using the drugs for a few days and they know that they will test clean, they become available and resume training at their regular facility.

Most athletes are tested approximately two times each year on a random out-of-competition basis. If a tester shows up and the athlete is not where they are supposed to be, then the athlete will receive a "missed test". This is the equivalent to receiving "strike one" when up to bat in a baseball game. The current anti-doping rules allow an athlete to have two missed tests in any given eighteen-month period without a penalty or consequence. So, the disadvantage for an athlete having a missed test is that they have one strike against them. The advantage of that missed test is the athlete has now received the benefit of a cycle of steroids. Long story short, an athlete can continue to duck and dive until they have two missed tests, which basically means that they can continue to use drugs until that time.

In summary, it's my opinion that more than fifty percent of the drug tests performed each year should be during the off season or the fourth quarter. This is when the track athletes are duckin' and divin' and using anabolic steroids and other drugs. Let me provide some rather startling information for your consideration. If you check the testing statistics on the USADA website, you will find that the number of out-of-competition drug tests performed during each quarter of 2007 are as follows: in the first quarter there were 1208, second quarter 1295, third quarter 1141 and in the fourth quarter there were only 642.

In late 2003 I advised USADA about the importance of random testing during the fourth quarter of the year. They did initially seem to follow my advice because they increased the number of fourth-quarter tests in 2004, 2005 and 2006.

However, they failed to continue this practice in 2007. Why would USADA decide to perform only 15% of their annual out-of-competition tests during the fourth quarter? Let's not forget that this is the off season before the upcoming summer Olympic Games. This is equivalent to a fisherman knowing that the fish are ready to bite and then consciously deciding that it is time to reel in his line and hook, lean his fishing pole up against a tree and take a nap.

On several occasions, I have provided detailed information to both USADA and WADA in an attempt to help them establish more effective testing policies and procedures.

I certainly have more information that I would like the opportunity to provide to you and UK Sport, but I will leave that for another time.

Hopefully, this information will be helpful and I am available to assist you further upon request.

Yours sincerely,

Victor Conte

Sadly, I don't have a magic solution to the drugs problem endemic in our sport today. But I sincerely believe that by working together we can eradicate it or at least change the mindset of young athletes all over the world. Drugs in sport isn't a new phenomenon. Like I said in an earlier chapter, twenty years ago four of the five fastest men in the world would go on to test positive at some point in their career. In the 1970s drug taking was rife and yet even as far back as the Ancient Olympics athletes were taking performance-enhancing substances. In the past, governments have not only advocated the use of performance-enhancing drugs but they have supplied them as well.

In 1977 one of East Germany's best sprinters, Renate Neufeld, absconded and fled to the West. She would rock the sporting world with her allegations.[3] See her testimony below:

At 17, I joined the East Berlin Sports Institute. My speciality was the 80m hurdles. We swore that we would never speak to anyone about our training methods, including our parents. The training was very hard. We were all watched. We signed a register each time we left the dormitory and we had to say where we were going and what time we would return. One day, my trainer, Günter Clam, advised me to take pills to improve my performance: I was running 200m in 24 seconds. My trainer told me the pills were vitamins, but I soon had cramp in my legs, my voice became gruff and sometimes I couldn't talk any more. Then I started to grow a moustache and my periods stopped. I then refused to take these pills. One morning in October 1977, the secret police took me at 7am and questioned me about my refusal to take pills prescribed by the trainer. I then decided to flee, with my fiancé.

She brought these so called 'vitamins' with her to the West. They were later identified as anabolic steroids. That's how big the problem was. I'm glad to say most of those regimes have long gone but with good reason. Some governments of the world still adopt the win-at-all-costs attitude and turn a blind eye to their top athletes taking banned performance-enhancing substances. In a nutshell, drugs in sport is old news, and some countries even to this day are transparently corrupt. We know who they are, WADA knows who they are, and the World Athletics and Olympic committees know who they are, but still we allow them to compete unhindered with a 'trackside' test occasionally knowing full well that any trace of banned substance will have long since disappeared from the body. What is frustrating is that I firmly believe the majority of countries, authorities and athletes genuinely want to clean up the sport.

Time and time again I have offered to help both the UK and the world doping authorities and time and time again they have shown some interest but their sincerity is lacking. What more can I do other than to hold up my hands, admit to my mistakes, and not only ask to be allowed to get on with my life but to actually offer my assistance in improving the situation? I don't know what it is with UK Athletics and the British Olympic Association and why they are declining my help because, from where I am standing, there is no person better placed to help them improve drugs detection and increase the deterrents than someone in my position. I flouted their detection methods with ease for a year and a half. In the real world professional security companies employ ex-burglars in order make their security systems as watertight as possible. Reformed bank robbers and pickpockets assist the police, disclosing the secrets that have enabled them to make a living from crime. I feel I am in the same position. I want to be forgiven and as part of my penance, if you like, I am only too willing to help. Why else would I have admitted to taking drugs for a full eighteen-month period? It would have been so easy for me to advise the committee I was sitting in front of that I had only been on performance drugs for a short period of time. But no. Not me. I figured that I should be as honest as possible. I figured that if I was, it would assist me in my eventual appeal in overturning my lifetime Olympic ban. I knew that by disclosing the duration of my offence the world authorities would strip me of all my titles, annul my times, force me to return my medals and my prize money, and this they duly did. I also lost all my sponsorship and although financially this put me on the breadline, I figured I had wiped my slate clean and it would stand me in good stead after the ban finished and I returned to competitive sport. At this time I sought advice from several legal sources. They all advised that Olympic lifetime bans had been overturned in the past and therefore in being honest and upfront with the authorities there was no reason to suggest that my ban could not be overturned. I would place my faith in the system and give them everything they required. In return I did not want to be become a millionaire or an all-conquering hero nor did I want to be exonerated in any way. I simply wanted the chance to run in the vest of Great Britain if my times on the track warranted it.

In the two years of my ban, I kept a low profile in the press and stayed away from the athletics meetings and Grand Prix events. And of course I watched the Athens Olympics on television. For me November 2005 could not come quick enough.

In July 2005 to my immense delight it was announced that the 2012 Olympics would be held in London. The greatest sports show on earth would be held in my own backyard.

On September 4th 2005 Leonie gave birth to our first son, Skye. It was by far the greatest moment of my life at that point. I remember walking out of the hospital in a daze and thinking that within a few short months my life would be on track again.

How wrong I was.

In athletics there are only a few ways to make a reasonable living. Unlike Premiership footballers that draw a weekly wage, a professional athlete does not receive a salary. One income stream is from sponsorship and another is from the big Grand Prix events around the globe. This is where the big money is made and winning the gold medal at these events can sometimes mean twenty-five to thirty thousand in your bank account. The other of course is to become an Olympic gold medallist and reap the rewards of the contracts and promotions that will inevitably follow. I therefore counted down the days until my ban was effectively over.

On November **7,** my ban expired but I had to comply with World Anti-Doping Agency (WADA) regulations that prevented me returning to competition until I had undertaken three mandatory tests three months apart. If they were clear I was eligible for competition. The results were fine and I began making preparations to start competing again. I waited by the telephone for the invites to the Grand Prix meetings later in the year.

The telephone never rang.

It was early June when I realised something sinister was going on. I didn't exactly expect Adidas to appear with another two hundred thousand a year contract but I did expect some sort of income via promotions to support me in the coming season. My exclusion from the Olympics meant I would no longer receive lottery funding. Strangely enough I thought that everything was sweet as that same month the IAAF had accepted my offer to reimburse them with the appearance fees and prize money I'd won during the period I was using THG and I was cleared by UK Athletics to make my comeback. But with no money and no offers of money, no sponsorship or funding, it was going to be tough. It was in June 2006 that the awful truth dawned on me that perhaps a two-year ban didn't mean two years after all. Here I was out of the ban and yet I still felt I was being penalised.

I had started training in Jamaica under Glen Mills, the coach of Caribbean sprinters Kim Collins and Usain Bolt. In my opinion the Jamaicans head the world in sprinting because of their attention to detail and technique. Bolt was not so special back then but I think he's worked hard at his game. I've been asked many questions of Usain Bolt since his awesome display in the Olympics and is he beatable? Yes he is, he's only human. Usain can do the 100 metres in forty-one strides, I would take forty-three or forty-four. But I have better stride frequency: 4.96 per second compared to 4.65. To beat him I need to maintain my frequency and improve my stride. Beijing was his time to shine, let's just say I'm looking forward to meeting him in 2009.

I returned to competition on 11 June 2006 in the Norwich Union British Grand Prix at Gateshead. In the 100m final I finished third in 10.07, behind Asafa Powell who equalled his own world record. My training regime in Jamaica had helped me make a strong return despite a long absence from competition. I had run the fastest time by a European sprinter in 2006. I wouldn't be celebrating too long though. My admission of drug use meant I had violated a technical rule in the IAAF handbook. The IAAF would see to that as they annulled even more of my performances. In a knee-jerk reaction the governing body extended the nullification up to the beginning of 2002. This took away my European 100m gold medal and invalidated my European record of 9.87.

My times in 2006 were poor. There is an argument that states once you have taken a course of steroids over a long duration the results will stay with you. This is plain nonsense as my times that year proved. In August of the same year, to my great relief, I was selected to represent Great Britain at the European Championships in Gothenburg. I didn't function at all well in the individual event. I recorded times of 10.24 first round, 10.39 second round, 10.25 semi-final and 10.24 in the final, in which I finished fifth. The results were not good and well below my personal best. Although I was a little disillusioned I was running clean and therefore happy within myself.

I then joined up with Mark Lewis-Francis, Darren Campbell and Marlon Devonish in the 4x100m sprint relay squad. Previously I had decided to arrange a meeting with team management about my position in the team. I had made it very clear that I wanted to play no part in the men's 4 x100m relay team. I felt that the team were more than capable of winning without me. Nevertheless they made their intentions known and selected me. I then went into a team meeting with the team coach and all members of the relay team. I had expressed to the boys that I was sorry for what had gone on and I asked them to forgive me. It was a clear-the-air session and I felt that they had accepted my apologies. Everyone was given the opportunity to speak their mind and more than one person told me what a silly bastard I had been. I held my hands up acknowledging that I had and I regretted it but, if possible, I wanted to look forward, not back.

Once everyone had said their piece all seemed fine; well, so I thought. Later that evening a member of team management told me that Darren Campbell had just left his room. He went on to explain that Darren was spitting fire and moaning about the fact that I was involved with the team. This threw me as only a few hours ago I had asked all the boys to speak their mind and if they didn't want me in the team then that was the time to tell me. In the 4x100 metre final I was on first leg. Darren was on second leg. The gun fired and I set off. I ran a powerful leg. I managed to get the baton into his hands... but only just.

I wanted to yell at him! What had happened? The GB team took the gold medal; it was a really special moment for me winning a gold medal for my country after all I'd been through. Darren Campbell however was determined to spoil the moment and divide the team. He sulked on the other side of the track as far away from me as possible. When the team finally came together for our lap of honour, Darren came over towards us with one hand on his hip. We asked him to join in the victory lap. He turned his back on us and walked off. Injured, my ass! He wanted to make a statement. He couldn't wait to get into the press room and tell them that he would have been a hypocrite to go on a lap of honour with me as he disagreed with my inclusion in the team.

If that was the case why run the relay at all? Step aside and let another man that wants to run, run. Furthermore he should have opened his mouth when he had the chance.

I reflected on the 2006 season. Apart from that moment of glory in the relay it had been a poor season and even that moment had been spoiled by Darren Campbell. The big money invites hadn't arrived and neither had the sponsors come knocking on my door. The British Olympic bandwagon for 2012 had also begun to take shape and the committee headed by a certain Lord Sebastian Coe were actively seeking funding.

My name began to appear more in the press as I had made my intention clear to fight my lifelong Olympic ban. By the end of the year my name was dirt again. It seemed everyone was jumping on the Dwain Chambers' bandwagon. Chief among the accusers were Coe, Moynihan and my fellow athletes past and present. I could be forgiven for thinking it was an orchestrated campaign against me. The voices would be heard right through 2007 and 2008 and be at their loudest a few weeks before the final hearing in which my fate would be decided and a judge would decide whether I would be running in Beijing.

PEOPLE IN GLASSHOUSES SHOULDN'T THROW STONES

Steve Redgrave, Malcolm Arnold, Sebastian Coe, Steve Cram, Kelly Holmes, Niels de Vos, Colin Moynihan, Frank Dick.

Yes… they've all stood up and condemned me, put the boot into a man on the ground. Sadly they are the sort of people that do influence others. They are names. Highly respected athletes and coaches, people with prominent positions in the athletics world and of course two of them sit in the House of Lords: Lord Coe and Lord Moynihan. They influence promoters and the television networks and organizers of the big athletic events. They have helped cost me the chance to compete, the chance to put food on the table for my family. They've even organized petitions against me. Yet Carl Myerscough has been invited to meetings that I haven't. Can I remind you, Carl Myerscough received exactly the same two-year ban that I did; he also took a cocktail of drugs which have not come into question. The relevant sports authorities hammered me down for my list of drugs and put it all over the news but not once did I see any reference to Carl Myerscough's list of drugs. His wife Melissa Myerscough was found guilty of the same drug as I tested positive for. THG was found in her system at the 2003 American Championships. When I was named (after a fight, I hasten to add) in the British team competing indoors in Valencia there was a public outcry. The names spoke out again, condemning Chambers the cheat. They said I was tarnishing the British team, I would upset the equilibrium of the team, my fellow athletes would feel uncomfortable.

And yet Myerscough was selected with barely a whisper from anyone. Not one person published a single statement saying they were against his selection.

Anyone who has not quite made their mind up on whether I deserve to be given a second chance cannot help being influenced by these people as they are by the newspapers and media coverage alike. It's a sad fact in this country: the press and media love the sporting headlines, the records and the medals. But if you fall out of favour with them after they have placed you on that pedestal they'll turn on you like a pack of hungry wolves.

While training in 2003 for the 2004 Summer Olympics at a French training camp, Kelly Holmes suffered a number of leg injuries. Falling deep into depression, she began to meditate using an English lantern, a scented candle used in Buddhist meditation techniques. "I made one cut for every day that I had been injured," Holmes stated in an interview with the News of the World newspaper. At least once she considered suicide, but she eventually sought help from a doctor and was diagnosed with clinical depression. While she could not use anti-depressants because it would affect her performance, she began using herbal serotin tablets. In 2005, after her achievements at the 2004 Summer Olympics, Holmes chose to talk about her self-harm to show others that being a professional athlete is an extremely difficult thing to do and places the athlete under tremendous amounts of stress. I can relate to everything she said.

Some of my fiercest critics are far from perfect themselves. Lord Coe's attitude towards me changed almost overnight. One minute I was speaking to his children and being invited to his house, the next I was something he had scraped off his shoe.

I remember a meeting at Crystal Palace where I was merely a spectator. It was during my ban and I was talking to his son. The friendly stuff, how was he enjoying the athletics, who did he want to watch the most, that sort of thing. The next thing I looked up and Sebastian Coe was walking over. I was a little bit nervous, I'd read so much about him, watched those wonderful videos of Coe against Steve Ovett and Cram, his wonderful comeback after the defeat by Ovett in the 1980 Olympics.

I was in awe of the man walking towards me. He shook my hand, offered me words of comfort, reassurance. He told me to be positive. It was a defining moment for me: Sebastian Coe was supporting me. Or so it seemed at the time. We had a good chat and he told me it would be nice if I could come over to his house sometime for a bite to eat, meet the family. Sadly his support would soon disappear out of the window. I wasn't even born when

Sebastian Coe made his British International Athletics debut in 1976 but I've seen the footage from the World Cup and those unforgettable Olympics in Moscow in 1980 and Los Angeles in 1984. Four Olympic medals and quite incredibly he set an impressive eight world records. In this golden age of Great British middle distance it seemed whenever any athlete broke Coe's records he would always have the reserves to pull out a little more. What an athlete, what a man.

Athletics has been good to Sebastian Coe. Some would say he's been a little fortunate; I would say he's worked hard for what he has achieved. He was roundly criticised when it was disclosed he was receiving a salary of £285,000 as chairman of the 2012 Olympic Committee as the project went three times over budget but he was quickly defended by a member of his team who said he deserved it. He was working a staggering sixty hours a week on the project. What a man, what stamina. His career after athletics is as impressive as his career on the track, of that there's no doubt. He has been a Member of Parliament and Parliamentary Private Secretary to Roger Freeman, Nicholas Soames and Michael Heseltine and his good friend William Hague. He is a regular contributor to BBC Radio 5 Sport, sits on the Sport for All Commission and the International Olympic Committee, chairman of Fast Track Ltd, President of the Amateur Athletics Association and a member of the House of Lords. He has an appointment with FIFA the world football governing body, sits on the Ethics Committee or something like that. Phew...what a schedule, just how on earth does he manage to fit those sixty hours work in for the 2012 Olympic Committee? Oh yeah, I nearly forgot, he is also an accomplished after-dinner speaker charging between £10,000 and £25,000 according to Jeremy Lee's website, the agent who arranges his speaking engagements. Sebastian Coe is a multi-millionaire; no wonder, just look at how many positions he has. Details of his earnings can be found at Companies House; he channels most of his earnings into Sebastian Coe Limited, company number 05396806. They are available for public viewing as are all limited companies. See also The Complete Leisure Group, an umbrella company set up by Coe. They make interesting reading.

If I had the opportunity to talk to Lord Sebastian Coe I would simply ask him to leave me alone. Let me get on with my life and give me a chance to provide for my family the same way he has provided for his. I was given a two-year ban. What a complete joke. Nearly six years on, I am still being victimised and ostracised. And, sad to say, it's the likes of Lord Coe who keep stoking the fire. Lord Coe has called me a cheat on more than one occasion, one of his more oft-quoted comments is, "I don't think there is any place in sport for cheats like Chambers."[4]

I made a mistake... one mistake and I have admitted it. It was the biggest mistake of my life... I'm sorry... I repent. I cheated myself.

In 2004 the Sunday Mirror and The Mail On Sunday broke the news that Sebastian Coe had had a ten-year affair. Vanessa Lander, Coe's former mistress, decided to spill the beans. She wrote that Coe had paid the hospital bill to terminate the life of their secret child. At first Coe tried to gag the paper claiming it was a breach of his private life. This is what the rich are able to do. Fortunately or unfortunately, depending on where you are looking in from, he lost and the paper was able to print every detail. Mr Justice Fulford found that as a public figure Lord Coe could not expect the right to privacy, and some of the details were in the public domain anyway. It was also well known that he had had an extra-marital affair. He respected Coe's right to privacy but also said Miss Lander had a right to disclose and the press also had a right to publish. In October 2006 the eminent journalist Rob McGibbon conducted a fantastic interview with Sebastian Coe in which he questioned him about the affair. It is worth googling Rob McGibbon/Seb Coe and taking a few minutes out to read the full transcript.

Lord Coe also threw the lawyers at Channel Four television when they attempted to screen a documentary about his position as chairman of the Olympic Committee for personal gain.

The programme went on air but, with only twenty minutes to go, Channel 4 Dispatches were being still warned by heavyweight lawyers Carter Ruck, hired by Coe. They had threatened them with all manner of retribution if they put one step wrong. The programme alleged that Coe had earned £200,000 in the two months after London won the bid, alleged it was some sort of bonus or reward for winning the Games. A spokesman for the 2012 Committee claimed it was a payment stretching back nearly twenty years representing back-payments from a long range of business arrangements and to his days as a world champion athlete. Personally I prefer to be paid monthly. I don't think my bank manager would be too happy with a job description that paid me a salary every twenty years. Anyway, I digress.

Getting back to Vanessa, she told how Coe never stayed overnight at her house for fear of being caught, she told of his stamina during lovemaking, a true athlete. (That's why he can work sixty hours a week and hold down all those other positions as well.)

Sadly, Vanessa told how, after the abortion, she realised they would never be together and that she was a physical and emotional wreck, exhausted by all the secrecy, deceit and cheating. The relationship ended. Vanessa claimed they made love once more but incredibly at his Surrey cottage at the same time as he was dating his then girlfriend Carole Arnett. Her estranged husband, Andrew, also accused Coe of stealing his wife and breaking up their happy family. He alleged they were seeing each other behind everybody's backs for about a year before his wife walked out on him.

Lord Coe is entitled to express his views about me but there will be many people who have equally strong views about all this.

I don't mind the criticisms that have been levelled at me over the years after my positive test. Some would say I deserved it. At times I wished I had the sort of money Lord Coe has, to defend the downright lies that have been written and televised about me. What saddens me is that Lord Coe appears to have stolen the moral high ground, branding me a cheat whenever he gets the chance. I don't mind, I have broad shoulders, I can take it. But what saddened me most was the simple shift in attitude as soon as the London 2012 bid became high profile and in the news.

"There will be no room for cheats in the British team as long as I am involved with the BOA."[5]

So said Lord Colin Moynihan, Chairman of the British Olympic Association. Lord Colin Moynihan, Olympic winning medallist, former Conservative minister and chief mouthpiece of the BOA during my fight against my Olympic lifetime ban.

All too often those at the head of various sporting bodies and authorities do not in my opinion have the experience or know what makes those athletes and sportsmen they are in charge of actually tick. For example, The Football Premiership seems to have it right from a managing and coaching point of view. Every one of the football managers in the Premiership has played football professionally, generally at the highest level. They realize the pressure and temptations players are under to perform consistently and at the top of their game. They also gain the respect of the players they are managing especially the younger ones.

The same cannot be said however for those at the top, namely the chief executives. The English Football Association in recent years seems happy to appoint former journalists and accountants rather than someone with a real 'hands-on' knowledge of football. Some may argue that it's no accident why our national team have underperformed at the highest level.

Alas, the same cannot be said for Lord Colin Moynihan. Lord Moynihan, you see, is an Olympic silver medallist; Lord Moynihan was a dedicated athlete.

Back in 1980 he was part of the British rowing team that were deprived of a gold medal by an East German team that were allegedly part of a regime promoting the use of banned substances to their young athletes.

Yes, Lord Moynihan is an athlete. The who's who of the BOA committee describes him as such:

Lord Moynihan won a silver medal in Rowing at the Moscow 1980 Games.

Of that there is no doubt, but isn't that statement a little misleading? Anyone under the age of about thirty-five probably won't even remember the Moscow Olympics and anyone over the age of thirty-five reading the BOA's own description of Lord Moynihan's Olympic achievement can be forgiven for thinking the man was an actual rower. Others may remember Charles Wiggin and the Chris Mahoneys and Alan Whitwells but will struggle to remember a certain Colin Moynihan powering his way through the water with gritted teeth and rippling muscles on the verge of collapse as his team crossed the line to snatch the silver medal from the Russians. That's because Colin Moynihan was the coxswain, (correct title, but not possible to have a laugh and a joke) or the cox, the smallest member of the *team* who sits at the rear of the boat shouting at the oarsmen. Won a silver medal for rowing? Well, he did, but he never actually rowed a single metre down the course, did he?

Lord Moynihan has been vociferous in his condemnation of me since I tested positive for a banned substance in 2003. Latterly, some would say he has been the principal voice of criticism and one of the main obstacles in my attempts to overcome my Olympic ban. Lord Moynihan is the chief of the British Olympic team, the chairman of the British Olympic Association. As you would expect, and quite rightly, he has taken a strong stand against 'drug cheats'.

It seems Lord Moynihan has taken every opportunity with every form of media and communication, be it television, radio, broadsheets and tabloids, after-dinner speeches, and even in the street, to vent a seemingly personal crusade on why the drugs cheat Dwain Chambers should not participate in the 2008 Summer Olympics. Lord Moynihan has shouted from the rooftops to anyone who will listen:

"Victory for the convicted doper would lead to the British team being labelled a team of drugs cheats.

"Chambers would cause cash backers to pull out of the 2012 Olympic Games in London."[6] (Please note, this is the start of his crusade to keep me out of the next Olympics in my own backyard.)

In fact, Google quite a specific search along the lines of *Lord Moynihan quotes Dwain Chambers* and you will find over 350 links. Google *Lord Moynihan drugs cheat Dwain Chambers* and you will find 550. I won't list every one but they make interesting reading and anyone forming an opinion would conclude that I'm not on Lord Colin Moynihan's Christmas card list.

However I will give you one of the more stirring quotes from Lord Moynihan. He said:

"There will be no room for cheats in the British team as long as

I am involved with the BOA."[5]

In a nutshell he does not want anyone who has taken drugs in the past to be associated with the British team. Right?

Well no actually, wrong.

No room for cheats in the British team, he said, and yet, in Moynihan's own chosen sport, rowing, the BOA are happy to employ as the British rowing team's head coach, one Jürgen Grobler. A certain Mr Grobler admitted encouraging young East German athletes to take banned substances during his many years as an East German rowing coach in the 1970s and 1980s. During the period between 1972 and 1988 East Germany dominated rowing winning an incredible forty-five Olympic medals, thirty-one of them gold. During a BBC investigation in 1998 Jürgen Grobler's name appears on documents which have been unearthed.[7]

In 1989 the East German secret police, the Stasi, destroyed thousands of files containing sensitive material but documents about the use of drugs survived.

Dr Giselher Spitzer, who investigated doping for the German government, said: "It was a state-controlled programme to use performance-enhancing drugs within the sports of the GDR. Rowing was a centre of research. If people asked what the pills were they were told they were vitamins. If someone asked too much they were thrown out of the sport." He says, "Mr Grobler was within the 'inner circle' which ran East Germany's rowing schools, where children as young as ten were given anabolic steroids."

Dirk Schildhauer, a former East German sculler and double junior silver medallist, backed up the claim and said the use of Turinabol, an anabolic drug made in East Germany, was mandatory.

Once a cheat always a cheat, I think you once said, Lord Moynihan?

When asked recently about Mr Grobler, Lord Moynihan said:

"The ARA (Amateur Rowing Association) have complete confidence in Mr Grobler, the BOA is not involved with coach selection."

But, Mr Moynihan, you said, *"There will be no room for cheats in the British team as long as I am involved with the BOA."* Aren't the coaches part of the team? Don't they wear team tracksuits and take part in the opening and closing ceremonies. Look at your own bye-law:

'The BOA....does not regard it appropriate that Team GB should include athletes or other individuals (including but not limited to coaches, medical and administrative staff) who have doped or been found guilty of a doping offence including but not limited to the supply or trafficking of prohibited substances.'

It's there as clear as bottled water. The BOA have broken their own bye-law. By the time you, my dear reader, ponder this blatant breach of BOA rules by the BOA, the Olympics will be over and it will be too late to turn back the clock. Grobler will have been to the Olympics and enjoyed the moment. Dwain Chambers will have watched it on television.

Frank Dick is a nice guy and I've valued his advice over the years. And there is no question that he's a first-rate coach. Latterly however, particularly as the date of the hearing loomed close, he seemed to pop up in the media urging me to think again and claiming I was damaging the sport I loved. He even wrote me an open letter. I wondered why he didn't send me a normal letter privately or even an e-mail. He has access to both addresses. Anyway, in this *open letter* he felt compelled to share with the world's press he stated:

'Congratulations on your performance to date this season. I hope you will read and reflect on this letter.

It is written to you; for the sport I believe you love and for the people in the sport whom you respect and who respect you.

I don't believe it is your wish to damage the sport so it makes little sense to pursue a course of action which would do so.

Such gives the press and media headline-grabbing material that lowers the sport into the mud of drugs and your association with them.

Rather, the headlines should be those athletes who have perhaps one chance only in their life to enjoy the limelight of being selected for the Olympics and of the Olympic experience itself.

Surely you would not wish to deny them that.'

What about coaches, Frank? What about the right of good British coaches who have worked tirelessly for years urging kids and young adults to run, row, swim and compete cleanly? And why if you want to avoid the wrong headlines did you send this *open letter* to the press? Frank Dick was instrumental in appointing the disgraced East German coach Dr Ekkart Arbeit to assist Denise

Lewis in her comeback after having a baby.

Arbeit was arguably the major player in supplying anabolic steroids to East German athletes during his eight years in senior posts within the East German team.[8] He was described as the architect of one of the largest pharmacological programmes in history.[9] (That's drugs to you and me.)

Because of his past in which he freely admitted supplying drugs to the athletes he was turned down by both the Australian and South African Athletics Associations. He then applied for accreditation to Great Britain in order to coach Denise Lewis. UK Athletics Performance Director, Max Jones, admitted the 'board' had discussed his none too rosy background but had decided to treat him as a normal coach so as not to disadvantage Denise Lewis.[10] UK Athletics President Lynn Davies insisted that the governing body felt comfortable with giving Dr Arbeit accreditation.

Many of these athletes suffer major health problems to this day. When asked how he felt about that, Arbeit responded:

"Nobody asked them to take the drugs, they weren't pushed, they could have walked away." [11]

Really, Dr Arbeit? Remember the case of one of East Germany's best sprinters, Renate Neufeld?

They weren't pushed, they could have walked away? Renate Neufeld did just that, she fled to the West as quickly as her legs would carry her. Dr Arbeit has expressed regret over his involvement in the East German doping programme but claimed he deserved another chance. He has never hidden the fact that he supplied young athletes with performance-enhancing and potentially life-threatening drugs. But probably the best statement regarding Dick and Arbeit is left to Jonathan Edwards. He said:

"With a Christian-like approach, it's now time to move on. It's time for rehabilitation rather than recrimination. It was Frank's decision to surround himself with a team of experts and he rates Arbeit as probably the world's leading strength authority."[12]

There you have it... the world's leading strength authority, as long as we can forget he's admitted supplying drugs in the past.

As a footnote and after a change of heart, Athletics South Africa appointed Dr Arbeit as head coach to the South African team.

I for one was more than happy when Denise Lewis dropped Dick and Arbeit and renewed her previous relationship with her former coach Charles van Commenee.

The names of Grobler and Arbeit and Myerscough who have all admitted their involvement in the past with drugs and seem to be treated oh so differently to me penetrate my thoughts often. People ask if I feel I have been victimized; am I angry? I say to them, for every hour I remain angry I lose sixty minutes of joy; I lose sixty minutes of pleasure I can share with the people I love, people like my little boys Skye and Rocco Star, with Jayon and Leonie.

I fight the anger; I take Skye and Rocco to the swimming pool or play football with Jayon in the park. Their trust in me and the unconditional love that I see in their eyes every minute of every day helps me enormously. I try not to be a bitter man but sometimes it's difficult, but with the help and support of my dear friends and my family I will succeed. I try not to look back and regret the things I've done. What's the point? I can't turn back the clock. You should try hard not to regret things in the past. What's done is done.

And I say good luck to Arbeit, Grobler and Myerscough. By the time this book hits the shelves Arbeit and Grobler will have returned from an incredible experience at the Beijing Olympics. Myerscough was not so fortunate but at least all three have been given a second chance and all three are supporting their families. That is all I've ever asked for but for some reason I've been denied that right for over four years.

As 2006 drew to a close I was aware that athletics was losing its appeal financially. Christmas was coming and I had a family to feed and presents to buy. Sadly, this Christmas, Santa would be conspicuous by his absence. I swore to myself the next year would be different. If athletics wouldn't allow me to provide for my family I would need to earn a living elsewhere.

A TEMPORARY CHANGE OF DIRECTION

The love for American football started when I was a child. I would watch Jerry Rice and the San Francisco 49ers on my black and white television in my bedroom. My mum would be watching Bonanza or Hawaii Five O on the colour television whilst cooking in the kitchen. I had so many idols in my life I didn't know which sport to choose. American football wasn't really played in the UK; it had only just started being televised in the UK but was gaining a little in popularity. The only junior leagues were being played in the States. I had to find another passion.

My second biggest idol was Boris Becker and I just loved watching tennis. My parents weren't exactly in a financial position to send me to Wimbledon to link up with the likes of Tim Henman so American football and tennis both had to be thrown out of the window. However, I still had a soft spot in my heart for American football.

When I was serving my ban I mistakenly thought I could simply turn to another sport. I was wrong. The severity of my suspension not only meant track and field but a worldwide suspension from all sports, so finding another sport to participate in became a dead end. I'd got back in touch with Remi and Victor as a means of help. We were all in the shit, but I needed help from somewhere as a means to continue earning money for the next two years. Remi got in touch with a junior college called Chabot. This was my training ground during my winter and midsummer season when I was in America training. The principal of the college and his officials knew how fast I was and that nobody in the college could get anywhere near me. They put me through my paces and raced me with the fastest guys on the campus over forty, sixty, eighty and one hundred yards. I beat them all. They accepted me on a sort of scholarship obviously looking ahead to the time when my ban would be over. For the first few weeks I was in NFL study classes only, where I had to learn defensive formations. Those two weeks of my life were a nightmare. I just couldn't get to grips with it. Defensive Coverages 1, 2 and 3, zone, man to man; it was as bad as learning another bloody language and so complicated. Remember my classmates had been brought up on this as juniors and knew it back to front. It got worse when it came to offence. We had to identify coverages on the defence. If they were in cover two you were required to identify cover two man or cover two zone. Depending on the coverage of the defence, your allocated route would change while on the run and you have to fake a move to the defender who is itching to knock you out. With all this mayhem you still have to run like the wind, turn around, focus on the quarterback and catch the ball!

When the class had finished I'd travel home to study, and travel back for practice, all the time remembering the drills. Nevertheless I was determined to stick it out and over time the patterns of play and the technical aspects of the game seemed to sink in. Just when I thought I was getting somewhere I was called up to the principal's office. He sat stony-faced as he announced they had to let me go. At first I thought it was of my lack of knowledge of the game. It wasn't; it was far simpler than that. I had been denied a work visa.

I must say the staff and students were amazing. They were very humble and sympathetic towards my situation. Everyone I spoke to wanted me to stay on. When they asked questions I told them the truth. With this I earned their respect.

I decided to stay on in America for a further week. I loved my time at Chabot and for a few short weeks I began to look ahead and thought a career in American football was a real possibility. Then yet again, as would happen quite often over the next few years, just when I thought an opportunity had appeared, another door was slammed in my face. I couldn't fight the depression. All alone in America yet again. I contemplated taking my life, but I was too afraid to go ahead. I sat in my room with a bottle of brandy that I had been drinking throughout the day. It was going straight to my head, I was so gone. Never had I been so depressed, never had I been so drunk. My mind drifted back to those training days with Remi and the first meetings with Victor. It was like a bad dream, a nightmare and I just wanted to wake up from it. I wanted to sleep; sleep was the answer, a good sleep then I'll wake up from this living hell.

I put the brandy to one side and tried to focus on doing something... anything. I decided to try and motivate myself to go down to the coin-operated laundry service two floors down and do my washing. Just a little thing but something that took me nearly three hours to do. I finally staggered up from the couch and dragged my dirty clothes with me. As I was walking down towards the washing facilities I was met head-on by two members of the IRS (I discovered later).

"Are you Dwain Chambers?"

"Yes," I replied.

(I have changed the names in the next few sentences for legal reasons.)

One of them spoke: "My name is special agent Geoff Novell and this is my partner, special agent Clint Rogers."

He flashed his badge right in my face and asked me if he could ask me some questions. I have never sobered up so quickly in my life. We walked into the laundry facility and I sat on top of the washing machine while the two officers stood in front of me. I must admit they were very polite but as they talked I was under the impression that I was going to be given a court order to testify in court or, worse, be taken into custody. I was in their company for no more than ten minutes. They explained the procedure for their visit as well as telling me that should I lie to them when answering any of the questions they asked I would be arrested and made to appear before a court of law. They were asking me about Victor and BALCO and I answered their questions without hesitation. Once they had left, I walked back up to my room, flung my dirty washing on the ground and continued drinking. After that ordeal I decided to travel back home to the UK straightaway. I wanted out of there; America was not my favourite place at that time.

My time in Chabot College stood me in good stead when I contacted a member of the NFL Europe team management. I was invited to the national camp. I travelled around Europe practising with other guys who also wanted to make it to the NFL. I played most of my American football at Crystal Palace National Sports Centre as well as travelling to Spain and Frankfurt. As in Chabot I was the fastest man on the field. My performances and understanding of the game earned me a place in an NFL Europe selection. Those of us that were selected to represent an NFL Europe team still had to fight and earn their place on a team but I was confident my pace and knowledge would carry me through. Everyone knew who I was, that I'd cheated on drugs, but they didn't hold it against me. They were giving me a second chance; why couldn't my own sport, the sport I loved, do likewise? Despite my ability to play on a national level, it was a different kettle of fish when it came to competing against the Americans, Japanese and other guys from around Europe. All of these guys had been playing football from the age of four. I was twenty-nine years old and this was the first time I had ever been thrown into a full-on American football game.

The top players from the mix were invited to a training camp in Tampa, Florida for a period of six weeks. I breathed a sigh of relief when my name was read out. I had earned my place on merit but it had been tough and exhausting and, of course, this was only the first part of the jigsaw. I still needed to earn a place in one of the European teams.

Once again I was faced with the nightmare of studying defensive and offensive patterns of play but this time it sank in a little more easily.

Being an athlete, I used my experience to help pull me through each day, but I was frustrated with myself as on the field my speed didn't count for shit. The defensive players had been taught how to deal with guys like me, i.e. sprinters, and every time I took off on a run I seemed to get blocked or hit by an express train. As time went by I would often go back to the apartment and stay on my own and sulk and lick my wounds. I was rooming with three other Brits: Scott McCready, Adan Durdy and Jermain Allen. They helped me out big time in terms of studying the formations and general strategy of the game. The more information I obtained the more complicated things seemed to become but I persevered. I stayed in my room on my own so I could study, no other reason. At times this caused a little friction with my roommates as they thought I didn't like them. Nothing could have been further from the truth. I loved those guys; they were the best roommates in the world.

On one occasion Leonie called to speak to me and one of my roommates picked up the phone. He complained to her about me not being sociable. Leonie explained to me that I was drifting back into old habits. This sometimes happened when I was depressed and yet I really was enjoying my time in Tampa. Perhaps I was fearful that I wouldn't make the cut. Leonie's words got through to me and I opened up to my friends.

Our time in Tampa was coming to an end and we were about to be transferred to our allocated team location or sent home. My speed must have been the only thing that helped with being selected and my subsequent transfer to the Hamburg Sea Devils, as during training camp my ability to catch the ball and think at the same time had been challenging to say the least. Nevertheless I'd been given a chance and was determined not to waste it. Athletics didn't want me but it appeared that American football had given me a break.

In Hamburg things changed for the worse. We were back in Europe and the culture was a little different to America. Some of the guys seemed hell-bent on drinking and partying hard. To me this was crazy but gradually I was sucked in. Normally I would never do this during the season but it was so much fun. Whether we won or lost a game we would still hit the clubs and nearly always the club promoters and DJs would announce that the Hamburg Sea Devils were in town. People would buy us drinks or the club would line up freebies as a way of keeping us on the premises. Some of the guys would be drinking straight vodka and dancing on top of the bar or the tables.

We would stay out late but still train in the mornings. This must have relaxed me as I started catching the ball more often and began to get noticed. Although I wasn't drinking as hard as the other guys my body was still wrecked in training. I found it tough, but mentally I battled through the pain barrier. God knows what the hard drinkers felt like.

It was around this time I gave the much reported interview with Matthew Pinsent. I was having a good time when I met with Matthew for the Inside Sport programme. People quite rightly jumped on some of the things I said. What people must realise is that I had a new career (or so I thought). I was more than just a little bitter towards the officialdom of athletics. I wanted to ruffle a few feathers; I wanted to cause a ripple. I certainly did just that. Matthew and I were in an Olympic village together and although he said after the interview that he found me aloof and unapproachable we got on okay off-camera. I said some stupid things, words that I wish I could retract. I said I cheated deliberately, that much was true, but I also said that athletes not on drugs could only beat those on drugs if they were having a really bad day. That wasn't true and I knew it. But still I said it and smiled at the camera. Matthew was none too pleased. I'd upset him. He asked me about Darren Campbell and I was none too complimentary about him. That much was true too… we don't like each other but I must try to be better than that. I apologise on record now to Matthew for some of the things I said. They were said in haste by a bitter man. Some would say who could blame me.

Hamburg Sea Devils were beginning to build a reputation and winning was everything. When we lost games the guys would argue like mad and I liked that. Winning is sweet, of that there is no doubt. There was an incident where we had lost a game and we were being hammered at training for our mistakes. It was a punishment and I took it like that. Some of the guys took it personally. When we finally got back to our hotel for food there was a mad rush. Guys were pushing and barging one another, all in an attempt to get some food. Cliff and another guy called Barry were shouting and squaring up to each other ready to fight over a portion of chicken wings. If it wasn't so serious it would have been comical. Two six foot four teammates ready to kick off over a piece of chicken. No wonder wars start.

One of my teammates was JD Washington, Denzel Washington's son. JD was so humble. All he wanted to do was play football and become an actor, but an actor in his own right and not on the back of the success of his father. If asked about his father from a member of the press association he would answer questions in a polite and respectful manner but you could tell it wound him up. He was always placed in the shadow of his father by the media. Even if JD had made a match-winning run or scored a touchdown the press would still want to know something about his father rather than find out more about JD. He had a real bolt of energy to him; he brought so much life and enjoyment to our team.

My time on the playing field was good and the team thrived and when I got my chance on the field I made damn sure I did the best I could.

My season ended prematurely due to an unexpected stress fracture but my team did go on to win the World Bowl 37-28 to Frankfurt Galaxy. It was a fantastic achievement and the team was on a high. Let's not underestimate the victory. The great Hamburg

Sea Devils had won the World Bowl Championships and I have my NFL Europe ring to show for it. It's not the Superbowl, but to me it was the next best thing. Things were good and I was pulled to one side and told to take a well-earned rest and report for training next season. I was absolutely ecstatic. Although I hadn't played in the final they hadn't forgotten about me, and my hard work and commitment had been noticed. I was being rewarded with a new contract and suddenly my long-term financial security looked a little brighter.

It was not to be.

The European League was closed down before the season began and I never even had the chance to discuss my contract. The National Football League (NFL) in America said they were losing $30 million a year on the European League and couldn't continue. I was scheduled to go back to Hamburg for my second season but it never happened. Players who had been in the NFL system for three to four years were all out of a job. Dwain Chambers was one of them. I was back on the scrap heap again.

HOSTILITY ABOUNDS

I had no option but to continue training and make known my intention to return to athletics. In January 2008, UK Athletics chief executive officer Niels de Vos made his feelings clear. He said I would be barred from making a comeback because I had not undergone drug testing since November 2006 when I left the sport. Niels de Vos failed to do his homework. I had been taken off the doping register as I wasn't competing. Throughout my time in Hamburg I had notified UKA and the IAAF of my whereabouts. The IAAF overruled him saying I was eligible to run because I had never officially retired from athletics.

In February I qualified for the World Indoor Trials in Sheffield by winning the 60m at the Birmingham Games in 6.60. I was allowed to compete in Sheffield after the UKA grudgingly accepted my entry but only after my solicitors prepared to launch a High Court injunction against them. On February 10th I won the 60 metres in Sheffield thus making it difficult for the selectors handing out the invites for the following month's World Indoor Championships in Valencia.

Despite vocal opposition I was selected for the championships in Valencia in March of 2008. The selectors had pointed out on more than one occasion that they didn't want to pick me. Talk about running under pressure. I prayed I would do well and that those with a voice in the sport would just keep quiet. This had happened constantly since my ban had come to an end. I'd tried to get on with my running and competed well. Invites slowly started coming through and then the likes of Niels de Vos and Moynihan, Seb Coe and Dame Kelly Holmes voiced their opinions and the invites dried up. At this time Niels de Vos seemed to be on some sort of personal campaign against me, saying on a Radio Two interview at the 'outrage' levelled against me and hoping that it would continue long and hard and allow the rules to change in favour of a longer ban. He argued that a two-year ban was no worse than a serious knee injury. De Vos made clear his opposition to me running in Valencia on more than one occasion. What was significant however was his deafening silence when Carl Myerscough was also selected for Valencia. Myerscough had also served the same two-year ban for a banned substance. As the date for Valencia approached I just prayed that de Vos would keep his mouth shut.

I won the silver medal in the World Indoor Championships in

Valencia securing a personal best. When I took this medal in Valencia, I felt that that moment was my proudest in athletics. I'd bounced back. I'd bounced back clean and was only denied the gold medal by the Nigerian Olusoji Fasuba. I was almost on the verge of tears, I was so proud. I thought about Leonie and Skye and Jayon. I could look them in the eye honestly without the slightest pang of guilt. Surely the country would forgive me now? Surely the doubters and the voices would see that I'd been honest, advocated running clean. Surely this medal I'd won for my country would tip the balance in my favour and I'd be allowed to resume the career that I loved. I was thirty years old and time was running out.

God sadly on that occasion did not answer my prayers. I came back from Valencia to the sort of headlines and newspaper articles that sickened me to the core. They were there again. 'Disgraced sprinter' and 'drugs cheat Chambers' and the *voices* were talking about organising petitions and lobbying the BOA. Never had I come down to earth so quickly. I was elated in Valencia. Most of the crowd were on my side, the Spanish press praised my achievement and the people treated me with respect. Now in my own country I was back at rock bottom again. I sat with Leonie on the verge of tears. How stupid I had been to think that they'd give me a second chance. How naïve I was to think I could still make a living from athletics. I sat with my family that evening as the television played to itself in the corner. My son Skye climbed on my knee and I thought about what I'd been able to provide for him in the first two years of his life. I'd given him nothing but love. No holidays, no presents, no clothes. Leonie had paid for everything even to the point of lending me money for bus fares at times. I discussed it with Leonie until the early hours of the morning. We talked about a previous offer of rugby league, an offer that I'd put on the back burner because of my love for athletics. That night it seemed the only option left – so many doors seemed to be closing one after another. I just had to find a way to compete at something. We talked about moving home and providing a better education for Skye. I had to get out, I had to try something else, and I made up my mind to ring Nick Collins the following day to talk about Rugby League.

It was now six years since I had made that mistake, nearly three years since my ban had finished and, despite winning a silver medal for my country, I was still 'Chambers the Cheat'. I was disillusioned and angry.

It seemed that once again I was being tempted to turn my back on athletics.

CASTLEFORD BOYS

Up north they used to say that if you wanted a rugby league team then all you had to do was shout the kick-off time down a pit shaft. The enthusiasm for the game in those areas was such that children grew to adolescence without knowing that some people actually kicked footballs rather than ran with them. But when the miners surfaced to don their jerseys they lost their pay. The crowds however were being entertained and more than happy to reimburse the lads their lost wages from the gate money. But in the late nineteenth century this went against the idealism of the Rugby Football Union whose class-ridden administrators duly expelled the so-called 'professionals' and so union and league divided. Rugby League remained the unfashionable professional estranged brother of Union. In a league team there is no need to field the giraffe for the line-outs, no need for a row of buffaloes to populate the front row. There is a need for strength and speed. There was always an association between the game and the professional sprinters who used to race off head to head like greyhounds while punters bet on the result. In the 1960s Welshman Berwyn Jones turned professional with Wakefield Trinity just before he was due to represent Great Britain in the Commonwealth Games Sprints. His career, eventually, was distinguished by those same class-ridden bureaucrats.

Nowadays Rugby League is called Super League. Its players, complete, well-defined athletes, but still as 'hard as nails'. So when I signed for Castleford Tigers I knew what to expect. The reality however, once I donned the famous yellow and black shirt, still came as a real shock.

Me... rugby league?

That was my reaction when the proposal was first put to me. I discussed the possibility with Martin Offiah who is a legend in the game. My agent Simon Dent who is also a friend of Martin's had arranged a meeting with him. Simon had been making some enquiries and apparently there were a few clubs interested in me. I'd watched and enjoyed both codes of rugby in the past but admitted to siding with league. It just seemed more honest and faster, steeped in history and, of course, berated by the establishment. (I could relate to that.) Simon and my solicitor Nick Collins were talking decent money for a rugby league contract: £50,000 plus per year. Although at one point in my athletics career I could earn that from one good race, those days seemed to be over. The reality was that beggars couldn't be choosers.

It was at Castleford that I reinforced my view that you do not need to take drugs to compete at the highest level. Those boys were the hardest fittest bastards I have ever had the pleasure to meet. I was tempted by mention of £60,000 a year contract, nothing more, nothing less. I was skint, didn't have a pot to piss in, so to speak. I'd lost everything including my house and car because I had to pay back money to the IAAF as well as UK Athletics. The money in rugby was good but could I cut it? Martin Offiah explained the working-class roots of the sport and how one or two of the lads might resent me a little bit. He explained how he was a target man, as soon as he made a name for himself. Hurt Offiah, stop him in his tracks and the opposition player who did would get his fifteen minutes of fame.

I decided to give it a try, I had nothing to lose.

I was to meet with Mick Robinson from Castleford and Nick Collins at the Oulton Hall Hotel on the outskirts of Leeds. I would also be meeting Ron Hill who had promised to finance the trial if we all agreed to go for it. Mick 'Robbo' Robinson made quite an impression on me. Remember I had never met him before and as I walked through the hotel doors I looked around for a table with three gentlemen. I remember a table on the far side of reception with a family enjoying an early morning pot of tea and a group of girls giggling by reception.

I heard a shout from the far side of the room and was stunned to see a rugby ball flying towards me. This was a sedate hotel reception area; rugby balls were alien to this environment! What was it doing heading in my direction and what was I going to do to prevent it smashing into my face? I dropped the bag I was holding and instinctively reached up to grab it. It nestled perfectly in my hands barely two inches from my face.

Robbo sauntered over as if a hotel foyer was the most perfect arena in the world to practise rugby.

"Not a bad catch," he called out. "I heard you played a bit for the NFL."

He was grinning, I got the impression I'd passed the first part of the initiation test. What would he have done if I'd fumbled the ball or it had broken my nose? I got the impression he wouldn't have cared. Robbo was the Castleford manager and a more than straight-talking guy. Immediately he offered me the trial. He told me he would love to see me take on the establishment and that he felt I'd been treated appallingly. He told me as far as he was concerned I'd served my time and deserved to be allowed to get on with my life. Athletics' loss was rugby's gain, he said. I warmed to Robbo straight away; he told me about his upbringing and we had a lot in common. He explained that rugby league was the place to be, it was tougher and faster than the rival code and there was no snobbery. Within ten minutes of entering the hotel and talking with Robbo, Ron and Nick, I'd agreed the trial and we were making the financial and living arrangements.

The newspapers loved it.

Christopher Irvine of the Times announced: "Dwain Chambers, *the disgraced* British sprinter, is to make a dramatic career switch to rugby league." The Telegraph announced that Castleford had moved for the *disgraced* former European 100 metres sprint champion. The Mail and the Daily Record, The Sun and The Guardian, The Yorkshire Post and The Mirror simply called me a rugby league *drugs cheat* and Sky Sports and CNN and the BBC all ran with a suggestion that it was a publicity stunt by Castleford and *Chambers the drugs cheat* had no place in the sport.

The press boys were all there as I jogged into the training ground that morning. They wished me luck, and asked for interviews and exclusives as the flash bulbs fired off. I once accused a certain member of the press of being two-faced. I will spare him the embarrassment of naming him.

"Two faces... me, Dwain? No... I've got twenty-two faces."

I think that sums it up. These were the same members of the press who wished me luck on the Friday a few months later when Judge Mackay delivered his verdict and then slaughtered me in their respective newspapers that weekend.

I was scared as I stepped foot onto the training ground. I shouted to the assembled press, "No more spikes and vests." It was a nervous reaction, some would call it cocky... arrogant. It wasn't. I was a bundle of nerves.

I was introduced to my new mates. They looked like hard men, and I was glad they were on my side. I *hoped* they were on my side. I wondered if there would be any resentment at the mention of a possible £60,000 salary. I was a sprinter, not a rugby player; I'd never played the game before. What right had I to command one of the biggest salaries at the club? Still I was there and I was going to give it all I had. At least I was working class and had stood up to the school ties and the establishment. I suppose it was good grounding for Rugby League.

I needn't have worried. The lads were great. Fair and tough but honest, they worked hard and played hard too. They were dedicated athletes and yet they lived their lives too. I remember on my birthday, April 5th, they took me to Frankie and Benny's at the local Escape Retail Park and forced a few beers down me. After three pints I was wrecked. By all accounts my teammates just kept going and going as their latest recruit, propped up between two of them in the corner, grinned. I remembered nothing the next morning and struggled through a particularly gruelling session. These lads who had drunk three times the amount I had didn't bat an eyelid. You'd have thought that they'd been tucked up at ten the previous evening with a cup of cocoa. I then realized just how fit they were and I was determined to be one of them. I struck up some great friendships there particularly with the likes of Brent Sherwin, Robbo, Ryan McGoldrick, Tom Haberecht, Adam Fletcher, Michael Korkidas and Stuart Donlan.

We worked on agility and stamina, something I had never before encountered in athletics. I thought 200 metres was a long way. Here we were, pounding the roads and up and down the rugby field time after time; sometimes a jog, sometimes a hard run, sometimes a sprint, but the distances seemed so long. At the end of two weeks I was mashed. My body felt as if I'd been run over by a train. I'd taken the hits, the knocks, and I wondered what sort of men my teammates were who could do this week after week, year after year. I lay in a hot relaxing bath in my hotel room paid for by Castleford Tigers and I wondered what the hell I was doing there. I wanted to give up, wanted to climb from the bath and ring Leonie there and then and tell her I was coming back.

The water was hot, the relaxing crystals all but melted though a little gritty on the bottom. I pressed my index finger into my thigh; bloody hell it hurt. I pressed it into the other one too; same effect. I lifted my foot clean out of the water and massaged my calf muscle. That hurt too. My back ached… in fact everything hurt, the only part of my body that didn't was my head. Something was happening in my head. I felt an inner peace, a calm. It was difficult to describe but for the first time in my life I'd worked hard at an honest job. £60,000 a year. It didn't seem a lot, but to me it was a million pounds. I drifted off to sleep with thoughts of Skye and woke up about an hour later in a cold bath.

I climbed out and dried myself. As I wandered through to the bedroom, Sky News was telling its viewers about Frank Lampard's new contract offer reportedly worth £120,000 a week. I laughed at the irony. Rugby League footballers and the Premiership boys are a million miles apart. For some strange reason I delayed the phone call to Leonie. I would call her in the morning.

I slept like a baby and awoke with an immense feeling of satisfaction and determination. I wouldn't give up and go back home to London. I liked it here, I liked my teammates, my coach and, above all, the fans. They hadn't prejudged me like some people do. I owed it to them to at least stick the month out. I owed it to my family.

I worked with a determination and inner strength I never knew I had. The training was like a drug and I had to have more. It's difficult to explain but my performance seemed to improve. It registered in those last two weeks that drugs in sport was not the answer. Here I was running through the pain barrier every day with my teammates. We were as one, comrades in a war and I loved it. I gelled with the whole team; to a man not one of them showed any animosity or resentment and I bonded especially with Ryan McGoldrick. The coach Terry Matterson, during a pitchside interview with a television crew, described me as the quickest rugby player he'd ever worked with.

I worked harder in those last two weeks and looked forward to the practice game they'd arranged with York. I remembered watching from the sidelines during my first week in training when the lads pulled off a shock win against St Helens in blizzard conditions and had to admit I hadn't had a real urge to pull on a jersey and get out there. But now it was different. After only three weeks at Castleford I had the rugby league bug. Castleford had arranged a reserve team friendly with York and Terry Matterson had told me I would be on the bench.

The game couldn't come quick enough for me and I felt a twinge of disappointment as I took my place among the other subs. On eleven minutes I was thrown into the fray; I got a great roar from the 3,500 fans that had turned up for the game and a surge of adrenalin coursed through my body. This was where I wanted to be. I wanted that contract badly and was making plans in my head to move the family up North. I had even spoken to Simon about the move and had been looking for schools.

My rugby league debut lasted all of thirty-nine minutes before I was brought off. I felt I did okay. I produced a try-saving tackle and felt my pace was always a worry to the opposition. My game was raw and of course I ran a little green when it came to positioning and the well-planned moves but felt it was something I could work on and, with good coaching, get to the standard needed.

My month was up and the vibes were good. Before I returned to London my new mates wished me well; a couple of them confidently suggested they would be seeing me soon and Terry Matterson shook my hand warmly and told me he would discuss the position with the chairman and Robbo after the weekend's games. The Castleford boys were heading south that weekend too. They were off to Cardiff for Millennium Madness, a two-day festival of rugby league. I strolled out of the training ground and looked back. I felt confident I would soon be returning.

I had a nice lunch with Leonie and Skye when I got back to London. We went out to our local restaurant and Leonie hardly got a word in edgeways. I told her about my newfound friends and the fans and the sights of the Yorkshire Dales and the wide open spaces and how it would be a better place to bring up Skye. The Yorkshire people were warm and trusting and altogether more pleasant to deal with than the average Londoner. Sad but true. And although she warned me on more than one occasion that the contract might not happen I was so full of confidence I wouldn't listen. The words of Terry Matterson kept coming back to me: *Quickest I've ever worked with.*

I watched the results from Cardiff coming through that weekend on the BBC Sports internet site and they didn't make for pleasant viewing. Castleford Tigers had been humiliated by their neighbours Wakefield Trinity. Out of curiosity I Googled Dwain Chambers/Castleford Tigers.

I wish I hadn't.

I read the headlines of each site listed: *'Publicity stunt'*, *'drugs cheat'*, *'disgrace'*, *'no place in the sport'* and *'athletics bad boy'*. Some of the press boys were ridiculing my performance against York and yet everyone at the club said I'd done more than enough. Suddenly I wasn't so sure. I desperately wanted this contract; it had nothing to do with athletics and yet the knives were out for me again.

By the time the call came a few days later I knew. Terry as always was great. He explained I suppose by way of a compliment that at first he'd thought it was a publicity stunt but he said I'd worked very hard at it and after the second week he knew how much I really wanted that contract. Although Terry didn't say as much, I got the impression he wanted to take me on. The chairman had suggested they had lots of young players breaking through into the first team and at the age of thirty, they didn't have the time or the patience (not to mention the money) to get me to a level where I would be able to play first team rugby. I respected their decision and felt they hadn't hidden or shirked from what must have been a difficult decision. Nor did they lie or flannel me or mention the drugs issue. They had given me a genuine chance and I'd taken the opportunity and given it my best shot. I was too old and not quite at the level they required. One thing irked me a little though: the game of rugby league is based on pace and yet they'd rejected the fastest man in Europe, the quickest man the Castleford coach had ever worked with.

I was back in a depression, back on the bottom again and with no control over my own destiny. That was the worst thing, I suppose, looking back. Leonie sensed this and left me to my own devices. I went for a long walk, came back home and watched a little television. I couldn't tell you what I watched as I just stared straight through the TV again. I climbed the stairs in the early hours of the morning and spent another restless night thinking about what I could have done differently to have won that contract.

RUNNING UNDER PRESSURE

There have been many times when I have wondered whether pursuing my dream to run in the Olympics has been the right thing to do. Running, particularly in the 100 metres, is not just about being physically fit. A huge part of the race is won and lost in the head. Mental focus is all-important. At all times a professional athlete needs to be completely focused and switched on to the task ahead. There were many days when I returned from a good training session with a healthy positive attitude only to be knocked back down because of a report on Sky television or a comment from a former athlete. The latter was always the worst and I can't tell the individuals involved just how much they hurt me, just how much they affected me. Perhaps that was their intention, I don't know.

I knuckled down yet again and began preparing for my hearing in which I would appeal my lifetime Olympic ban, but to make it all worthwhile I would need to make the Olympic 'A' times. It was no good winning my case if I couldn't achieve the times needed to get me to Beijing. My appeal was scheduled for July. I didn't have an awful lot of time left and I prayed to myself I would keep clear of injury. I warmed up at the beginning of June with my first 100m win since August 2006. Then I focused on a race at Crystal Palace to make the qualifying time of 10.21. Although I didn't know it at the time I had to do the 'A' time twice. I had three meetings in which to do it: Crystal Palace, Birberach in Germany and the Aviva Championships at Birmingham that was the qualifying event for the British Olympic team. I lay in my bed one evening thinking how easy it would be for the BOA if I just didn't make the times. I thanked my lucky stars I wasn't living in a pre-Iron Curtain country where certain influences could have been applied.

As I warmed up for my heat run at Crystal Palace I was called over by an official. He looked a little flustered and more than a bit embarrassed. To my utter astonishment he proceeded to try and tell me that he'd lost the official clock.

"What do you mean, you've lost the clock?" I asked.

"Errr... well... we know where it is but we just can't find the key."

"Find the key?"

"To the office."

"It's in an office?"

"Yes, but we can't find the key."

I looked at him and snarled, "Then break the fucking door down, just get that clock out here."

"Can't be doing that," he commented as he walked away. "Don't worry, we'll time you by hand."

Time me by hand? I thought to myself, what the hell was going on?

I ran well that day at Crystal Palace. A sprinter knows when he has run well and he knows when he has run close to ten seconds flat. I ran close to ten flat on two occasions that day, I'm convinced of it, but surprise, surprise, my times, timed by hand, were said to be aided by the wind and therefore just outside the Olympic 'A' qualifying time. Now how can you tell whether a performance is wind-aided if you have no electronic equipment in use? No electronic wind gauge, no electronic clock, this is some bullshit! Ironically some of the other heats I didn't run in were said to have been run with a plus-wind so the times of those athletes' runs were actually altered in their favour. I could have been forgiven for thinking someone was out to cheat me. The Crystal Palace meet was being held over a two-day period. The following day, being a Sunday, the case of the lost keys was resolved as the electronic clock and wind gauge were in full use. The day I was running in an attempt to obtain the qualifying mark there was no electronic clock, the next day the clock was there.

I had two meets left and needed to run under the 'A' time both times in order to be fast enough to be up for selection for the 2008 Beijing Olympics. On June 26th I flew into Germany to prepare for the meet in Birberach a couple of days later. Running in a foreign country was altogether more relaxing. There were a few cameramen and reporters there but nothing compared to the British meets. It wasn't always like that. Prior to 2003 it was only the athletics or sports press boys there. After I'd tested positive for drugs it seemed that every man and his dog wanted a picture.

Running in Birberach was pleasant and the relaxing atmosphere rubbed off on me. Although I was still under pressure it was a nice pressure, a pressure that would push me just enough to do what I had to do. I made the qualifying time easily with a lot more in reserve. For the first time in years I felt invincible and dared to dream of a medal in Beijing. The officials and the crowd in Germany congratulated me... they were smiling and it was all so alien to me. When I returned to the hotel the staff were smiling too; a few of them had even been along to watch me and they took great pleasure in shaking my hand.

I began preparing for Birmingham in two weeks' time. Five days after Birmingham my appeal would be heard at the High Court in London.

On the day I returned home to London it was announced that two hundred past and present athletes including Dame Kelly Holmes and Sir Steven Redgrave had signed a petition against me being picked for the Beijing Olympic Games.

I met with my legal team at least a dozen times before that all-important race in Birmingham. My normal training routine was shot to pieces but still I believed in myself and knew I would simply have to win. I owed it to my friends and my family but above all to my legal team of Nick Collins and Jonathan Crystal and my hard-working agent Simon Dent. I started having sleepless nights daring to let the negative thoughts enter my head... what if?

What if I didn't make it? What if I got a bad start? What if I pulled a muscle or got the cramps? The hard work, the trust and the faith that all of these people had placed in me would be wasted.

It was four in the morning on July 3rd. I couldn't sleep as this was the day my legal team would launch court proceedings. I sat at the kitchen table writing about my feelings in general and my thoughts on going back to the High Court. I was due to travel up to Birmingham in preparation for the big race, but I then had an unexpected change of plan. With the launch of court proceedings I had to put on a suit and travel down to the Royal Courts of Justice and sit in an open court room. Jonathan Crystal my barrister suggested it would be a good idea to show my face as it would show good intentions of being serious about the appeal. The judge was pleasant, he suggested that I go ahead and compete and win! Should I lose the Olympic trials then there would be no reason to continue with proceedings. So, without further ado, I hopped on a train back to Enfield, chucked my things in my car and drove up to Birmingham.

I was to have another sleepless night as I lay in my bed in a hotel just off the M6 near Birmingham. Friday night's heats had gone well despite the pressure and I'd qualified for the semi-final. It was make or break. I went to bed early, around 9.30. I was physically exhausted and as soon as my head hit the pillow I was out!

Around midnight, I was woken by a loud banging on my bedroom door. I was disoriented in the dark, not sure where I was in this strange environment. I managed to make my way over to the noise, the light from the passageway shining under the door lighting my way. I threw the door open wondering what was going on. There was nobody there and as I looked along the passageway it was empty. I yawned and climbed back into bed thinking it was just somebody with one or two many beers inside them. It took a little longer to get to sleep but eventually tiredness took over and off I went.

My hotel phone woke me up at three o'clock then again at five. Each time I answered it there was no one there.

I arrived at the track on Saturday afternoon at a distinct disadvantage to my fellow competitors. One of them commented, "*Wah Gwan,* Dwain, you look so tired." (*Wah Gwan* being Jamaican slang.) As I said earlier, sprinting is all to do with mental attitude. It would have been so easy to feel sorry for myself that day in the Alexander Stadium particularly when a certain section of the crowd started booing me. It was strange; they weren't athletics fans, I could tell. I have been to enough meets in my life to know what genuine fans look like. I can't describe them but, believe me, I can tell. I was looking at rent-a-mob. They weren't going to beat me. The people who kept me awake through the night weren't going to beat me either. If anything I was more determined than ever as I began my mental preparation and walked over to my lane.

I'd qualified for the final, and was now one step further than I expected to be. Should I fail to qualify for the Beijing games all would be lost. All I can recall is the sound of the gun; the rest of the race was very vague. I can't describe the relief and sheer pleasure I felt as I stormed to victory that day in Birmingham and as the weight of the world was lifted from my shoulders. I'd made it hard for myself with another poor start as Simeon Williamson powered into the lead. But with a surge of adrenalin and determination not to get beaten, I powered past him to claim victory in a time of ten seconds dead. I was ecstatic and it showed as I dipped my chest across the finish line. The all too familiar words from Simeon shouting, "Fucking hell" as he too crossed the line in second place suddenly brought me back to reality. I was emotionally drained and yet all I could think of was the Beijing Olympics and what I could achieve if I got my act together and improved my start. I was capable of an even faster time. I was improving with each race and would peak perfectly at the Olympics. I was capable of a gold medal. I collapsed in a heap on the track, I was on the verge of tears, trembling with a million different emotions running through my body. My fellow competitor Mark Findlay was also in the race. He managed to find the courage to put his emotions to one side, as he failed to qualify for the Olympic games, and congratulate me on my performance. Picking me up, he said, "You've done it, Dwain man, you've done it." He kept repeating himself as he lifted me bodily from the track. I wanted to smile, I wanted to laugh and I wanted to cry as I looked into his eyes and at the big stupid smile etched onto his face. He was on the verge of tears too. How we managed to control our emotions I just don't know.

As Craig Pickering, Simeon Williamson and I stood on the podium with our medals around our necks I was rewarded with a standing ovation from the crowd. I then heard boos from a certain section of the audience and the fake athletics supporters. They were the only members who weren't clapping.

I reminded myself I still had one more race to win... at the High Court the following week.

MY LONGEST DAY AND UNFAIR INFLUENCES

The Hearing

There is a saying in British justice that the people who pay for the best lawyers win. I can relate to that. My team consisted of Jonathan Crystal and Nick Collins. They worked for free, they knew I was broke, they are my friends. They are two honourable men who believed in the cause. They believed in my right to run and right to compete but also, and more importantly, my right to earn a living. Both Jonathan and Nick had viewed the evidence since my ban had been lifted. I was not able to compete on an equal footing. Most of the high-paying Grand Prix meetings are by invitation only. Those invites did not materialise. Lesser athletes than me were receiving corporate sponsorship and invites to open sports stores and supermarkets, a very lucrative part of an athlete's overall earnings. In a nutshell I was being blackballed long after my punishment had come to an end.

Like I have said, Jonathan and Nick believed in me and believed in British justice. That is why they worked so hard, fee free. Both Jonathan and Nick could have applied themselves to other work which would have paid well. However, we all stood our corner and prepared to fight. I remember sitting in Jonathan's Chambers one afternoon when he announced that the BOA had secured the services of David Pannick QC.

He did not look too happy.

"Who is David Pannick?" I asked.

Jonathan simply replied, "He's one of the best in the business, Dwain. The most expensive and we have a real battle on our hands."

Nevertheless we all agreed to press on and Jonathan and Nick prepared to present the basis of the case.

CHAMBERS V BOA
17th July 2008
Introductory Presentation
Historical Context

1. The very first race of the Modern Olympics held in Athens in 1896 was the opening heat of the 100 metres. 104 years later Dwain Chambers lined up in the final of the 100 metres in Sydney. He missed out on a medal – finishing fourth. His margin of failure was 4/100ths of a second. Had he recorded the same time as last Saturday he would have secured a Bronze medal just 1/100th of a

second behind the Silver medal winner from Trinidad and Tobago.
2. GB has secured three gold, two silver and three bronze medals in the 100 metres over the last 110 years. There have been two fourth places: Mr Chambers and at the 1948 London Olympic Games. Of the last five winners of the race, 1 was disqualified for doping and 2 subsequently suspended for doping. The disqualified runner was suspended but returned to run in the next Olympics.
3. In his masterful book of Olympics, David Wallechinsky records that:

"The use of performance-enhancing drugs and concoctions by Olympic athletes is nothing new."

He recalls that it dates back to 1904. The views of the IOC as to who should participate in the Games are therefore not to be lightly rejected.

Mr Chambers' current position

4. The following opening submissions are made on Mr Chambers' behalf.

4.1   He is eligible and welcome by the IOC to participate in Beijing 2008.

4.2   He is eligible, though probably less welcome, to represent GB other than in the Olympics – since returning to athletics he has contributed a Gold medal in 2006 and a Silver medal earlier this year.

4.3   He represents our best chance of a podium finish in the 100 metres in Beijing. There would be no restriction to his selection for any nation (save possibly Denmark). After the selection announced on Monday no athlete in direct competition with him will miss out going to Beijing so that he is not "taking someone else's place on the plane."

4.4 He has completed the sanction imposed on him – two years' ineligibility in conformity with the World Anti-Doping Code. This application does not set out "to beat the sanction system".

4.5 He has demonstrated laudable qualities since returning to athletics:

(i) Acknowledging his guilt and wrongdoing and expressing regret for his actions;

(ii) Promoting the anti–doping message and cooperating with the authorities to strengthen its vigilance against doping;

(iii) Demonstrating courage by carrying on as an athlete without financial and medical support or coaching;

(iv) Producing remarkable times and finishes in the face of pressure and adversity;

(v) Facing up to his financial responsibilities by trialling for other sports;

(vi) In the face of vociferous detractors both on and off the track, striving to take part in the Olympics and bring home success.

5. There is no instance of a suspended athlete returning to competition being denied participation in the Olympic Games other than by inadequate performance. Amongst many, Randy Barnes, the US shotputter, returned after suspension and secured the Gold medal in 1996.

6. He demonstrated five days ago what he could achieve as a

"clean athlete". No stronger message could be sent to those doping or considering it.

The challenge and the basis for it

7. Controversy surrounding selection for the Olympics is not new. Seb Coe's non-selection for the 1988 Olympic Games evoked strong conflicting views.

8. His challenge is to disapply the Bye-Law so as to make him eligible for nomination by the BOA for Beijing 2008. UK Athletics have confirmed that they "would not seek to rely on the BOA Bye-Law in the event that the Court were to restrain the BOA from enforcing it."

9. He requires an interim Order from the Court restraining the BOA from applying the Bye-Law until a substantive trial in March 2009. The Bye-Law is attacked on three bases:

(i)   It is an unreasonable restraint of trade;

(ii)   It offends against competition law and

(iii) It is arbitrary, capricious and irrational.

10. The Bye-Law (we say) is more than necessary to pursue such legitimate aims as the BOA can claim. It cannot be objectively justified by the BOA as proportionate. Furthermore it promotes inconsistency and denies rehabilitation.

11. As a matter of "practical reality" Mr Chambers should be nominated to run in Beijing.

J Crystal

The night before the hearing Jonathan invited me and my family for dinner with Nick Collins and Simon. We drove to his house in central London. I was feeling apprehensive, a little nervous even. Simon is a lawyer too. I was dining with four bloody lawyers as Jonathan's wife is a lawyer as well!

I needn't have worried. We had a relaxing dinner and chatted about what to expect the next day. I kept asking what my chances were. The consensus of opinion was that it was about 50/50. This concerned me a little; I expected better odds than that. They were just being cautious, I reassured myself in the car on the way home.

I didn't sleep well the night prior to Thursday 17th July. This was the day I thought my fate would be decided by the High Court. My barrister Jonathan Crystal had applied for a temporary injunction. In simple terms he would ask the judge to postpone any hearing until after the Olympics if he felt there was a reasonable chance of winning. This would give me a place on the plane to Beijing.

I awoke around 5.45 that morning giving up on my personal battle to get more sleep. Before I went downstairs I looked in on Skye, my little boy, nearly three years of age. He is not normally a good sleeper; he has bundles of energy. Of course he knows nothing of my chequered past. One day I will tell him. I will try and convince him not to make the same mistakes that I have made. I boiled the kettle and made a cup of tea. As I took it through to the sitting room I noticed the dim red light shining out of the darkness. I picked up the TV remote control from the coffee table in front of me and pressed the standby button.

The television burst into life. It automatically configures to the last channel from the night before. Sky News and the face of Mark Longhurst filled my world. The grim-faced presenter reached for a sheet of A4 paper and announced *Chambers Battle*. It's very important for a TV presenter to alter their emotional state as each story is read out. Any mention of drugs requires a grim face or even a scowl of disapproval.

D-day for drugs cheat Chambers and the info bar along the bottom of the screen displayed likewise. I am always the cheat, never the sprinter or the athlete. I am the drugs cheat Chambers. Sky News boasts "Breaking news every 15 minutes". On this particular day that wasn't entirely accurate as the channel covered the same facts albeit in a slightly different manner every ten minutes throughout the day. There were four main stories that day that ran over and over again depending on what time you viewed proceedings. I was either second or third, sandwiched in between the release of two north London girls from a jail in Ghana for attempting to smuggle six kilos of cocaine into the UK, and a certain Mrs Darwin and the infamous canoe trial. Mrs Darwin was being tried for fraud and deception. It was claimed Mrs Darwin's husband had died over five years before after a canoeing accident. In fact he had been alive all these years living on the other side of the world and Mrs Darwin was aware of the fact all along and incredibly had kept it from her two sons.

At times I have felt very unfairly treated by the press and media of this country but my treatment pales into insignificance at the treatment meted out to one Robert Murat who coincidentally was at the High Court on the same day as I was. His trial or rather lack of it lasted a mere five minutes in which ten newspapers admitted writing over one hundred stories connecting Robert Murat with the disappearance of Madeline McCann. Robert Murat stood outside the High Court having received a full apology in open court and told waiting reporters of the total destruction the media had caused to his life. Amongst other things, he was being likened to the Soham killer Ian Huntley and also accused of being a paedophile. One can only imagine what this man must have gone through and although he was awarded £600,000 I think the ten newspapers got off very lightly. One must never underestimate the power of the media. I don't.

A different headline on Sky this time, *Self-confessed drugs cheat.* Oh well, it's a little different just as long as they get the word cheat in there. Eamonn Holmes took over from Mark Longhurst and the same stories were played over. Eamonn too is careful to grimace as he mentions Dwain Chambers and drugs in the same sentence. I realise it isn't personal. Eamonn Holmes is a model professional and has a job to do. I respect him immensely. It was Eamonn during a moment off camera that explained my almost permanent smile could be interpreted as arrogance. It isn't. It was never meant to be. In reality it's probably a sign of nervousness. Eamonn has interviewed thousands of people and he took me to one side and told me a few home truths. He judged me well, knew I wasn't the arrogant cocky celebrity that some people made out and yet he explained very well just how I could come across on camera. I try now not to smile too much on camera. Sad, I know, but it seems to keep the vultures at bay the next morning in the newspapers.

Sky opened up their sports section at 6.20am. You have guessed it: number one sporting issue of the day ? *Chambers the cheat.* It made no difference that they had covered exactly the same story only ten minutes earlier on their breaking news spot.

It was the start of the British Open Golf Tournament and the day Freddie Flintoff returned to English cricket. Chambers the cheat relegated the golf and cricket to second and third spot respectively.

After a light breakfast I dropped Skye off at the nursery. I explained to him as best I could that I was going to court. As you could expect he replied by saying, "Uhh!" I never expected him to understand. I smiled at him and kissed him goodbye. His little smiley face warmed my heart as I walked out of the nursery. Leonie, Gabe, a friend who recorded the whole event from my house to the Royal Courts of Justice on a camcorder, and I made our way to Tottenham Hale Station. Leonie had decided she wanted to be there for me and had taken the day off work. Never had I been so glad to have a hand to hold. My emotions were now somewhere between terrified and hysterical. Leonie commented on how hot and sweaty my hand was but still refused to let go. We took the tube to Holborn Station at 9am and met with Simon Dent and Nick Collins. It would have been nice to take a taxi but the truth of the matter was we couldn't afford to. In a way I was glad. I was recognized on the tube and at least three or four people wished me luck. I appreciated their comments, they meant a lot to me. I had been reading in the paper a few days before the hearing that public opinion was against me. On the street and in the tube stations, in the parks and cafés of London all I heard were messages of support and good wishes. The papers had got it wrong or were they just trying to manipulate the hearts and souls of the public once again? Before the hearing the papers seemed to be siding with the BOA. I was hardly surprised. Simon had tried to generate some support in the media but told me it was very difficult. It was as if an invisible barrier had been erected. Down-to-earth genuine journalists seemed only too eager to print a story of something positive I had done, but the stories never made it to print.

Simon did however manage to organise a petition in the Londonpaper. In one week two thousand people had signed it and I had received some fantastic messages of support which I still have in a scrapbook. Every time I hit the street running up to the hearing, people were always encouraging me, urging me to challenge the BOA. You may find this difficult to believe but prior to the hearing not one person ever came up to me and said that I was a disgrace, no one ever approached me and called me a cheat to my face. They are happy to write about it, of course, and the letters pages of the papers and the internet blogs are full of accusations and advice that I should crawl under the nearest stone and die. But on the street, where it matters, I feel wanted. And I must thank people like Karen Doku and Joel Campbell who helped with the petition and gave up their time to rally support for me. Your work was not in vain.

The short walk to the High Court was a nightmare. Press photographers, journalists and members of the public jostled and wrestled with each other. The fact that Leonie was nearly six months pregnant made no difference at all. Long lens cameras, voice recorders and microphones were thrust into our faces and at one point a brawl broke out between two photographers vying for the best position. They were a disgrace to their profession.

Sky's coverage of the Dwain Chambers appeal would saturate television screens up and down Great Britain for the rest of the day. One cannot fault their commitment to a story.

Among many individuals interviewed that day were a specialist sports barrister, the former chief of the Anti-Doping Committee, two respected journalists in Duncan McKay and Richard Lewis, and several athletics coaches including Frank Dick.

At 11.44am Sky reported that the judge Mr Justice Mackay had announced there would be no decision made in the High Court that day. He wanted to ponder the decision, sleep on it and return to court the following day. Sky News went straight to Ian Doveston who suggested that the judge was listening very seriously to Dwain Chambers' argument and that this particular race was heading for a very tight finish. Ian Doveston presented a seemingly unbiased report taking care to document both sides of the argument, but as always, as seems to be par for the course with Sky News, he ended on a negative. He pulled at the heartstrings of the great British public when he mentioned Tyrone Edgar and Craig Pickering, the two athletes that might miss out as a result of this appeal.

On that day Sky News also opened up a viewers' blog. Again they were very balanced in the opinions they aired that particular day. However my good friend Joel was watching events unfold

One of the steadying influences in my life, my physio Sarah Connors

My two closest friends Darren Thompson and
Christian Malcolm

The love of my life and me at a friend's wedding

DC and Skye enjoying a special moment in Barbados

With Prince Philip at Buckingham Palace, my proud mum and Celia Facey

Skye's Christening 2006. My son, Jayon, in the foreground

Photograph: By kind permission of Mark Aspland

Me and my son Rocco Star just a few weeks after his birth

and could not help noticing that the final word would always be given over to an individual without an ounce of sympathy for my predicament. A fourth sports news story surfaced later that afternoon. Ricardo Rico became the third cyclist in the 2008 Tour De France to fail a drugs test.

Inside the court things were going as well as could be expected. In layman's terms I was challenging the legality of the bye-law. I had already been banned from one Olympics and, yes, I thought the decision was unfair. Meanwhile the barristers were discussing principles.

The first principle of sports law is that governing bodies are not public authorities whose decisions are subject to judicial review. The second principle as it was read out concerned me. It stated that the decision of the BOA may be challenged in private law proceedings. However, because such judicial control has been developed in the context of restraint of trade, in order to protect the right to work from unreasonable restrictions, the courts will not entertain a legal challenge concerning an amateur event even if there would be indirect commercial benefits for the competitor. In the eyes of the law, the Olympics is an amateur event even though some countries do reward their athletes in the way of expenses. The Americans even offer a financial rewards system for medals secured.

The court heard that in 1988, the Court of Appeal ruled that a professional tennis player and coach had no legal redress against the Essex Lawn Tennis Association for leaving him out of the team, however unfair the selection decision might be. This was an amateur event and it was immaterial that the plaintiff hoped and expected that success for the Essex team would improve his chances of securing sponsorship and promoting his coaching career. The BOA also stated I was fighting an exclusion from an event for which there was no prize money and the hope that success might bring indirect financial rewards was legally irrelevant.

It was also announced that the courts would not be prepared to intervene at the last moment to grant an injunction to compel a regulatory body to allow an individual or team to participate in a sporting event if there has been delay in bringing the case to court. If an athlete is concerned about a regulatory barrier to participation (e.g. the life ban) he cannot wait until he has satisfied the sporting criteria for eligibility as I did before bringing the legal challenge. This amounted to a slap on the wrist for me and my legal counsel for bringing the appeal to the court so late.

David Pannick, QC, led the BOA's legal team. Adam Lewis was also part of the team. He said that the main challenge in the case was to convey why a difficult question of selection policy determined by a sports body, based on its experience and expertise, should be overruled by a court. Pannick explained that the BOA was in the best position to strike the balance between redemption and the interests of an individual athlete on the one hand and the need to protect Olympic ideals and clean sport, and the interests of all athletes, on the other. The decision was likely to be relied upon to prevent attempts to persuade the courts to intervene in other sports bodies' decisions, particularly where the application is left to the eleventh hour. At this point I had a real feeling that perhaps we should have acted a little more quickly. Hindsight is a wonderful thing and of course earlier that year I'd been trying to earn a living other ways. Because of time constraints and the way the British judicial system works we had applied for interim relief from the bye-law. That is, we required the BOA to select me to compete at the Beijing Olympics notwithstanding that the bye-law has not been ruled illegal. In a nutshell, we knew that a ruling on the bye-law would come after the Beijing Olympics and therefore I should be allowed to compete if there were a realistic possibility of winning. Should the court find in favour of the BOA after the Olympics then any medals won could be taken away from me and my performance struck from the record.

BOA in their case contended that if my application for interim relief succeeded, this would be mandatory and alter the status quo.

They argued that I had a very weak case in that I couldn't show that sportsmen and women are significantly restrained in their trade by the bye-law which only concerns eligibility for an amateur event which takes place every four years and for which there is no prize money. At this point the balance swung back to us. No one sitting in that court room honestly believed that the Olympic Games, the greatest show on earth, wouldn't financially benefit the athletes that took part and, more importantly, those who won medals. It was an amateur event back in ancient Greece, but not any more.

Time and time again the BOA brought up the fact that the appeal was lodged far too late and said I had threatened to bring these proceedings from 5th Feb 2008. The BOA say that they wrote to me on 13th February to tell me that I had to notify them of my appeal by 15th February – a deadline set by BOA in a letter of 22nd August 2006 sent to all sports governing bodies. With that 22nd August 2006 letter, BOA appended a note requesting the governing bodies to inform all relevant athletes of the deadline to appeal Olympic bans. This letter was never received by me or my legal team until a *copy* was sent on the 11th February 2008!

My solicitors said they wrote to the BOA immediately on receipt stating there simply wasn't enough time to respond by the 15th. They also stated that I was not going to come to any decision until after the World Indoor Championships the following month. I felt this was a realistic request. How on earth could I appeal an Olympic ban until I genuinely believed I was good enough and had the times to warrant going?

Get on with it! I wanted to scream at the BOA. Here we were in a court of law attempting to discuss the legalities of a bye-law and we were wasting time arguing whether we should even be here at all! I realise now that it was all part of their tactics. We had a limited time to discuss the bye-law and the more time we spent on other issues, the better for them.

Ford and Warren (my solicitors) had also written complaining that Lord Moynihan's statements in the press indicated that any appeal under bye-law would be pre-determined. *"There will be no room for cheats in the British team as long as I am involved with the BOA...we will pay whatever is necessary to have top lawyers represent us and put the strongest case in support of that ban. We will send a clean team to Beijing and there will be no room for doping cheats."*

At last, as the hearing progressed late into the day we began to address the bye-law. The BOA argued that grant of interim relief would have a significant and unjust effect on third parties and on the good administration by the BOA of the British Olympic team. It would deprive another athlete of his place in the team. The bye-law, they claimed, introduced in 1992, was not an anti-doping rule which prevented a person from competing in other sporting events, only the Olympic Games. It is worth noting that since 1992 there have been 31 appeals of which 28 have been allowed.

I laughed inwardly as the BOA referred to the 100 metres relay and claimed that the athletes likely to form part of that squad had been undertaking relay training together over the last two years and the squad would be weakened by the inclusion of someone who had not done so. Had they forgotten I had been part of the GB team that had won a gold relay medal and had been competing in relay races since the age of fourteen?

To me the BOA seemed to be clutching at straws as they argued that if I competed well and ran in the final of the 100 metres, the lane advantage that I secured may have a detrimental effect on the chances of success of other athletes. What? This was an unbelievable statement! What other athletes? The competition, the Americans and Jamaicans? Were they stating that they would rather the others won? It got better... they said that if I ran exceptionally well, my performance may deprive another athlete of a medal. What! It would also involve irreparable losses to other athletes. In my opinion they contradicted themselves here. Early on in the proceedings they were claiming the Olympics was an amateur event and didn't necessarily mean financial gain for athletes and now they were clearly talking about irreparable losses to athletes.

The BOA concluded this session by claiming they were very concerned about the impact on the reputation of Team GB and the BOA if it were compelled to include persons who have deliberately cheated. Moynihan believed it would have an adverse impact on the ability to raise funds through donors and sponsors to support the 2012 Games.

The proceedings closed for the day and Mr Justice Mackay instructed us to return the following day at ten o'clock when he would deliver his verdict. We were all a little surprised as we expected him to give his verdict there and then. I wondered why he had to sleep on it. He'd heard both sides of the argument and listened to people talking all day.

Nevertheless, the feeling in our camp was one of quiet confidence. To me the BOA argument just didn't stack up. I wanted to earn a living and felt that my legal team had made that abundantly clear. Jonathan had explained in detail my attempts to try and do this in other sports and my lack of inclusion in Grand Prix events after my ban had finished. There was no doubt that if I was given the green light to run in the Olympics my profile would be raised and if I managed to win a medal I would be back in the public fold again and perhaps... just perhaps, I would begin to be accepted again.

I returned home that evening satisfied that at last justice would prevail. I looked in on Skye who had just gone to bed and I sat with Jayon and Leonie and watched a little TV. I was back with my family again, a family I prayed I would be able to provide for once more. I looked forward to the following day.

The next day, we followed the same procedure as the day before. If I thought the media scrum the day before was bad, this was ten times worse. There were more members of the public and the photographers fought with each other yet again. Demonstrators were waving placards that to this day I don't know what they said. People were shouting, and the press were asking the most ridiculous of questions actually believing I could stop outside and give an interview. At one point I was genuinely frightened for our safety as I felt myself being pushed and jostled from all angles. I breathed a sigh of relief as we managed to make the relevant calm of the court building

We walked into Court Number 70 of The Royal Courts of Justice and all heads turned. A few pleasant nods and smiles were exchanged, the two teams were like two prizefighters who had slugged it out for twelve rounds and were waiting for the referee's decision. It was clear that there would be no more debate. Mr Justice Mackay started to speak. Suddenly I didn't feel so confident. I listened carefully to the man who held my life in his hands and could feel my heart beating so so loudly, I wondered if anyone else could hear it too. To be honest I didn't know which way the verdict looked like going early into Mr Justice Mackay's address, but ten minutes after he started speaking Jonathan Crystal turned towards me and whispered, "We've lost."

I wanted to tell him he was wrong, I tried to raise a smile, shake my head. I looked at my team; they had the same glum expression as Jonathan. It was over. We had lost.

I tried to focus on what the judge was saying. Perhaps Jonathan was mistaken, perhaps that's what judges do when they are summing a case up, give two sides of the story and then the final verdict. Within three quarters of an hour everybody in the court room knew the result and the journalists were filtering the news outside to the assembled media and television crews waiting with bated breath.

Mr Justice Mackay upheld the right of the BOA under a bye-law to exclude me from Team GB at the Beijing Olympic Games. He then went on to detail the reason behind his decision. Meanwhile outside the courts Sky television was speaking live by telephone to John Regis. He commented that he was reasonably happy with the verdict. I was a nice kid who made a bad choice but I had cheated and you have to understand that cheaters never prosper. After the judge finished we waited behind. The BOA announced they would not pursue costs if I did not appeal the decision. Pursue costs? I had nothing to give them and they knew it. We had no option but to agree. Moynihan walked over to me and shook my hand, said it was nothing personal. I was in a daze, I can't even remember if I answered him.

We regrouped in Jonathan's Chambers, decided to hold our heads up high and face the music outside. The vultures would be circling; of that there was no doubt.

We waited behind for at least thirty minutes and went out to face the press. There were more smiles than there had been that morning; it was all quite bizarre, more teeth on display. It's funny the things you remember; someone was punched again. I remember the fist swinging through the air in an arc, as if in slow motion connecting with the poor unfortunate on the receiving end.

In the end we took a cab back to Enfield. It seemed like a long way. We sat in the back of the cab and nobody said anything for what seemed like a long time. Leonie tried to get me to make conversation but she had a hard task. Simon tried to remain positive, talked about the long-term plan and the book and kept saying it wasn't the end of the world. For me... it felt like the end of world.

Many people have asked me why we brought the claim so late. In not so many words, we brought it late because we decided it would be absolutely pointless appealing the ban if I couldn't make the qualifying time of 10.21 seconds necessary to get to the Olympics in the first place. I could see the sense in this but unfortunately could not race anywhere. After the World Indoors they blocked me all over Europe so I couldn't compete. Otherwise we would have achieved the time and brought the case a lot earlier.

RUNNING AWAY TO SPAIN

The press accused me of fleeing to Spain. *Chambers runs to the sun* claimed one Spanish-based newspaper. I had no complaints; for once the press boys were right. I'd had enough. I needed a break, my family needed a break. Events leading up to the trial had taken me on a roller coaster of emotions. One day we were on a high and confident, the next day it didn't look so good. Everything hinged on the judge's decision. I was trying hard to look confident, stay cool. On the surface I seemed okay, the press would again brand me as arrogant; underneath I was a quivering nervous wreck.

When the judgement came I was shattered. I didn't expect it. I always believed that I deserved a second chance, believed that the justice system of my country would give me just that.

I returned home from the High Court to the press camping outside my house, hassling Jayon and Leonie. Even Skye was frightened at the number of bodies and cameras pitched outside his home. "Give us a comment, Dwain," they shouted as I walked through the gate. "How are you feeling now?"

Fuck off and die, I wanted to say, give me a break, give my family a break, you got what you wanted. Now they wanted more.

I wanted to get away from London, away from my own home, my own street. It was impossible, we had no money and a none too impressive overdraft. I remembered my grandfather's words: something will always turn up.

I received a phone call from Simon Dent later that evening. He'd been talking to my publisher and they'd hatched a plan. Libros International are based in Spain. They have a small independent apartment for their authors to go and chill out or to seek a little inspiration. It was free and they suggested I bring the family out for a week; they would also cover the cost of the flights. I had a book to write and Libros International were hoping it would be in the shops for Christmas so we had to get moving. How could we refuse? Leonie made the necessary telephone call to work and we cleared it with Jayon's dad. The following morning we began to pack our cases and Skye started to get excited. He had been on holiday before but only as a tiny baby. I explained that the 'little house', as he called it, had a swimming pool just outside the back door and the sun shone all day and every day. The English summer had been poor so far and Skye had been cooped up in the house all too often. Even on the nice days recently there seemed to be a photographer or a member of the press permanently ensconced outside our door. I looked forward to taking Skye in the pool, perhaps teaching him to swim. I looked forward to the peace and tranquillity and taking him to the beach. But most of all I wanted to find out whether I could write.

"It won't work if you don't, Dwain," Ken Scott, my ghostwriter, said as he thrust a notebook and pen at me. It was not alien to me. I'd taken notes for many years, writing down things that I felt were important. During the trial I'd scribbled continuously. I'd jotted down thoughts on the tube as I travelled to meet with Jonathan and Simon and I'd sit in Simon's shop sometimes for hours lost in my thoughts whilst transferring them onto paper. "It has to be Chambers' story," Ken explained, "not Ken Scott's."

That week with Ken made me realise I could write. It made me realise that this was my big chance to tell the world how it was. The written word is all-powerful and for years it has been used to discredit and dishonour me. Now it was my chance to set the record straight. I wrote for England that week I really did.

It was a beautiful feeling waking up to the sun each morning. It was so quiet out there, so idyllic and so peaceful. We were staying south of Valencia in a small town called Altea La Vella. It's five minutes from the beach at the foot of a mountain; what a beautiful place to live.

We ventured into a town called Calpe with a stunning sandy beach. It was so nice not to be recognized, not to be hounded or chased. Leonie commented on how chilled I'd become in just a matter of a few days. We sat overlooking the sea as we ate grilled fish and meat with huge bowls of fresh vegetables and salad and fresh Spanish bread. It was heaven and altogether different from the dining experiences back home. We have a fair-sized back garden back home in Enfield but the one barbecue we had planned in the summer ended early with a torrential downpour.

One evening I was even persuaded to drink a few beers. My God, I must have been relaxed.

The one and only time I had to work at promotion was one evening when I went to a place called Albir to do some speed training with a couple of local kids' football teams. I was only too happy to do this as I love working with kids. I hope this is something that the establishment will allow me to do in the future. The television cameras were there and the local Spanish, English and Dutch press.

Apparently there had been a bit of trouble the week before when it was announced to the parents that I would be helping with the training. Although the football club is multi-national with a real mixture of Spanish, English, Norwegian and Dutch kids, one of the English mothers was none too pleased that I would be helping with the session. She said that it was not right to parade me as a role model and that I was a drugs cheat. Someone spoke up defending me, saying my ban had finished and I should be given another chance. The woman wouldn't have it. Fifteen minutes later her husband turned up to voice the same opinion. At one point the argument had looked like it was getting out of hand. The lady never turned up on the evening I trained the boys and girls. If she had I would have explained that I was in fact the perfect role model for the children. I've been there, got the T-shirt and now advocate clean running. What better example to give to children than one of experience combined with forgiveness? Regardless, the children had a fantastic session and revelled in the presence of the cameras.

After the training session I had been asked to take part in a question and answer session at a local bar. I felt a little nervous as I walked into the bar and there was a muted silence as people began to notice me. It was standing room only, not a spare seat to be had anywhere. I'm not a good speaker, I know that, but I realise in my profession as a top athlete it's a necessary evil. People will always want interviews, always ask me questions. As soon as I walked in, the children were up out of their seats asking for photographs and autographs. Most of the families were on holiday and consequently everyone seemed to have a camera. I didn't mind, I never refuse a child a picture or a signature. But with every photo I allow and for every autograph I sign, I just pray that the individual wants to be seen with me for who I am as an athlete, the fastest man in Europe, and not because of my notoriety. It's different with children: the majority of them are there because they've seen me run on TV. With their parents I'm not so sure. I suspect half of them were there that night to hear what I had to say about drugs. It was half an hour before I took my place at the question table. The press were there too and the questions began.

As always the first few were nice enough: What was your greatest race? What was it like winning the trial? Questions I quite naturally expected but then, as the evening wore on and the customers found their voices and as the beer flowed, the questions about drugs inevitably rose to the surface. I answered them as I always do... with honesty. I held up my hands and as I looked into the eyes of the children fresh-faced and suntanned, on holiday with their parents, I told them about my big mistake, told them how wrong I was and that it's better to run clean. The questions rained down on me for an hour. Nikki Luxford, a reporter from the Costa Blanca News, posed the question of the night:

"There are children here tonight, Dwain. What would you say to the budding athletes here tonight about winning at all costs? Is it better to run clean and second or is winning everything?"

I knew exactly what she meant and again I answered her honestly. "I would rather come second," I replied and the crowd seemed to appreciate my response.

The hard work of writing my book continued for the rest of the week. In one of my conversations with Ken Scott he mentioned the name Horace Greasley. Ken had nearly finished ghostwriting the memoirs of this World War Two ex-prisoner of war. "Horace was beaten and battered into submission by the Germans, Dwain, but he survived." Ken grinned. "It's simply the best wartime story I've ever heard. It's been a pleasure to write it."

And so it was my pleasure to meet up with Horace and his wife Brenda and to hear some of his story. Slowly, as the story of the camps, the torture and brutality came out, I began to suspect why I was there. Once or twice Horace took a deep breath, fighting hard to control his emotions. Ken would explain later that Horace had eventually found closure to the horrors he'd endured by pouring his story out. He had wanted to tell it for over sixty years. Horace retired to Spain twenty years ago moving to Javea thirty miles up the coast.

He and his wife forged a particularly special relationship with their next-door neighbours enjoying paella parties and barbecues, and they shared birthdays and anniversaries together.

"What were their names, Horace?" Ken asked.

"Joachen and Helga," Horace answered.

It clicked. Horace and Brenda's best friends were German.

Forgiveness. Now it all made sense.

The week was just about over, it had flown by and a certain mini-depression washed over me as I made my way to the airport. My life was on hold but I had a new purpose. I had the book to concentrate on.

BEIJING AND BEYOND

The great thing about England, advised my barrister Jonathan Crystal when I started writing this book, is that no one can sue you for having an opinion. Freedom of speech is denied in many countries but not, it seems, in our green and pleasant land.

As I watched the Olympics in China I was reminded of their record on human rights and the brutal put-down of the student movement in Tiananmen Square not so many years ago. I watched the demonstrations on Sky News and the Free Tibet Organization. I watched as world leaders like George Bush voiced off in a worldwide reported speech about just that, before he took up his position at the opening ceremony, no doubt anxious and looking forward to watching his fellow countrymen win gold after gold.

In my opinion half the American athletes you have enjoyed watching at the 2008 Olympic Games have used performance-enhancing drugs in the past. Dramatic statement, I know, but a statement I'm convinced is correct.

Don't forget I've been there. I've met America's greatest athletes and their coaches and at one point been ridiculed by those very athletes when I challenged their morals. Everyone is on it, they laughed; you can't be the best without help.

Now I know they spoke the truth; now I know how easy it is to cheat the system. I watch with dismay as genuinely clean athletes cannot get near to their competitors. It's a joke! The authorities are simply not serious about the drugs issue in our sport; they are merely paying lip-service to it.

The women's 10,000 metres world record is held by Wang Junxia of China, set back in 1993. Who? You have a right to ask; her career was mysteriously short-lived. A good long-distance athlete's career can span ten to fifteen years; just look at Paula Radcliffe. On September 8th 1993 Wang Junxia won the 10,000 metres Chinese Games final in a world record of 29:31.78 which was faster than the former record by forty-two seconds. FORTY-TWO SECONDS!

The next day she claimed the 3000 metres in another world record time of 8:06.11. She also won the World Cup Marathon Championships later in the year. Her coach Ma Junren claimed that a mysterious fungus helped improve her physical condition. The critics claimed the Chinese had not given the random samples requested at the time and yet the records achieved back then stood and still stand to this day. The times and performances of those Chinese athletes during that period of time were undoubtedly enhanced by someone or something and yet the world authorities did nothing. In fact they rewarded them by allowing them to stage the Beijing Olympics. China only holds three world records in outdoor athletics as I write this chapter. Three were achieved in September 1993 and still stand to this day.

As a footnote, prior to the Olympic Games in Sydney, six athletes coached by Ma Junren (Junxia's coach) were tested positive for performance-enhancing drugs. Some people may say it smells a little of double standards and cover-ups and does not give a clear indication that the world authorities are serious about ridding the sport of drugs. The truth is it's about money and sponsorship. The crowds want to see fast times and records broken by seconds, not hundredths of seconds. They want to see athletes pushing their well-conditioned bodies to the limit and the authorities want to see full stadiums. They want paying customers and the ability to sell lucrative TV rights and sponsorship.

It would be nice if everyone competed clean but they know that won't ever happen. The chemists will always be one step ahead of the authorities and those such as Victor Conte are very rich men on the back of their chosen profession. The world athletics' governing bodies' solution is random drug testing, occasionally catching a cheat and parading him or her in front of the world's media. A scapegoat is nice now and again; a top athlete, maybe someone with a little character, slightly arrogant perhaps. And when they do catch someone after a random test, it's important to keep them in the limelight as long as possible. It's all about tactics, you see; taking the moral high ground so that the sponsors are happy to associate their sponsorship with the so-called *clean* athletes. Britain, unfortunately for me, not only want to take the moral high ground; they also want to lead the world, want to be a shining beacon in the fight against drugs. A cynic may tell you it didn't do their 2012 bid any harm. The cynic would be right. Despite my ban finishing over two years ago I have played into the BOA's hands and kept myself in the spotlight because of my desire to compete in the Olympics. Don't forget my ban prevented me from competing at the last Olympics in Athens too. Ironically Chambers the cheat may have played his own small part in securing the 2012 Olympic Games for London. I certainly hope so. Gentlemen... I was glad to be of service.

In the summer of 2008 the International Olympic Committee (IOC) introduced a new rule. The rule is as clear as day and one that I would advocate the BOA takes on board. They say that any athlete who gets a ban of six months or longer will miss the first Olympic Games after their ban has finished. That's fair enough and would have meant I was banned from Beijing anyway. I could have lived with that and got on with my preparations for London 2012. There would have been no court appearances, no need for lawyers and barristers, no doubts in my mind, and no feelings of persecution, bitterness or animosity. But will the BOA take this on board and allow British athletes a level playing field? No, I suspect not. I suspect Coe and Moynihan and de Vos will still wish to go that little step further to show the watching world that Great Britain won't bend an inch. The only two other countries in the world who insist on an Olympic lifetime ban are Norway and... wait for it... don't laugh... China. China... land of the strange fungus.

Now that Britain has won the right to stage the 2012 Olympic Games it is even more important that the BOA take the moral high ground. The London Games are already three times over budget; it is now even more essential that Lords Coe and Moynihan are able to attract the right sponsors to alleviate that deficit just a little. No doubt at this very moment Niels de Vos and Moynihan and Coe et al are out courting the big sponsors. They attended the Beijing Olympics, hoping to rub shoulders in the corporate lounges and tents with the big boys writing the cheques, the television companies and advertisers. This of course is normal practice and expected of the people at the very forefront of the bid. After all it is their job, I suppose.

As I write this chapter the British rowing team has struck gold in the men's fours. What an incredible race and a wonderful achievement. I enjoyed it immensely as I sat perched on the edge of my seat and willed their boat past the Aussie crew in the last few hundred metres. Their head coach Jürgen Grobler has been mentioned by the commentators several times. The East German has the Midas touch, says the female pundit on Eurosport. She tells of his wonderful coaching methods and the fact he has now coached the men's fours to three successive gold medals at three separate Olympics. The mention of his name saddens me. It exposes another double standard by the BOA and again there is inconsistency written all over it. Linford Christie and Jürgen Grobler share similar backgrounds. Both men have been awarded an OBE, both men have coached Olympians. Jürgen Grobler has never denied his chequered past; Linford Christie put his neck on the line for his family, then his country. He not only won medals for Great Britain but he played a huge part in keeping our country on the map for years and yet the BOA chose to refuse Linford accreditation for Beijing.

Linford Christie is currently coaching Christian Malcolm who is the only Brit to make the 200 metre Olympic final. He is there without his coach. The BOA had a fit when Ken Livingston announced that Linford Christie would be carrying the Olympic torch through London. If Ken Livingston can accept Linford, why can't the BOA? Please explain to me why a man that has admitted encouraging athletes to take illegal drugs can go to Beijing but a man like Linford can't. Linford has always protested his innocence. In fact, when he failed the test in 1999, he was actually cleared by UK Athletics. However that verdict was later overturned by the IAAF. What is beyond dispute though is that Linford had been retired for two years. He was running at a meaningless indoor meeting in Germany; there was simply no point in taking anything. Whatever his reasons might have been for taking steroids at that time knowingly or otherwise it had nothing to do with winning gold medals or that he was once the fastest man on earth. Everyone seems to have forgotten (especially the BOA) he was Commonwealth, European, Olympic and World 100 metre champion. They all have short memories. Arguably Linford did more for UK athletics than any athlete alive.

A few days later I watched the television as the men's 100 metre heats are announced. The cameras are on the athletes as they make their way down the tunnel and onto the track. My heart is beating like mad. I want to calm down, but I can't. This is the same type of rush you get when you're on the start line. Everything has suddenly intensified. Your pulse rate goes sky-high, your brain is telling you to walk away, you feel like vomiting all over the place. This is all a result of the pressure and uncertainty which can prove too much to handle.

Sitting watching the 100 metre heats on TV hurt me more than when the judge told me that I would not be going to Beijing. Seeing Tyrone Edgar, Craig Pickering and Simone Williamson running there when I knew I could beat every one of them felt like a knife through my heart. I was disappointed that no Brits made the 100 metre final and yet I wanted to stick two fingers up at the BOA and say, I told you so. Why couldn't they give me that second chance?

Christine Ohuruogu was given a second chance and look what she's gone on to achieve. I compare Christine's missed test to that of Rio Ferdinand too. Rio Ferdinand is a professional footballer, his wages are a reported £100,000 per week. Ferdinand was asked to take a test at United's Carrington training headquarters in 2003 but left without undergoing the procedure. The testers were there at the ground and so was Rio Ferdinand and he'd been notified he needed to undergo a test. Rio drove off stating it simply slipped his mind. A drug test is a big thing. I sincerely believe that when told you have been selected it simply cannot slip your mind. Even when clean it's a major concern. What about that cold cure I've taken? What about that nutrition bar, those vitamins? What if someone has slipped something into a drink or tampered with your food? It's all what ifs and, believe me, if you are at a training facility with the testers in attendance and they say it's your turn, sir, you just don't forget – whatever's on your mind!

When they tried to contact Rio to ask him return to the ground his mobile phone was switched off. He was uncontactable for two days. Nobody could catch up with him. Rio's missed test was around the same time as my positive test. He fared slightly better in the treatment he received. At the subsequent drugs commission he was banned for eight months. He effectively missed only half a season and although he was fined £50,000, Manchester United continued to pay him full wages. They commented, "It is a particularly savage and unprecedented sentence which makes an appeal inevitable."

Not only did Rio have the full support of Manchester United, his professional union the PFA backed him too. Accepting the verdict of the commission, the FA said, "Clearly the commission regarded not taking a drugs test as a very serious matter and have taken their action accordingly." But Professional Footballers Association chief executive Gordon Taylor labelled the decision as draconian.

"We knew there had to be a penalty, bearing in mind the world pressure, but he has quite clearly not been given the benefit of the doubt," Taylor told BBC Radio Five Live.

It is worth noting the view of World Anti-Doping Agency president Dick Pound however; he said he thought Ferdinand should have received a longer suspension.

I know I would have been right up in the mix fighting for a place in that final.

I get ready with my pen and notebook as Usain Bolt prepares himself.

My event; the one place in the world I wanted to be if only I'd been given the sort of chance Rio and Christine were afforded.

I wasn't going to watch it but I couldn't help myself. Ken, the man who has helped so much with this book, rings me from Spain just as they line up for the final. I tell him I won't be watching. Somehow he knows I'm lying and tells me to write about my feelings as I watch the race. I pick up my notepad and pen and scribble a few lines.

Bolt wins in a canter, leaning back, he pounds his chest as he crosses the line in a new world record time of 9.69. His lace is loose too and yet he is still two metres clear of his nearest rival. It is a breathtaking performance from the Jamaican and the commentator likens his performance to that of Ben Johnson all those years ago. It's easy to say as an armchair supporter that I would have made the podium and I'm sure I could have been there but sadly no one will ever know and I will never have the chance to find out. One thing I will say is 9.69 seconds is an amazing time. I remember an interview I did with Michael Johnson whilst banned. Michael asked me, "How fast will a human being be able to run over the 100 metres?"

"A human will be able to run 9.65 seconds," I replied.

"Not in my lifetime," Michael retorted. He obviously thought I was mad.

But Usain Bolt has proved that what I said to Michael Johnson is distinctly possible. I ain't ready for those times but a place in the top three at the Beijing Olympics was a huge possibility.

The race has fired me up for the 2009 World Championships. I've shown over the past few months that I can handle the pressure. Let's not forget that I was still competing throughout all the madness of the hearing and the hurtful headlines. As far as I'm concerned, if you can handle all of those outside distractions, then you've got what it takes to pull out the results in the majors.

I'm still passionate about my sport and I want to line up against the likes of Bolt, Powell and Gay, and anybody else that wants to race against me.

An hour later I am out for a stroll and I am asked by a friendly member of the public if I think Bolt is clean.

"I certainly hope so," I tell him. "I certainly hope so."

I have my notebook with me, I write down the story. My notes have words like *awesome* and *unbelievable* scribbled across the page when referring to the final. Prior to the trial I was telling people I was a genuine gold medal contender. After watching *that* race I know that Usain Bolt is on another planet and in 100 metre terms Bolt is miles clear of the rest of us. Mind you, I would have fancied my chances for the silver medal. That time was certainly within reach for me.

I return home and flick through the sports channels looking for Olympic highlights. I watch the race again and again and again and record it for posterity.

"The result won't change," Leonie calls from the kitchen as those 9.69 seconds of action begin to bore her a little. The action doesn't bore me; I watch it another three times during the course of the evening. I simply can't believe what I'm seeing; it's as if Bolt was out for a jog. Just what sort of time is he capable of? Will he be the first man in history to break 9.5 seconds? And just when will the records stop falling?

They won't.

The world governing bodies' lack of involvement in educating young athletes against drugs is nothing short of criminal. Not once, since fourteen years of age, have I been given a lecture, a talk or even a detailed information pamphlet on what substances are banned, which are legal and, more importantly, the penalties attached.

And did you know I have not received anything in writing detailing my ban? It's nothing short of scandalous. As I sit here writing I do not actually know which competitions I am eligible for and which I am not. Much has been made of the fact that I knew the consequences of an Olympic ban before I took the drugs. Let me state here and now that I didn't know the details of an Olympic lifetime ban and a bye-law back in 2002.

I have taken the opportunity to go onto the official site of UKA, the organization that banned me. Sure enough there is a PDF available for download. Its title is UK ANTI-DOPING RULES.

Great, I thought, that's where it must be. It's sixty-one pages long, full of jargon, and despite going over the document three times, I cannot find any information about the Olympic Lifetime Ban. I took the opportunity to search for Olympic Lifetime Ban on their site... no results found. I searched for bye-law and eligibility bye-law. No results found.

I've held my hands up and been honest ever since that fateful day when I received *that* phone call. Officialdom have never once admitted their own shortcomings. They've simply put the boot in again and again and again. They are inept and their actions smell of double standards, a turn-the-other-cheek-if-it-suits attitude when it suits them. They implement bye-laws and ignore them at will.

ANOTHER VIEW FROM PETER HILDRETH
Journalist and 1952 GB Olympian

Wiseacres intent on putting drugs in sport into a neat historical perspective always start by naming 'disgraced Canadian drugs cheat Ben Johnson'. For twenty years that has been the well-worn thesis. Only this year did Johnson reveal to the *Daily Mail* that he was not actually on drugs when he shocked the world at Seoul in 1988. Well-coached athletes never are on drugs at a big event where they know they may be tested. They study the clearance time of the drugs they use in periods of intensive training and discontinue them punctually in time to be clean when they are due at the Olympic Games.

Ben Johnson was by no means universally reviled after the Seoul debacle. An un-named Soviet coach told a newsman from *The New York Times*: "I feel sorry for Ben Johnson. All sportsmen – not all, but maybe ninety per cent, including our own – use drugs." Common sense tells us that if there is something that makes a big difference, people hoping to be seriously competitive at the business end of international sport can't possibly afford to leave it out, not because they want to steal an advantage but because they don't want to look like amateurs in a professional arena.

Doctors and coaches have had a long time to master the game of 'drug cheats'. It is on record that steroids were in place in athletics and other sports over half a century ago. I was competing then and they were not in use in the UK. I began to hear rumours just before I retired in 1964. One amusing legend was about an Australian sprinter who built himself up with steroids and became a shot-putter instead. I thought that was a hoot. By that time I was reporting athletics for the *Sunday Telegraph*, often sitting in the press box at tracks where I used to compete.

The most riveting observation came from Geoff Capes who retired after the Moscow Olympics in 1980 and did a book with Neil Wilson. Britain's mightiest shot-putter apparently used to feed Dianabol, a banned steroid in athletics, to his parakeet and tried to teach the bird to say, "Polly wants a cracker – now." In his book *Big Shot* [1981] Geoff described himself as "somebody who has been part of the drugs generation." He added, "If the new generation has to beat the old standards, of course they are going to take drugs. There is no way anybody can reach beyond those levels without them." Capes retired after the 1980 Olympic Games with two Commonwealth gold medals in1974 and 1978 (the year Dwain Chambers was born) and a national shot record which remained unbroken until 2003. He embarked on a career in the entertainment industry with successes in the televised strongman circuit and Scottish Highland Games competition. At the Rosneath and Clynder Games in 1987 he tested positive for amphetamines which had been prescribed by his doctor to reduce high blood pressure brought on by obesity. "I informed the Scottish Highland Games Association of the medication before the test," he said, "but they still fined me £200."

Coe himself went on record in an *Athletics Weekly* interview in 1985 saying the dope test was easy to beat. "It is generally accepted," he said, "that you must be badly managed or have very stupid doctors to fail the drug test." This was borne out by Tony Ward, Public Relations Officer for British Athletics, in his book *Athletics the Golden Decade* [1991]. "Testing procedures were slack and easily avoidable," Ward wrote. "Promoters were as relaxed about drug-taking as about money. If part of the deal for an athlete to appear was that he or she would not be tested, no problem."

Andrew Jennings explains in his book *The New Lords of the Rings* [1996] how officialdom made sure at the Moscow Olympics that not a single positive test in any sport was reported. Jennings later interviewed a KGB officer now retired who had been on duty at those Games. This stalwart told Jennings he was obeying orders to ensure that no positive tests were reported although there were several, he insisted, without naming them.

Ben Johnson was to be the star of what is probably the most exhaustive study ever of drugs in sport. It was staged by the Canadian government in 1989. Mr Justice Charles L Dubin sat through 91 days of public hearings in which 122 witnesses gave sworn testimony, compiling 86 volumes of printed record. Although the Johnson scandal gave rise to the Inquiry it was not just about him at all. There were 45 other Canadian athletes who admitted they had used drugs, and the judge said in his report: 'A total of 46 Canadian athletes from a wide spectrum of athletic disciplines admitted their own anabolic steroid use. This number was merely a sample and in no way suggests that the number of athletes using banned substances is limited to those who testified.' Dubin also said that the use of drugs in sport had reached 'epidemic proportions'. He said: 'The general public has long been led to assume that if only one athlete tested positive; the others are not also using drugs. We now know, as the IOC and the IAAF have known for many years, that this assumption is false and that steps must be taken to remedy the situation.'

A number of highly qualified and experienced witnesses testified to Dubin. Dr Robert S Kerr of San Gabriel, California said that drugs were a way of life in American sport. He stated that he had prescribed steroids to thousands of athletes for the past twenty years with impressive results. Among his patients were twenty medallists at the 1984 Olympic Games. Nor was he alone. Kerr said there were seventy doctors in the Los Angeles area giving similar medical care to athletes.

Dr Jamie Astaphan, who supplied Johnson's drugs, testified that he had also supplied athletes from a dozen other countries including the USA, Italy, Holland, Australia, Sweden, Finland, East and West Germany, Bulgaria, several African countries and the UK. Astaphan also helped athletes in cycling, skiing, volleyball, football (amateur and professional), weightlifting, power lifting, bodybuilding and cricket.

Italy may have been one of the best markets for Astaphan's exports. Evidence for this came from the very summit of athletics officialdom. Acclaimed in his own press handout as 'a guardian of tradition', Dr Primo Nebiolo rightly claimed credit for the fact that after he took over in 1969 as president of the Italian governing body (FIDAL), Italian athletics soon developed to such an extent that it drew the attention of the entire athletics world.

The dynamics behind this startling transformation were brought to the world's attention by Sandro Donati, a track coach, who discovered the secret of Italian prowess in 1984 when he visited the offices of FIDAL in Rome. Inside the technical department Donati and a friend found a stock of over 1,000 50mg steroid tablets imported from a company in New York. When confronted with this smoking gun evidence Nebiolo, who had also been president of the world governing body (IAAF) since 1981, told Donati: "You must take a broader view of the activity of the federation. I put a lot of effort into trying to promote track and field. It used to have a low image in the media and with the public. Ours is a great circus in which if we stretch the tent walls too far the roof will fall in. We have to look at the global thing, not one aspect. We don't want the roof to fall in." Reports concerning the links between FIDAL and Dr Francesco Conconi, an expert in blood doping and testosterone, were also confirmed in Donati's book. However, I must give Dr Conconi the benefit of the doubt as although he was accused of administering EPO and other drugs to over four hundred athletes including several Tour de France and Giro d'Italia winners, he has denied it strenuously: "These accusations are erroneous. I am completely innocent. I have never given forbidden products to anyone."

Further penetrating insights into aspects of Italian coaching came in 1986 from Romano Tordelli, a leading middle distance coach, who produced documents, tapes and invoices in support of lurid allegations about blood doping and drug use. Nebiolo blandly dismissed demands for an inquiry saying: "The problem exists all over the world and we are clearing it up. However, our athletes are very honest and in this respect we deny everything." In 1998 Nebiolo targeted tennis, volleyball and cycling as sports that should be excluded from the Olympic Games on account of their poor record in doping control.

Although I had heard little about blood doping and its supposed benefits, it was in use in the early seventies. Mikko Ala-Leppilampi, who placed tenth for Finland in the 1972 Olympic 3000m steeplechase, admitted to the gossip magazine HYMY in 1981 that he had used it. He quoted the doctor who gave him the treatment as saying: "If you tell others about our system, I as a doctor can destroy your family." Blood doping was not formally banned by the IOC until 1986. It is a medical technique which involves extracting blood plasma from the athlete, allowing the body to replace it, then injecting the removed plasma back into the bloodstream. The increased red blood cell count brings more oxygen to the working muscles which gives enhanced endurance to the distance runner. It can be dangerous.

More information about Finnish methods came from Dr Marko Allen of Jyvaskyla University in 1985. He said that the previous year 13 Finnish Olympic medallists had used banned drugs and that 71 Finnish Olympic athletes used illegal stimulants in training for those games.

The most devastatingly effective system of doping control ever seen at a major international competition was set up by Dr Manfred Donike, a West German biochemist, at the 1983 Pan American Games in Caracas. The laboratory working under his supervision found that as many as fifty competitors had used banned drugs, nineteen of them testing positive after competing. A further nine volunteer subjects tested before the competition also came up positive and did not compete in the Games while thirteen Americans went home without competing, presumably to avoid detection. A total of twenty-one medals, seven gold, were stripped from offenders. Sports involved were cycling, fencing, track and field athletics, volleyball, weightlifting and wrestling.

After his success at Caracas, Donike was a natural choice to take charge of doping control at the 1987 World Championships, but he and the British expert, Dr Arnold Beckett, were replaced by less qualified staff weeks before the Championships opened, and only one positive test was recorded.

In 1989 Bernd Heller, a former international pole vaulter and now a West German TV commentator, testified at the Dubin Inquiry that Donike told him of a study of the endocrine profile of samples collected at the 1988 Olympic Games and later re-tested showed that eighty per cent of the athletes tested had used steroids in the previous five to eight years. Donike later testified that Heller was mistaken but Dubin said Donike's study revealed a much higher rate of prior steroid use by male athletes tested at Seoul than was indicated by the official results.

Donike's steroid profile test, which measured the concentration ratio of testosterone to epitestosterone in the sample, created another sensation in 1990 when fifty-seven un-named weightlifters were banned from the forthcoming World Championships in Budapest. All fifty-seven had passed drugs tests at the Championships the previous year.

A former professional cyclist, Donike is believed to have used legal stimulants himself. His perception of modern training methods was sound and as long ago as 1975 he had recommended out-of-competition testing: 'Anabolic steroids are not used to increase performance at the day of competition – like stimulants – but they are ingested months before during the building-up phase of training… Therefore doping control for anabolic steroids must be performed not only at the day of competition but months before…' He was also alert to the side effects of doping. In 1988 he told me: "One effect of the use of anabolic steroids is a weakening of the tissue connecting the tendons, and notably the Achilles tendon, to the neighbouring bones. By microscopic examination it is possible to measure those changes and to establish new methods to monitor long-term administration of certain drugs." Donike died in 1995 and his ideas were allowed to fall into the discard but there were others familiar with side effects of doping.

Dr Robert Voy, former Chief Medical Officer for the United States Olympic Committee (USOC) said in his book ***Drugs, Sport and Politics*** [1991] that drugs are abused every day at the elite levels of sport. He said that among other injuries, steroids lead to stress fractures because they block the release of calcium to the bone which can lead to brittleness. Voy is also eloquent on behaviour changes. Tina Plakinger, a former national body-building champion, 'grabbed her husband and forcefully jacked him up against a wall one night. The reason? He was late for dinner.' Nor did Voy forget long-term after-effects, including death. 'The casualty list of athletes who died from performance-enhancing or "recreational" drug abuse goes on and on.'

Dr Armin Klumper was a more controversial contempory of Dr Donike. Founder of the renowned Sport Traumatology Clinic in Freiburg, Klumper was one of a group of German sports physicians in 1976 who advocated that anabolic steroids should be used under medical supervision. As a practitioner of cellular therapy he enjoyed a good reputation among athletes, earning the tabloid nickname of 'The Needle Doctor' owing to his use of the hypodermic in the treatment of injuries. His Klumper Cocktail was said to contain secret ingredients apart from cortisone, antibiotics, animal cells and amino acids.

In 1984 after 17 out of 61 West German athletes were forced to withdraw injured from the Olympic Games Klumper said, "Many athletes and coaches ignored my warnings of the enormous burden imposed by a third successive year of major competitions. The high number of withdrawals is also related to... inadequate medical care."

Despite his personal charisma and clinical success, Klumper's methods were called into question after the death in 1987 of his celebrated heptathlete, Birgit Dressel, aged only twenty-six, to whom he had administered at least four hundred injections. He was temporarily banished by the sports medical establishment and left state service after twenty years to open a private clinic for elite athletes in 1989. There is no suggestion that Dr Klumper ever prescribed illegal performance-enhancing drugs to sportsmen and women under his care; indeed he should be commended for his close attention to appropriate levels of medical care, not to mention his concerns that the athletes were overburdened with competitions.

One of Klumper's pupils is Dr Hans-Wilhelm Muller-Wohlfahrt, cell therapist and 'miracle healer' to a galaxy of stars of sport and show business as well as politicians and captains of industry. The big names of sport that have been to his clinic in Munich include: Boris Becker, Roger Black, Jason Gardiner, Tyson Gay, Kelly Holmes, Colin Jackson, Maradona, Jose Maria Olazabal, Michael Owen, Asafa Powell, Paula Radcliffe, Ronaldo, Daley Thompson and Zinedine Zidane.

My observation of the changing scene made me wonder sometimes why there was so much sky-punching behaviour in sport that wasn't there before. Stars of sport had become entertainers, playing noisily to the crowd. I was perhaps slow to grasp that manipulating the body's natural processes with drugs almost certainly affects the mind as well.

Dr David Katz gave a talk on the psychiatric effects of doping with steroids at Monte Carlo in 1989. A lecturer on psychiatry at Harvard Medical School, Katz reported the results of a study conducted with Dr Harrison Pope based on interviews with 41 bodybuilders and football players who used steroids. They found that 22% of their subjects displayed a full affective syndrome and 12% suffered full psychotic symptoms including auditory hallucinations and delusions of reference and of grandiosity.

Following publication of their report in1988, Katz and Pope began to receive calls from lawyers and district attorneys around the USA describing individuals who had apparently committed violent crimes while taking steroids; one bodybuilder, intoxicated with his enhanced strength, celebrated by tipping over fifteen cars in a suburban street.

The Daily Mail's US correspondent reported the case of a bodybuilder in Maryland who burgled six houses setting fire to them to cover the evidence. In court seven doctors gave evidence that over-use of steroids had given him an 'organic personality syndrome' that 'impaired his ability to appreciate the criminality of his acts'. His sentence was nothing more than an order for psychological examinations.

I was not a boxing writer but I had no doubt that the superstar who came closest to the Katz diagnosis about delusions of grandiosity was Muhammad Ali. His cavernous mouth opened wide and often, giving voice to the histrionic claim 'I am the greatest'. This convinced many sportswriters that he really was the greatest sportsman of all time. Although he looked to be almost permanently on a cerebral high, Ali was a leading campaigner against drugs and only once admitted using a thyroid drug. This was in 1980 before his heavyweight title bout against Larry Holmes when Ali had been out of the ring for two years and needed to lose weight. However he did not object when, long after his retirement from the boxing ring, his name was still being used to sell performance-enhancing drugs. The advertising blurb carrying a 1994 copyright line of Instant Improvement Inc said of one of their products: 'Add more than three-fifths of a teaspoon and you may be able to shake the earth!' On the same page it recorded that: 'Muhammad Ali used it as a supplement to raise the strength when he fought for and regained his heavyweight title.' This was obviously a hormone drug of some potency because: 'factory workers who got it on their hands every day were perpetually erect, and were forced to see their doctors.' Again there is no suggestion that anything Instant Improvement Inc subscribed to was either performance-enhancing or illegal.

Dwain Chambers opened his mouth pretty wide too when winning a race. His mouth was not as big as Ali's, but like 'the greatest' he hoped for lasting fame. Dwain's hopes were dashed when he was banned for drugs, but I felt a certain respect for him because he did not shrink from going on record with the hard truth. People who understand what has happened to sport have known that had been the truth, at the elite end of sport, for a long time. Linford Christie, probably Britain's greatest ever sprinter, knew the truth too. This year Linford claimed that Dwain should be used as an 'ambassador' for the sport. "If we leave him to rot then he'll become a bitter person... If God can forgive us then we should go out and forgive others."

TO INFINITY... AND BEYOND

Writing this book has been difficult as has the last six years. As I have mentioned on more than one occasion getting caught was almost a relief. I held up my hands, knuckled down and prepared to take my two-year ban on the chin. This I did. I was vilified quite rightly but looked forward to rebuilding my life and my career once the ban had been served. The last four years however have been a living nightmare. I have not been allowed to get on with my life, and have been denied the basic right to feed and clothe my family. To say it has been a struggle would be an understatement and yes, at times, suicide seemed the easiest option. Thankfully I am not that selfish and thought about the friends and family I would have left behind. I'm probably too much of a coward too! It would have all been so easy though. At times I want to scream out to those people who have fought so hard to stop me competing about just how much athletics and Team GB means to me and that when they cut off my lifeblood they kill a piece of me. If they knew me, really knew me, they might have thought again.

My true friends have helped me along the way, encouraged me, helped me out financially and tried to steer me back on a true focused course. But there is something more sinister that no one knows about until now. Only in the last year or so have I become fully aware of just how many people want Dwain Chambers to fail, want the poor black boy to fade away into obscurity. The only trouble is no one knows who they are. Simon Dent my agent has worked tirelessly over the last year or so trying to get me work. He has done a great job but some strange things have happened that have left us speechless. Things we shrugged off at first, but then as they happened again and again and more frequently following the same pattern we began to get rather nervous, a little scared and then downright angry and determined.

Take for example this book deal. When we first announced that we were ready to do a book, three or four BIG publishers came knocking at the door. I remember sitting with one representative from a well-known London publisher in Simon's office who was talking sales in excess of 200,000 and a very attractive 'advance' if we put pen to paper. Then the small to medium independent publishers got wind of the book and they too came knocking.

But one by one they all fell away. They blamed the economic climate, the credit crunch, an excess of celebrity auto-biographies and slush piles (whatever they are); anything and everything. But one of the representatives was quite honest. I won't name him as he only told us in confidence if we kept his name out of it. He came to Simon's office in early March 2008. He'd already advised us that his publisher's verbal offer had been withdrawn. He was the gentlemen who had previously been talking advances and huge sales. Over a beer and a handshake, Simon and I had agreed to go with him as long as the proposal matched what he had been telling us.

I attended the meeting too; he'd asked me to be there. We asked John (not his real name) what the problem was. John was pale, clearly a little distressed, annoyed even. He told us everything had been agreed and the publishing proposal had found its way to director level. There was a buzz in the office, he told us; his immediate supervisor had congratulated him on what they thought was a done deal.

Then everything went pear-shaped when the board decided they were not going to offer Dwain Chambers a contract. A senior director had said that Chambers wasn't the sort of athlete he wanted associated with the company. Now this was very strange because John told me that that very director only a few weeks prior had given him every encouragement to 'reel Chambers in'. John's words not mine. John was at a loss to explain the change of direction at senior management level. He was highly critical of the change of direction that the company had taken but then he dropped a bombshell.

"They've been got at."

"What are you talking about?" Simon asked.

"They've been got at. It wasn't their decision, they were all behind your book last month. Directors just don't change their minds like that especially where money is concerned."

Simon and I sat back stunned. I still didn't know what he really meant. But as the conversation progressed it slowly sank in. John explained that his publishing company and their associated companies had published the memoirs of mass murderers, gangsters, drug dealers and disgraced MPs. They'd published blow-by-blow accounts of soccer hooligans, published books on extremism and pornography. And at board level the previous day they'd had the audacity to announce that because I'd made a mistake six years ago they didn't want to be associated with me. John was right... it just didn't add up.

He left soon after, apologising again and again, ranting on about the freedom of speech even as he walked through the door. Simon was upbeat. "We'll find another publisher, don't worry," he announced.

It was one hell of a bloody deal though, I thought to myself as I sat on the tube on the way home.

Simon called a few days later. He had found another publisher, we were in business. I really wanted to write this book, I was so happy.

It naturally follows that when a rather controversial book deal is done the press boys come knocking, offering serialisation rights to the book. Certain books sell papers, make headlines. My book, I was told, was just that sort of book. And come running they did. I sat with some of the Libros International staff in the Embassy Club on the 12th June at a launch party of one of their authors when a representative of a national daily offered a six-figure deal if I named names.

Just like the publishing company their offer was withdrawn at the last minute. The representative told me, "Someone somewhere doesn't want to hear what you have to say."

And so it went on: TV deals, work in the media, all promises made and promises broken. Sponsors came and sponsors went without putting the money on the table. After the Olympics it was arranged for me to do some sprint coaching with a number of the young England rugby players. No coaches or directors or board members were involved; it was simply a friend of a friend of some of the players who asked me for my services to help them improve their technique. One of them had seen me give a session to one of their children and was suitably impressed. I wasn't going to charge for this, I just wanted to help. I'm a patriotic man and I looked on it as an honour. We arranged the date and I put some handout sheets together on my PC ready to print off for the guys. We had been told we could use the training facilties at The Stoop, the home of the famous Harlequins. I was quite excited as the day drew nearer and I even bought an England rugby shirt as an ice-breaker before the training started. Three days before the session one of the guys rang me to say how appreciative they all were.

Two days before the session however, I got a call from Simon. One of the directors had found out about the training and blocked it. He didn't even have the nerve to call me himself; one of the players' agents rang Simon and let him know. It was clear that I was an undesirable and they didn't want me to be associated with the club. It was yet another example of being an outcast and a social leper. All this three years after my ban had officially ended.

The organizations that upset me the most however were the charities that I'd offered to work for for free. Whichever way you look at it, the name Dwain Chambers puts bums on seats, brings people through the door. And yet someone somewhere in certain charities which I won't name and shame (though I should) decided they didn't want the money or the association with a tainted man.

It is as clear as bottled water that something or someone higher up the chain is out to stop me. They are trying to stop me competing, stop me earning a living and of course trying to prevent me from attending the Olympics in 2012.

I have a message for them.

I want to race for Team GB in 2012. England is where I started my athletic career and it will end here! I wish to make it clear that I want to finish my athletics career right here in the UK under my national UK colours. I also aim to keep you all on the edge of your seats when it comes to any 100m final, and maybe, just maybe, you will see me on that starting line in the 100m final in London 2012!

What does the future hold in store for Dwain Chambers? Rumour has it we can't predict the future, but I can already see my dreams of the future coming true. I always said I wanted to inspire others, and now I'm actually seeing the positive effect of my work within the community, in my career and in my home life. I am altogether a more peaceful man.

In life you must stand firm in what you believe is right for you. Outsiders, friends and family members will always put in their twopence as a means of distraction; sometimes they think they are guiding you. This is where you must be strong and determined and follow your heart as well as your head.

With athletics I never really knew what I had until it was gone. The pain I experienced when I lost my chance to compete during 2004-2005 is something I would never wish upon my enemy. To have everything taken away from you because of a poor error of judgement was heart-rending. My soul was broken and I felt numb. I felt as though I no longer had a purpose in life. If I wasn't able to run then what else was there for me to do.

I was left with very few options, so I had to grow up real quick and figure out a way to get myself back on track. I continued to train and made time to get to know my friends and family, people who I hadn't really got to know over the years.

I started to read more books. A few that I would recommend are as follows: The Laws of Attraction by Michael J Losier, The Secret by Rhonda Byrne, and my favorite, Rich Dad, Poor Dad by Robert T Kiyosaki. I took on teaching classes within the sporting industry as a means to offer my knowledge and expertise to others. And I started to write down my feelings on paper. I also took time out to pursue what I love most: cooking. I find cooking very therapeutic especially when it comes to preparing Jamaican food. I learned a lot about food when I was involved in Hell's Kitchen. So whenever Ainsley Harriott, Gordon Ramsay, Jamie Oliver or Heston Blumenthal are on TV, I'm glued. I also enjoy music. I'm a great fan of music from the 1980s and 90s; this was when music was in its purest form. Songs by Color Me Bad, Lisa Stansfield, Spandau Ballet, Michael Jackson and Sade. I love my Bashment music, Funky house and R&B.

Two years is a long time but I would like to feel I used this time to help better myself as opposed to letting it destroy me. I often found myself standing on a cliff edge and a pack of hungry wolves wanting to eat me at the bottom. (You know who you are, gentlemen.) At times I felt I had no option but to jump. Sometimes I did. I would jump into situations not knowing where I would end up, yet I tried to figure it out, learn from my mistakes and aim to land on my feet.

The constant thought of failure would play heavily on my mind. I'd attempted a career in the NFL and in Rugby League but none of them came to anything. I'm sure you've read the chapters and made your own mind up. Somehow I found the will to survive. I kept on fighting my own mental demons that haunted me daily.

I've often heard people saying that what defines a man is the ability to pick themselves up from an almighty kick in the balls and keep on moving.

Mistakes occur all day every day, but where we've failed once we must improve the next time and learn from those mistakes. It's a learning process that all human beings must go through. We all have done stupid things in our lives, some more stupid than others. Our wrongs teach us to do right in the long term and for those individuals that don't believe in second chances for those who make mistakes, believe me, your next mistake is lurking around the next corner.

Many successful business men and women have failed at some stage of their lives but through hard work, determination and paying attention to the finer detail they have risen above those mistakes and moved onto another level. There is a saying that goes:

'A man who chooses to fall over the same rock twice deserves to get hurt.'

I can relate to that; perhaps it should be everyone's motto.

There are many positive things I would like to be remembered for. The one that comes to mind now is the fact that I took a wrong turn at a crossroads, got hit by a bus, was left for dead but somehow made a recovery. I got back on my feet and carried on walking. There were many that wanted to confine me to a lifetime in a wheelchair but I wouldn't let them.

God has been good to me. I've been blessed with a talent that has allowed me to continue running despite the negative obstacles that have been placed before me. I have become a father. I have three wonderful boys whom I hold close to my heart: Jayon, Skye and the new addition to our family, Rocco Star.

Behind every successful man there is a strong woman. I used to turn my nose up at the phrase; now I can see the relevance in that statement. Leonie has been my rock since the news of my positive test broke. Leonie has been the ackee and salt fish in this relationship. Ackee and salt fish is my favorite Jamaican dish. I love this dish which means I love Leonie to the max. Without Leonie's support I would have died. A dramatic statement perhaps… but nevertheless true.

Leonie has taught me more about myself than I was aware of. With this renewed insight into life I see things differently now. I'd always believed that people thought the same way about things which influenced our daily lives. I have now seen the light. There are two types of people in the world. Some are robots who do as they are programmed and some are aliens. Aliens are able to do as they please because they have the mindset to do so. They fly in and access the situation and decide whether what they see is worthwhile; they are not bound by rules and they know what they want from life and try to be unique… different. I'm not suggesting that we all become aliens overnight, nor is it that easy. But I do believe we all need to learn to embrace our own individualism. All too often we support the celebrity or sportsman when things are going well but the moment he steps out of line there are certain elements of our society that are ready to kill and bury him. Robots… you know who you are. Take a look at yourselves.

We are encouraging this behaviour and our children are absorbing it; they think it's normal, the done thing. You need to stop and think about what you are doing.

I went against the grain and owned up to my failings but still I'm not accepted by certain people and organizations. The real quality in a person is one where they can judge honesty and sincerity, reading when someone is genuinely sorry for what they have done. Don't be so keen to knock celebrities from their pedestal when they make a mistake. These are the very people we build up, encourage our children to be like when they grow up and then, one mistake and they are dirt. The more we feed lies and dishonesty to our people, the uglier this world will become. Remember that.

Where do I plan to go from here? Well, my family will always be my first priority. Quite simply everything else falls into second place. With regards to my career I still intend to compete up to the 2012 Olympics then I will retire.

Throughout this time I will continue to spread the word to the youth of the country that drugs in sport is bad news and there is a better way to achieve success without damaging your body. I enjoying touring the schools speaking to the normal kids on the street and I enjoyed immensely speaking to the Oxford Student Union. I can think of no better place than to address the future influential youth of the country than this famous amphitheatre of debate. The place is steeped in history. Presidents and prime ministers have addressed this impressive gathering over the years, even Kermit The Frog and yes, to be honest, I was as nervous as a Christmas turkey. As I entered the old oak-panelled library I thought of a hundred places I'd rather be but suddenly I was overcome at the reception I received. It helped quell the nerves just a little. This was my biggest stage so far and I could have killed my agent Simon Dent for putting me there.

"Just be honest with them," he said, "and it will work itself out."

I was and it did. I told them about my mistakes and my relationships with other athletes. I bared my soul and told them how I gave up the 200 metres because I couldn't bear to beat my dear friend Christian Malcolm, a specialist at the distance. This was a tough call. I couldn't look him in the eye when I beat him. Sometimes he won, sometimes I did but I felt I was trying to be too greedy competing at both. If Christian hadn't been so good at the distance I would have continued but I took the decision to concentrate on the 100 metres. No one was happier than me when Christian climbed aboard the plane for Beijing. He qualified for the final improving his time in each heat and the semi-final. A fifth place after a couple of disqualifications was a very credible performance. I was a little unkind to Darren Campbell once again at the Oxford Student Union but strangely enough it seemed to go down well.

I left to wild applause and thoroughly enjoyed my night. It was a sort of turning point, I suppose, being accepted and loved by a predominantly white, middle-class, young audience.

I'm in the process of forming a group of young athletes who I believe may be good enough to compete in London 2012 and beyond. I will be there for them and do my utmost to keep them on the straight and narrow. I will offer them the kind of support and advice that I never had; not from my father, my management company, UK Athletics, Coe, Moynihan, Niels de Vos or the others in the sport. I have however been pleasantly surprised at the comments and welcome mat thrown down by the new head coach of UK Athletics, Charles van Commenee. Even de Vos seems to have changed his tune a little. During a Radio Five Live interview in September 2008 he said on more than one occasion I have been and will be treated exactly the same as any other athlete. Nice thought.

I will continue supporting worthwhile charities and continue visiting schools, prisons, youth centres and town halls to take my message forward. That message is simple: I advocate clean sport as a way to escape the boredom of our inner cities and a way to steer clear of the gun and knife culture spreading like leprosy through our country. If only a few of the *names* mentioned in this book spent a fraction of their energy focusing on constructive worthwhile causes instead of pontificating, the country as a whole would be a better place and the youngsters would be training and competing with a goal in sight, putting their energy into something worthwhile.

For what it's worth, I have had a great time writing this book. I hope you, the reader, have enjoyed it as much as I've enjoyed writing it. I owe you all a big thank you for all the support over the years. Now that I have a clear mind and a purer heart I will continue my dream of inspiring others, and along my journey I hope to leave many positive breadcrumbs on the table so the masses will benefit. I regularly hold web chats on my Facebook fan site and it has become a brilliant platform for me to share information and advice with young and aspiring athletes.

In closing I wish to say a special thanks to Jonathan Crystal and Nick Collins. We all knew we were asking a lot in taking on the establishment and trying to win but at least we took them on. We took our message forward and reached out to the masses in the form of our friends in the media. They are now well and truly exposed for what they really are. If we had won perhaps that wouldn't have happened?

Four years on, our story and our message is still front-page news; perhaps the next front page will feature a picture of a medal for Team GB and the name Dwain Chambers in the caption underneath.

Additional notes

On 18 June 2004 **Kelli White** was stripped of her medals because she had tested positive for modafinil during a drug test. She admitted guilt and testified before the Court of Arbitration for Sport (CAS). All her performances since December 15, 2000 have been annulled. She was banned for two years by the United States Anti-Doping Agency, effective from 17 May 2004. She retired from professional athletics in 2006.

Chryste Gaines was also banned for two years for testing positive for modafinil. She attempted to return from her ban to find herself frozen out by the sport and she threatened legal action. She has been eligible to compete since June 2007 but has been unable to get races.

"We're being prevented from making an income. It's against the law in the US – I don't know about British law," Gaines told BBC Sport in February 2008. She claimed the BALCO athletes were being treated differently to everyone else and were given what amounted to lifetime bans.

Wilfried Meert, the vice-president of a body that represents the promoters of fifty-one European track meetings, appeared to validate Gaines' claim. He said no athletes with doping convictions would ever be invited to compete again. "All our meetings are invitational, so we can invite whoever we want," Meert, who promotes Brussels' Golden League event, told BBC Sport. "We have no obligation at all to send invitations out to particular athletes. That's why we can say we are no longer going to invite people who have been banned for drugs."

US Olympic 400m relay gold medallist **Alvin Harrison** accepted a four-year ban in October 2004 for drugs offences, according to the United States Anti-Doping Agency. A USADA statement said: "Harrison admitted to using numerous undetectable performance-enhancing drugs. These included anabolic steroids known as 'the clear' and 'the cream', EPO, insulin, growth hormone and modafinil." USADA confirmed the evidence against him did not include a drugs test failure.

Patrick Arnold, the chemist who created 'the clear', a previously undetectable steroid, was sentenced in August 2006 to three months in prison and three months' home confinement for his role in the BALCO drug scandal. He was the last of five defendants convicted of steroid-distribution charges connected to the Bay Area Laboratory Co-Operative, a nutritional supplement company federal authorities exposed as a steroid distribution ring for top athletes. Arnold said he was very regretful for what he had done and especially since what it had precipitated in sports and society. Arnold created the steroid in his Illinois laboratory.

The things they said...

My personal opinion is that he's a cheating bastard who shouldn't be allowed to compete.

Daley Thompson

These days there are no unhappy circumstances where athletes don't know what they're doing. This is not 30 years ago when a 14-year-old child behind the Iron Curtain is given something at breakfast and told that it was part and parcel of becoming an international athlete. With the amount of money being spent on education programmes, I do not accept there are any circumstances where athletes like Dwain Chambers can get sucked into something without being complicit.

Lord Coe

We need to multiply the deterrents. If there was a hint of criminal proceedings and a spell in the 'nick', that would dramatically increase the pressure on an athlete who may be tempted down the drugs route.

Niels de Vos

He is being treated in the way he deserves to be treated.

Dame Kelly Holmes

I'd be more convinced by the hand wringing on the part of the athletics' authorities if they hadn't swiftly reversed their ban on Christine Ohuruogu when it became clear she might actually win something. She broke the rules and was given a lifetime Olympics ban which was rescinded as soon as she won gold in the World Championships.

D.M. on an Olympic Internet Blog

We will pay whatever is necessary to have top lawyers represent us and put the strongest case in support of that ban.

Lord Moynihan

Dwain had a good coaching structure in this country and was running world-class times. He then goes off to charlatan coaches and sleazy chemists in the United States and runs a whole stack slower so I think there is a good lesson to be learnt there.

Lord Coe

There will be no room for cheats in the British team as long as I am involved with the BOA.

Lord Moynihan

I think a lot of us in the sport feel that a two-year ban is never enough for people committing that type of offence. And I would hope that as the next few months follow on, this isn't really just about Dwain Chambers at all, it's about the sport's attitude towards those who've committed serious drugs offences.

Olympic silver medallist Steve Cram

I will robustly and vigorously defend our bye-laws in the interest of all the athletes who seek to represent us both in this generation and future generations - and I'm not going to trade that in for any financial interest.

Lord Moynihan

He's served his ban, leave him alone and let him get on with it. He's been brought back into the sport and allowed back by the governing bodies and he understands that he has made a mistake. If he does well, get on with it.

1984 Olympic gold medallist Tessa Sanderson

Dwain has served his two-year ban. It's something that the rules stated at the time and he's done that. He won the national championships last weekend in a fine time so I can't see why they shouldn't pick him. Dwain made a wrong choice, a very, very bad choice, and paid the ultimate price. He's now said he's trying to come back and prove that it was a mistake. You can't keep punishing him.

Olympic 200m silver medallist John Regis

If they don't pick him then UK Athletics would be bending their own rules. He should be allowed to run and he should be representing Great Britain because he's the man for the job. He did serve his time and unless they are willing to change the rules and keep it 'once and you're out', he should be able to run.

2003 world 100m champion Kim Collins

The weak can never forgive. Forgiveness is the attribute of the strong.

Mahatma Gandhi

The one who pursues revenge should dig two graves.

Allen C Guelzo

He that cannot forgive others, breaks the bridge over which he himself must pass if he would reach heaven; for everyone has need to be forgiven.

Lance Morrow

Forgiveness is the fragrance that the violet sheds on the heel that has crushed it.

Mark Twain

Focusing your life solely on making a buck shows a certain poverty of ambition. It asks too little of yourself. Because it's only when you hitch your wagon to something larger than yourself that you realize your true potential.

Barack Obama

Timeline Dwain Chambers

1978: Born Islington, London, April 5.

1994: English Schools intermediates champion at 100m.

1995: Gold in 100m and sprint relay at European Juniors.

1997: Gold in 100m and sprint relay at European Juniors. Won 100m in 10.06, then a world junior record, the first by a British sprinter since Peter Radford in 1958.

1998: Took a silver medal in the European championship and was third in World Cup.

1999: Second to Bruny Surin in Nuremberg in 9.99 seconds. In doing so he becomes only the second European sprinter to break the 10-second barrier after Linford Christie.

Ran 9.97 to claim bronze at the World Championships.

2000: Fourth in Olympics final in Sydney.

2002: Bid for 100m gold at the Commonwealth Games, starts well with wins in preliminary rounds, but he gets off to a bad start in the final and pulled up with cramps, later attributed to lack of fluids.

Takes the gold medal in a championship best of 9.96 at the Europeans and adds a superb run to bring the British team home for gold in the 4x100m relay.

Reduces his 100m best to 9.94 in Zurich.

With a tailwind on the legal limit of 2.0 m/s, ties Linford Christie's European record of 9.87.

2003: August 25 - Finishes fourth in the World Championships 100m final in Paris in a time of 10.08.

October 22 - Revealed to have tested positive for newly discovered 'designer steroid' tetrahydrogestrinone (THG). Denies knowingly taking the drug.

November 7 - IAAF suspend Chambers pending disciplinary hearing, after B sample tests positive.

2004: February 12 - Chambers' coach Remi Korchemny among four men indicted by a federal grand jury in America on charges of distributing illegal steroids.

February 22 - Handed a two-year worldwide ban due to expire on November 7, 2005 and lifetime suspension from the Olympics action.

2005: November 7 - Ban expires but Chambers has to comply with World Anti-Doping Agency (WADA) regulations preventing him from returning to competition until he has undertaken three mandatory tests.

December 10 - Admits using THG for 18 months before failing his drug test including when he became double European champion in August 2002.

2006: June 9 - IAAF accept offer from Chambers to reimburse them with the appearance fees and prize money he won during the period he was using THG.

June 10 - Cleared by UK Athletics to make comeback.

June 11 - Returns to action at Gateshead, finishing third in 10.07 as Asafa Powell equalled his own world record of 9.77. His time is the fastest by a European in 2006.

June 26 - All performances since January 1, 2002 annulled including individual and relay gold at the European

Championships in Munich in 2002 and the European record of 9.87 he shared with Linford Christie after his admission to using THG prior to his failed drugs test.

August - Selected to represent Great Britain at the European Championships in Gothenburg.

Finishes seventh in the individual event before joining Mark Lewis-Francis, Darren Campbell and Marlon Devonish in the 4x100m sprint relay squad. The quartet won gold but their achievement was overshadowed by Campbell's refusal to celebrate on a lap of honour with his team-mates, saying it would be 'hypocritical'.

2007: March - Secured a contract with NFL Europa side Hamburg Sea Devils after completing a national training camp in Tampa, Florida.

2008: January - UK Athletics chief executive officer Niels de Vos claims Chambers will be barred from making a comeback because he has not undergone drug testing since November 2006 when he left the sport. The IAAF claim he is eligible to run because he never retired from athletics.

February 2 - Qualifies for the World Indoor Trials in Sheffield by winning the 60m at the Birmingham Games in 6.60.

February 5 - Chambers allowed to compete in Sheffield after UKA grudgingly accept his entry after the athlete's solicitors prepared to launch a High Court injunction against them.

February 10 - Storms to victory in the 60 metres in Sheffield to book himself a spot in the following month's World Indoor Championships in Valencia.

March 7 - Wins a silver medal in the World Indoor Championships.

March 28 - Chambers to visit Super League club Castleford for talks about a possible career in rugby league, according to his spokesman Damion Silk.

May 6 - After a month-long trial with Castleford, the club reveal he will not be offered a contract.

June 4 - Wins his first 100m race since August 2006 in Greece.

June 28 - Achieves the Olympic 'A' qualifying standard at a meeting in Birberach, Germany.

June 30 - 200 past and present athletes, including Dame Kelly Holmes and Sir Steven Redgrave, sign a petition against Chambers being picked for the Beijing Games after his lawyers confirm plans for a High Court appeal against the BOA's lifetime Olympics ban.

July 3 - Court proceedings are launched by Chambers' legal team.

July 12 - Wins the 100m at the Aviva UK National Championships, the qualifying event for the British Olympic team.

July 18 – Chambers' attempt to gain a temporary injunction against the BOA ban is rejected at the High Court to end hopes of competing in Beijing.

2009: January 31 – Chambers breaks 60m personal best at Birmingham games.

References

1.   I was waiting for my teammates to embrace me, and no one came. I told them, 'Come hug me, or the referee isn't going to allow it.' **Diego Maradona USA TODAY 23 August 2005**

2.   I think Dwain is going to be one of the best 100 metre sprinters Britain has ever seen. **Selwyn Philbert The Independent August 4 1996**

3.   At 17, I joined the East Berlin Sports Institute. My speciality was the 80m hurdles. We swore that we would never speak to anyone about our training methods, including our parents. The training was very hard. We were all watched. We signed a register each time we left the dormitory and we had to say where we were going and what time we would return. One day, my trainer, Günter Clam, advised me to take pills to improve my performance: I was running 200m in 24 seconds. My trainer told me the pills were vitamins, but I soon had cramp in my legs, my voice became gruff and sometimes I couldn't talk any more. Then I started to grow a moustache and my periods stopped. I then refused to take these pills. One morning in October 1977, the secret police took me at 7am and questioned me about my refusal to take pills prescribed by the trainer. I then decided to flee, with my fiancé. **Renate Neufeld, Fahrenheit World Press/ Wikipedia. Also Sport Information Dienst West Germany December 1978**

4.   I don't think there is any place in sport for drugs cheats like Chambers. **Lord Coe Daily Mirror 04/07/08**

5.   There will be no room for cheats in the British team as long as I am involved with the BOA...we will pay whatever is necessary to have top lawyers represent us and put the strongest case in support of that ban. We will send a clean team to Beijing and there will be no room for doping cheats. **Lord Moynihan BBC Sport 13 March 2008**

6.   Chambers would cause cash backers to pull out of the 2012 Olympic Games in London. **Lord Moynihan TIMESONLINE July 18 2008**

7.   During a BBC investigation in 1998 Jürgen Grobler's name appears on documents which have been unearthed. In 1989 the East German secret police, the Stasi, destroyed thousands of files containing sensitive material but documents about the use of drugs survived. Dr Giselher Spitzer, who investigated doping for the German government, said: "It was a state-controlled programme to used performance-enhancing drugs within the sports of the GDR. Rowing was a centre of research. If people asked what the pills were they were told they were vitamins. If someone asked too much they were thrown out of the sport." He says, "Mr Grobler was within the 'inner circle' which ran East Germany's rowing schools, where children as young as 10 were given anabolic steroids." Dirk Schildhauer, a former East German

sculler and double junior silver medallist, backed up the claim and said the use of Turinabol, an anabolic drug made in East Germany, was mandatory. **BBC News February 20 1998**

8.   The common theme among Dr Arbeit's apologists is the absence of a criminal prosecution against him and the assumption of his being a mere factotum for the harrowing drug regimen. This, The Daily Telegraph refute from new documentary evidence out of Germany that paints an entirely more sinister picture.

Transcripts of a police interrogation of Dr Manfred Hoppner, one of Dr Arbeit's medical associates and the former deputy director and chief physician of the GDR sports medical service, reveal the depth of Dr Arbeit's collusion with the largest sports pharmaceutical experiment in history.

Questioned on Oct 31 1997 as part of an on-going interrogation which would form the basis of a prosecution and subsequent receipt of a jail sentence, Dr Hoppner identified Dr Arbeit's handwriting from his Stasi file and commented on the coach's fanatical support for specific use of anabolic steroids. **Daily Telegraph 14 May 2003**

9.   Dr Eckhard Arbeit was a major person responsible for the use of anabolic steroids. **Dr Werner Franke, German Parliamentary investigator into East German sports drug abuse**

10.   Frank knew that Dr Arbeit's involvement would bring a lot of attention and when I met with Denise (Lewis) I discussed the

implications. At the end of the day, this was Frank's shout and he clearly thinks Arbeit is the best man for the job. **Max Jones, former UK Athletics' performance director**

11.   It was part of the time all over the world, and I was working also with athletes in the United States at the same time, everybody was taking drugs. Everybody took the same or more drugs than East Germany. **Dr Arbeit in an interview with The Associated press October 1997**

12.   With a Christian-like approach, it's now time to move on. It's time for rehabilitation rather than recrimination. It was Frank's decision to surround himself with a team of experts and he rates Arbeit as probably the world's leading strength authority. **Jonathan Edwards BBC Sports 22 June 2003**

Other books from Libros International

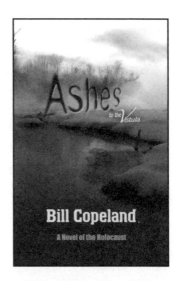

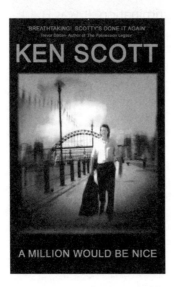

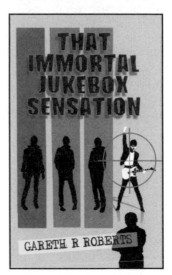

For more details, visit: www.librosinternational.com